THE COMPLETE INFLATABLE KAYAKER

THE COMPLETE INFLATABLE KAYAKER

JEFF BENNETT

Ragged Mountain Press
Camden, Maine

To Edward Simon . . .

See you downriver my friend.

Published by Ragged Mountain Press

10 9 8 7 6 5 4 3 2 1

Library of Congress Cataloging-in-Publication Data

Bennett, Jeff, 1961–

The complete inflatable kayaker / Jeff Bennett.

p. cm.

Includes bibliographical references and index.

ISBN 0-07-005428-2

1. Kayaking. 2. Kayaks. I. Title

GV783.B45 1995

797.1'224—dc20 95-20336

CIP

Questions regarding the content of this book should be addressed to:

Ragged Mountain Press
P.O. Box 220
Camden, ME 04843

Questions regarding the ordering of this book should be addressed to:

The McGraw-Hill Companies
Customer Service Department
P.O. Box 547
Blacklick, OH 43004
Retail customers: 1-800-822-8158
Bookstores: 1-800-722-4726

A portion of the profits from the sale of each Ragged Mountain Press book is donated to an environmental cause.

The Complete Inflatable Kayaker is printed on 60-pound Renew Opaque Vellum, an acid-free paper which contains 50 percent recycled waste paper (preconsumer) and 10 percent postconsumer waste paper.

Printed by Quebecor Printing, Fairfield, PA
Design and Production by Dan Kirchoff
Edited by Jonathan Eaton, Sydne Matus, and Tom McCarthy

All photos by Jeff Bennett and Tonya Bennett unless otherwise noted.

CONTENTS

INTRODUCTION

Paddle

From a rocky perch high upon the banks of Idaho's Snake River, I peered down upon a familiar scene. A thick green tongue of fast water slipped over a submerged shelf and swung headlong toward a minefield of boulders and churning hydraulics.

On past trips, I had run this rapid with a casual confidence that bordered on nonchalance. But this trip was different. Gone were the familiar confines of my opulent raft. In its place was a comparatively small craft known as an *inflatable kayak.*

I had spent little time in my inflatable kayak and had yet to gain any confidence in its ability to tackle big rapids. I was more accustomed to sitting high upon a raft tube and bobbing *over* rapids than sitting close to the water and crashing *through* them.

A remarkable metamorphosis was about to take place.

As I entered the top of the rapid, the kayak held steady and responded smoothly to every paddle stroke. Once past the first waves, the river ebbed and surged in a liquid landscape of frothy peaks and emerald valleys. I flirted with the shoulders of each mountainous wave until a clean route all but disappeared. Now ready for the meat of the rapid, I determinedly dug my paddle into the heart of the current and took a short, excited breath.

My kayak crested a giant wave perfectly and exploded into the air surrounded by a shimmering veil of liquid pearls. The next wave slammed me from the side, but a quick brace with my paddle kept me upright. Miraculously, the few gallons of water that had invaded my cockpit had already drained through the self-bailing floor, leaving me light and ready for the final moves. With a couple of fast forward strokes, I was able to paddle quickly around the final holes and complete my descent.

Resting in a calm pool beneath the tail of the rapid, I marveled at my accomplishment. Actually, I marveled at the capabilities of my inflatable kayak. It had tackled a tough rapid, and had done so with poise and grace. Plus, it had provided a level of intimacy with the river I had never experienced as a rafter. The metamorphosis was complete.

Today, the inflatable kayak is an important part of my river-running arsenal. More exciting than rafts, and more forgiving than traditional hardshell kayaks, the inflatable kayak allows me to explore rivers in ways I had never previously imagined. The inflatable kayak has proved perfect for low-water descents and for exploring steep creeks. It packs and travels with the simplicity of a large suitcase and can be carried into remote wilderness streams. It is equally at home on meandering rivers or Class V canyons... even on protected harbors, gentle seas, and crashing surf.

It is my hope that this handbook captures my love for inflatable kayaking and reveals those things rivers have taught me. It is not my intent to teach you to become a total kayaker, for only the river is the true teacher, of which we are all forever students. Instead, it is my intent to share with you my version of inflatable kayaking in the hope that it will enhance your own kayaking experiences.

Whether you are about to embark on your first inflatable kayaking adventure or have long since discovered the joys of inflatable kayaking, I wish you the very best with all your kayaking endeavors!

Inflatable kayaks can take you to magical places.

About the Author

When I first decided to try inflatable kayaking, it was to bridge a gap. Lacking the necessary skill to adequately paddle a hardshell kayak through wild rapids, yet still seeking a smaller craft than my trusty raft, I found the inflatable kayak to fit a perfect niche. It was stable, forgiving, and fun. Despite my many years of inflatable kayaking, my ultimate mastery of hardshell kayaking, and my constant association with whitewater rafting, I have yet to lose my fascination with inflatable kayaks.

As I look around me, a growing number of people share this sense of joy and fascination.

Everywhere, inflatable kayakers and sit-on-top kayakers are growing in numbers and are becoming a more powerful force in river-running communities. At the same time, quality literature describing inflatable kayaking techniques and equipment is sparse.

As a longtime whitewater instructor, river guide, and river author, I found this void to present a unique opportunity to share some ideas and concepts with fellow paddlers. Bear in mind, however, that this book is not the sole creation of the author. Instead, it is the culmination of a river-running evolution that has been going on for the last half-century. This book borrows tips and techniques from contemporary instructors and classic technique handbooks alike. Its roots spread broad throughout river-running circles and find their strength in the wealth of information available to river runners. However, this book remains unique in tailoring river-running techniques and equipment to you, the inflatable kayaker.

A Little Help from My Friends

I would like to give special thanks to those who have spent endless hours with me sharing river trips and tall

The author testing the limits of an early-model kayak on California's Cherry Creek during the 1980s. (Photo by Mike Doyle)

tales and those who have listened patiently while I babbled incoherently about river books and whitewater dreams. My helmet goes off to Les Bechdel, Eugene Buchanan, Fryar Calhoun, Bill Carlson, Bob Carlson, Jim Cassady, Bryan Cavaness, Dan Cole, John Connelly, Bill Cross, Dick DeChant, Scott Downey, Mike and Bonnie Doyle, Rich Freimuth, Dale Fuller, Casey Garland, David Gilmore, John Hall, Alan Hamilton, Dave and Carol Hammond, Ryan Hanegan, David Harrison, Lars Holbek, Mike Huddleston, Myrna Huddleston, Dan Jursnick, Robert Koch, Larry Laba, Mark Leder-Adams, Glenn Lewman, Mark Lisk, Doc and Vera Loomis, Brad McAllister, Dave Mullins, Jack Nelson, Steve O'Meare, Angela Peets, Dave Prange, Jill Radel, Greg Ramp, Craig Richter, Taylor Robertson, Beth Rundquist, Dave Sher, Morgan Smith, Jim Snyder, Don Stevens, Jim Stohlquist, Gary Stott, Dennis Stuhaug, Attila Szilagi, Scott Timmer, Charlie Walbridge, Kris Walker, Todd Walker, Mark Yawney, and everybody else credited throughout this book.

I would also like to thank the following manufacturers, retailers, outfitters, publications, and organizations for their support: AAA Rafting, AIRE, *Adventure West,* Alder Creek Kayak Supply, Alpenbooks, The American Whitewater Affiliation, B & A Distributing, Bend Whitewater Supply, Beyond Limits Adventures, *Canoe & Kayak,* Canyons Incorporated, Carlisle Paddles, Carlson Designs, Cascade Outfitters, Colorado Kayak, Columbia Sportswear, Down River Equipment Company, Downstream Products, Eastern River Expeditions, Extrasport, FlashBack Photographics, Hyside, Kokatat, Mountain and Surf Pro Shop, National Organization for River Sports, Northwest Design Works, Northwest River Supply, Ocean Kayaks, Orange Torpedoes, Pacific River Supply, *Paddler,* Patagonia, Perception, Power Bar, Predator, Preferred Modes, Project RAFT, Rapid Shooters, REI, Rescue 3 Northwest, Riken, Rivers and Mountains, Sawyer

Paddles and Oars, Sevylor, Sierra Designs, Sierra South, *Snow Country,* SOAR Inflatables, Wave Sports, Whitewater Manufacturing, and Yakima.

I pass along my special thanks to United States Wildwater Team member Bryan Tooley. Bryan not only spent a couple of hours in front of my camera demonstrating many of the techniques shown in Chapter 5, he patiently heightened my own knowledge of contemporary paddling techniques. Finally, I must thank my family—Paul, Bobbi, and Michelle Bennett—for having shared a singular vision of the world, one that knows no limitations, and bases quality of life on experience and adventure.

What Are You Getting Yourself Into?

The phrase inflatable kayaking evokes a broad canvas upon which different paddlers will paint different images. These versatile craft are vehicles for peaceful float trips or extreme descents, overnight getaways or a day on the beach. Whichever appeals to you, inflatable kayaking is an exhilarating way to travel across water.

If you have any friends who have gone inflatable kayaking, you've surely heard how fun this sport can be. Inflatable kayaks are stable and forgiving when used properly, and a majority of inflatable kayaks are designed to support first-time paddlers safely even in moderate whitewater.

If your penchant is for raucous whitewater, inflatable kayaks are the way to go! You can bring all your previous river-running skills into inflatable kayaking, or start from scratch and perfect your techniques as you progress from easy to more difficult rivers. If you give it your best, you can acquire enough skill in your first day or two to carry you comfortably from easy Class II rapids to more powerful Class III rapids. Then, as your confidence and ability grow, those same basic skills will guide you down more challenging rivers with only slight modification.

Ultimately, inflatable kayaking will become whatever you make of it. Your kayak can be a tool to bring you back in touch with the natural splendor of river canyons, or provide an opportunity to push river running to its limits. With the enormous flexibility of inflatable kayaking, you will always have a fantastic array of choices when you're inflatable kayaking, from the equipment you use to the type of rivers you paddle.

Why Inflatable Kayaks?

Inflatable kayaks are part raft, park kayak. Yet in many ways they exceed the capabilities of both craft. To the rafter, inflatable kayaks will feel like minirafts. The old, familiar buoyancy will be there, but the miniaturized tubes will impart a more intimate river experience. Neophyte hardshell kayakers turn to inflatable kayaks for stability and comfort. For these folks, inflatable kayaks open new opportunities to experience whitewater without having to learn an Eskimo roll. Finally, skilled kayakers revel in the inflatable kayak's ability to run steep drops without the same danger of entrapment, and also enjoy its portability when traveling.

Whether you're a city dweller seeking a craft that will store in a closet, a rafter seeking a craft to do low-water trips, or a maniacal paddler in search of the ultimate mode of river travel, inflatable kayaks are for you!

How to Use This Book

This book is arranged in a simple, user-friendly format that takes you from the showroom of your local paddle shop to the put-in of your favorite river. It is a complete course in river running, with each chapter designed to build on the ideas learned in the previous chapter. As you float through this book, you will embark on a journey that touches upon all aspects of inflatable kayaking.

After an introductory look at kayaking equipment and accessories, you will explore rivers themselves, probing underwater currents, surface hydraulics, and the many forces that make up whitewater rapids. Next, you will study actual river running, from basic maneuvers to the advanced techniques used on Class V rivers. Finally, we'll look at other options available to you, such as sea kayaking and inflatable canoeing. As you move from chapter to chapter, you'll learn about safety and rescue, how to pack gear for overnight trips, how to plan river-running expeditions, and much, much more.

If you have never paddled an inflatable kayak before, start with page 1 and keep reading. As you progress, you will learn new concepts and acquire new skills that will carry into future chapters. After a day on the river, come back to where you left off, read some more, then go paddle again. More experienced kayakers can jump to later chapters and pick up the information they need to break through learning plateaus or learn new skills.

Though this book teaches inflatable kayaking with descriptions, photos, and diagrams, it is ultimately just a book—little more than frozen glimpses of a fluid sport. The techniques taught here work best when you have competent guides or more experienced paddlers to demonstrate and coach you through each skill. It is up to you to *start easy* and to *progress slowly!*

Ultimately, this book will exercise the most important part of your body . . . *your brain*. Through imagery and explanation, *The Complete Inflatable Kayaker* will give you the mental tools you need to get down the river safely and efficiently. With the time you spend in your kayak—learning by both mistake and triumph—you will advance faster and more efficiently than you had ever dreamed possible.

1

GET WET

YOUR FIRST INFLATABLE KAYAKING ADVENTURE

Outfitters

One of the easiest ways to get your first taste of inflatable or sit-on-top kayaking is through a reputable commercial outfitter. Rafting companies abound in just about any state and province that has hills and streams. You can find these outfitters in the yellow pages under "River Trips," "Rafts," "Rafting," or "Guides." Many of these companies offer inflatable kayaking trips in addition to their normal rafting trips. Next, try contacting *America Outdoors* or one of the other outfitters organizations given in the appendix for a list of its members. Also, check out your local outdoor store. It will often have some brochures from local outfitters. Even government agencies such as the Bureau of Land Management, the National Forest Service, and local tourism departments maintain lists of qualified outfitters. If none of these prospects turn up a good outfitter, check out the advertisements in one of the popular outdoor magazines at your local bookstore.

Once you find an outfitter, inquire about the types of inflatable kayaking trips it offers. One easy way to figure out what types of rivers the outfitter offers is to read

Your inflatable kayaking adventures are just about to begin.

A commercially outfitted trip can be an excellent introduction to inflatable kayaking.
(Photo courtesy of Orange Torpedoes, Grants Pass, OR)

between the lines in its brochure. *Scenic float trips* are usually peaceful journeys along easy waterways with a few riffles to spice things up. *Fun for the whole family* often means the river has some whitewater, but that the rapids are forgiving enough for uncoordinated paddlers or misbegotten swimmers. Once the word *adventure* pops up—especially when combined with adjectives like *ultimate*—you're into more difficult whitewater. Unless you have paddled whitewater before or have the utmost confidence in your aquatic abilities, reorient your thinking and slide back to the family-class trips for your first whitewater voyage. Remember, don't overestimate your abilities! It is better to leave the river hungry for more challenging adventures than to scare yourself out of the sport on your first trip.

Clubs and Organizations

Local outdoor clubs, whitewater organizations, and college outdoor programs offer appealing alternatives to the *pay to play* option offered by outfitters. Clubs and organizations can usually save you a lot of money by asking you to contribute your own food, transportation, and personal gear, yet they frequently offer the identical rivers that outfitters advertise in their brochures.

Rentals

On some of North America's more popular rivers, it is possible to rent inflatable kayaks, lifejackets, helmets, and all the other gear necessary to undertake your own whitewater adventures. Since this gives intrepid greenhorns direct access to whitewater, it is best to have an experienced guide along when you rent a kayak!

2

EQUIPMENT

DON'T LEAVE HOME WITHOUT IT

Whether you're strolling the floor of your favorite paddle shop or watching boats pass you on the river, you will likely be amazed by the myriad inflatable kayaks available today. Manufacturers incorporate dozens of subtle design features, rugged components, and durable materials into their kayaks to produce quality, functional craft. Although it is easy to discuss each part of a kayak separately, it is the combination of parts and design features that determines how your kayak looks, feels, and performs.

In this chapter we'll explore kayak designs, gather the information you'll need to rent or purchase a kayak, and survey the accessories that will keep your whitewater adventures safe and exciting.

Basic Kayak Anatomy

Inflatable kayaks combine the inflatable tubes and air-supported shape of rafts with the sleek hull designs of kayaks. Remarkably diverse in design and function, there are inflatable kayaks built for the occasional Class II paddler and the hard-core Class V extremist alike. As the accompanying diagram shows, any fully assembled

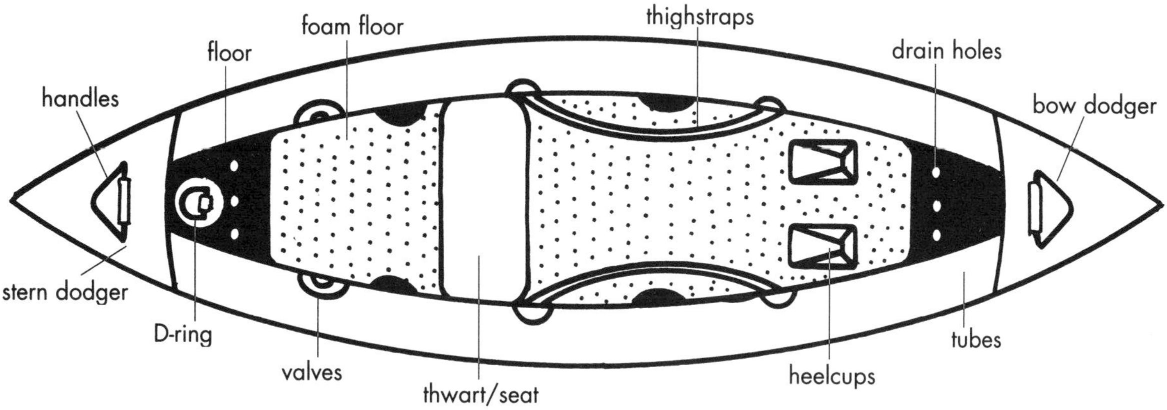

Anatomy of a typical inflatable kayak.

inflatable kayak consists of a multitude of independent components, each important to the kayak's performance. These include *tubes, floors, seats, thwarts, bow dodgers, thigh straps, footbraces, valves, seams, panels, D-rings,* and *carry handles.*

TUBES

Inflatable kayaks have two main tubes that give the kayak its distinctive banana shape. Tubes are frequently constructed independently, then built into the kayak so they meet at the bow and the stern. A few manufacturers build their tubes as a single unit, then separate the air chambers with a *baffle* or *diaphragm* inside the bow and the stern. (The independent air chambers keep the kayak afloat even if one chamber is punctured.)

One interesting twist on typical tube designs is the *bladder system*, which is similar to a car tire and inner tube. Rather than filling the outer tube with air, a bladder is inserted inside an outer tube, and the bladder is filled with air. If the inner bladder is damaged, it can often be removed and patched faster and more easily than a single-layer tube could be patched.

SEAMS AND PANELS

Tubes are manufactured from many separate pieces of material, and each *panel* is welded or glued together. The overlapping joints between different swaths of fabric are called *seams.*

Thermowelding—which is used to build many PVC and urethane kayaks—fuses the panels together without the use of toxic glues or solvents. This leaves a seam that is virtually indestructible. Gluing, on the other hand, is used to adhere two panels together. Gluing works best

Features like open cockpits and stable tubes distinguish inflatable kayaks (top) from hardshell kayaks (bottom).

on rubber-based fabrics such as Hypalon and neoprene and forms an excellent seam when done by top manufacturers.

VALVES

Each chamber has its own valve. Most kayaks have one of three types of valves: military-style, Halkey-Roberts, and AD-1. (A-7 valves are used on some kayaks.) You open and close military-style valves by twisting the outer assembly, and air flows freely in either direction when the valves are open. The Halkey-Roberts, AD-1, and A-7 valves have spring-loaded center posts that let you pump air one way into the kayak. To release the air, you just depress the post.

No matter which valve your kayak has, it should be durable, maintenance-free, and easily accessible.

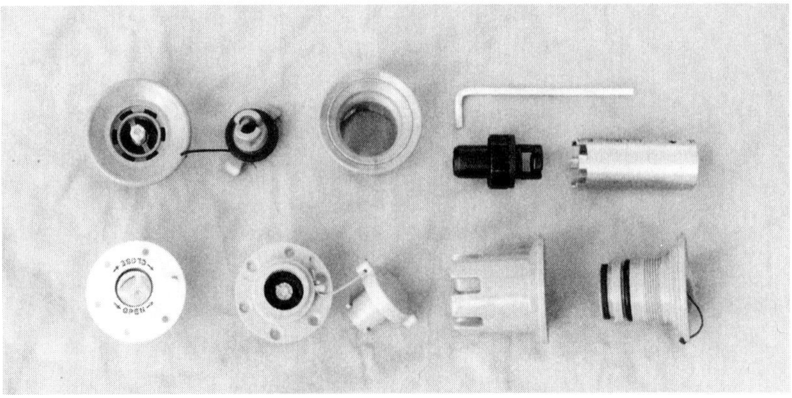

Kayak valves (clockwise from top left): Low-profile Halkey-Roberts valve parts and tools; full-size Halkey-Roberts valve parts; AD-1 valve; plastic military-style valve. (Equipment courtesy of Cascade Outfitters, Springfield, OR)

THWARTS AND SEATS

Thwarts are the inflated cross-tubes that run at right angles to the main tubes. Whether glued, welded, clipped, or strapped in place, thwarts help the kayak maintain its shape by holding the main tubes an equal distance apart, and act as a seat back by pressing against your lower back.

Permanently mounted thwarts are carefree and durable, but allow for little adjustment if you aren't comfortable with the kayak's cockpit configuration. With them, the only way to gain a few extra inches of leg room is to let a little air out of the thwart so that you can scoot your butt back. To get around that problem, many manufacturers use adjustable thwart mounts or independent seats.

A seat can be more comfortable than a thwart for some paddlers, but can pop free of the kayak unless it is strapped in place. Nonetheless, adjustable thwarts and removable seats let you customize your cockpit by placing the seat or thwart where *you* want it.

FLOORS

Inflatable kayaks are built with either *standard* or *self-bailing* floors. In a standard-floor kayak, the floor is glued to the tubes, in effect creating a giant bathtub. Standard-floor kayaks are economical and well suited to deep, gentle rivers. However, they offer little protection for your bottom unless they contain an air-filled or foam floor or seat, and can become heavy and unwieldy when full of water.

Self-bailing inflatable kayaks have buoyant foam or air-filled floors. When water enters the kayak, it lands on the surface of the floor, then pours out of the cockpit through a series of holes or slots.

Foam floors are durable, streamlined, and protect your tailbone. They show up on many high-tech kayaks and are increasing in popularity. Foam floors are also bulky and can add weight to your kayak—especially if they become waterlogged. *Air-filled floors* pack compactly at the end of the day and can reduce the overall weight of the kayak—great features for pack trips and apartment closets. The trade-off, of course, is that an air-filled floor can pop or deflate, leaving your butt too close to the rocks you're floating over. Although this may be of little concern for some paddlers, make sure that the floor is durable enough to withstand the level of abuse your kayak will see.

BOW AND STERN DODGERS

The bow and stern dodgers—also called the *spray shields*—are flaps of fabric that hold the ends of the tubes together and deflect water.

In self-bailing kayaks, water can splash over the tubes, but it runs off the side of the buoyant floor and back into the river through the floor's drain holes.

Kayak Accessories

THIGH STRAPS

Thigh straps are an inflatable kayak's version of a seat belt. They secure you tightly in the cockpit when your kayak is getting bounced around and increase the contact points between your lower body and your kayak. When used correctly, thigh straps improve your control. However, thigh straps can also pose a hazard if installed or used improperly.

When thigh straps were first introduced, fears of entrapment rang loud. Since most thigh straps allow your leg to slide through the strap loop, there is always a possibility that the strap will snare your leg. However, a majority of today's paddlers praise the increased kayak control that thigh straps allow. This, they argue, allows you to paddle more effectively and to steer clear of hazardous situations.

In any event, thigh straps should have a quick-release system so that you can free yourself from your kayak in an instant. (If the thigh straps don't have a quick-release system, carry a river knife on your lifejacket in case an emergency arises.) Also, the thigh straps should be tightened securely to lessen the likelihood that a leg will slip through the strap.

Most people can use thigh straps safely if they practice flipping and exiting the kayak in a safe, calm pool before taking the kayak out in whitewater.

D-RINGS

D-rings are heavy-duty steel rings mounted on short, fixed straps, which are then sewn and glued beneath a patch made of the same material as the kayak. D-rings provide a fixed point for strapping down gear, tying your kayak to a roof rack, or retaining a handline.

Thigh straps will keep you on board and in control even when your kayak is rocking to and fro.

HANDLES

Carrying handles on the bow and the stern are somewhat akin to the handles found on large suitcases. Whether constructed from solid plastic or the same material as the kayak, these handles make lifting and carrying a kayak much easier. (Bow and stern dodgers make great handles when your kayak has no added handles.)

FOOTBRACES

It's difficult to paddle an inflatable kayak if you're always sliding around the cockpit. That's where footbraces come into play. Footbraces give your feet something to push against and increase your contact with your kayak. They keep you in place when you're paddling steep falls and powerful hydraulics, and keep your legs in your thigh straps by keeping your knees bent.

The two most popular ways to brace your feet are *heelcups* and *footbraces*. Heelcups—small wells cut into the deck of foam floors—can be custom-cut at the point where your heels naturally touch the floor. When you sit down in your kayak, your heels will nestle in the heelcups, thus holding you in place. Footbraces—small platforms that press against the balls of your feet—have recently been borrowed from hardshell kayaks. They can be built on adjustable tracks so that the cockpit can be customized to each individual paddler.

Materials

Inflatable kayaks are constructed from a variety of materials, which vary in durability, life expectancy, stiffness, and overall *feel*. In order to give kayakers some idea of how materials compare, I'll describe many of the fabrics and coatings used when this book was written. Keep in mind, however, that technology is constantly changing. By the time the ink dries on these pages, there will be new materials on the market. The only way to keep up will be to read whitewater magazine reviews, obtain literature from manufacturers, and talk to local retailers. Still, the comparisons here will help you decipher manufacturers' claims and advertisements when new materials do show up.

Kayak materials have two parts: the *base fabric* and the *coating*. It is the base fabric that provides tear and puncture protection. The coating—which covers both sides of the base fabric—provides abrasion resistance, air retention, and resistance against ultraviolet rays.

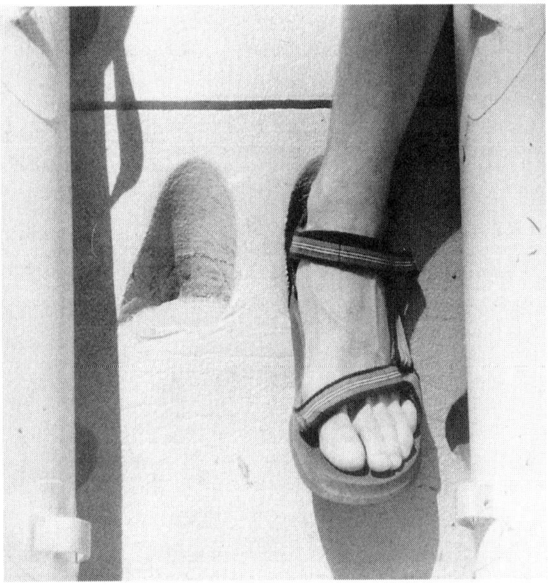

Heel cups—small wells cut into the deck of foam floors—will stop you from sliding forward inside the cockpit.

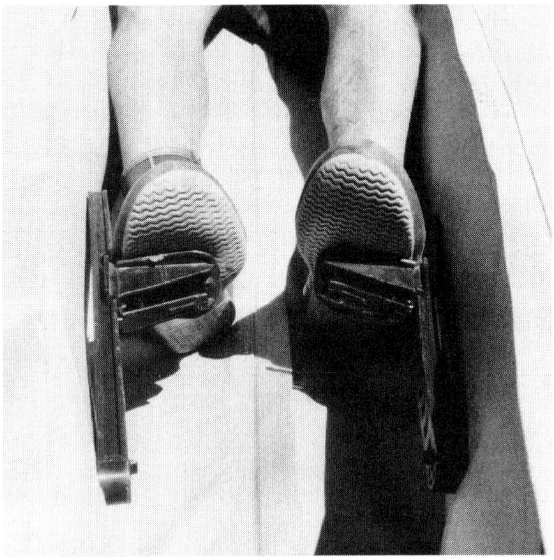

Footbraces—small, adjustable platforms that press against the balls of your feet—also keep you from sliding around your cockpit.

BASE FABRICS

Base fabrics consist of cloth sheets made from woven or knitted polyester or nylon threads. Single polyester threads are less stretchy, but tend to be weaker than single nylon threads. Single nylon threads, in turn, are stretchier but stronger. I've used the term *single threads* since the cloth's *weave* can also affect how much each thread stretches. In fact, it is possible to weave a nylon thread into cloth that is less stretchy than polyester cloth!

One of the most common terms you'll hear regarding material is *denier*, which is but one of many factors used to figure out material strength. Denier measures the weight of one 9,000-meter-long thread in grams—the heavier that thread, the higher the denier. Quality whitewater kayaks are usually constructed of materials with a minimum of 420 denier, and more-durable kayaks have deniers of 1,000 or more. If you see two numbers describing the denier (e.g., 420/840), the fabric is woven from yarns of two different deniers. Since polyester tends to be a little weaker than nylon, polyester-based materials generally use a higher-denier thread to achieve the same characteristics as a lower-denier nylon cloth.

The quality of the base cloth can also be measured by *thread count* and *fabric weight*. Thread count simply measures the number of threads per inch; fabric weight measures the weight of one square yard of cloth. As with denier, higher numbers tend to indicate better materials.

COATINGS

Most fabric coatings fall into two general categories: *rubber coatings* and *plastomers*. The most popular rubber coatings include *Hypalon* (polyethylene chlorosulfone) and *neoprene* (polychloroprene). Plastomer coatings include reinforced *vinyl*, *PVC* (polyvinyl chloride), and *urethane* (ether-based polyurethane). In turn, each coating may have different variations—for example, there are more than twenty neoprene compounds—but even the newest coatings will probably fall within these two groups. Common to all coatings are fillers such as stabilizers, UV inhibitors, antioxidants, and colored pigments.

Hypalon

Hypalon is a lightweight rubber coating developed by DuPont. It stands up well to abrasion and UV rays, is fully cured when applied to the base fabric, and bonds securely to the base fabric. In top-quality kayaks, Hypalon makes up almost 80 percent of the coating; cheaper Hypalon kayaks might have 25 to 50 percent Hypalon. Many kayakers like Hypalon for its durability, long shelf life, and ease of repair. Hypalon is also easy to store in a tight bundle. On the other hand, Hypalon kayaks are usually more flexible than PVC or urethane kayaks, and tend to stick to obstacles with greater frequency. Hypalon's sticky or rubbery feel is partly due to the nylon that usually constitutes base fabric. However, some manufacturers use stiffer base fabrics and higher-quality Hypalon coatings to give their kayaks a more solid, slick feel.

Neoprene

Neoprene—which has been around for decades—is similar to Hypalon. It can be glued easily and holds air extraordinarily well. On the other hand, neoprene is heavier and less abrasion resistant than Hypalon, which has led to a decrease in its popularity over the years.

Vinyl

Long before Hypalon, urethane, or PVC started appearing on inflatable kayaks, companies like Sevylor were using reinforced vinyl to build inexpensive kayaks. Sturdier than plain vinyl, reinforced vinyl has been used successfully on Class I to III rapids for many years. Its real forte is affordability. These craft are usually the least expensive on the market. On the other hand, reinforced vinyl is usually less durable than other coatings like Hypalon, PVC, and urethane.

PVC

While comparable to Hypalon in abrasion and UV resistance, PVC is a much lighter and stiffer coating than Hypalon—especially when used with polyester-based fabrics. PVC's light weight and increased rigidity lets kayaks glance off rocks and hold their shape in powerful hydraulics. This allows manufacturers to build high-performance kayaks that recapture some of the performance characteristics of hardshell kayaks.

The trade-off for this increased rigidity shows up the moment you try to roll up your kayak at the end of the day. PVC kayaks don't wrap up as tightly, and may crack if rolled up in very cold temperatures. Also, as a plastomer, PVC isn't fully cured when applied to the base fabric. Instead, PVC's plasticizers leach out slowly, leaving the PVC brittle and weak after many years of use.

Urethane

Urethane, another plastomer, is not only extremely rugged and long-lasting—perhaps more so than Hypalon and PVC—it recaptures some of the *hand* of Hypalon and can be welded like PVC. Urethane is used alone, or sprayed over other coatings like PVC as a protective outer layer. Urethane's ability to hold air is so well recognized that it is even used to build air-tight bladders in PVC kayaks.

Adhesion

The bonding of the coating to the base fabric has a remarkable effect on kayak materials. Since the coating adheres to the base fabric, the material works as a single unit. If there is too much adhesion between the coating and the base fabric, the threads will be locked in place, and the material's tear resistance will be lowered. On the other hand, too little adhesion leads to delamination and lower abrasion resistance. The way coatings are layered can also be important. Some manufacturers use one coating on top of another to combine the best performance characteristics from each coating.

Design Characteristics

Every inflatable kayak feels a little different than any other. Some plod downriver like small rafts, others dance on the water like a hardshell kayak. Some excel at carrying gear efficiently, some specialize in steep-creeking.

Once you have had an opportunity to test-drive a few kayaks, some noticeable patterns begin to emerge. For example, different fabrics react differently to rocks and hydraulics, and a kayak's overall shape affects how it travels straight *(tracks)* or spins.

This section discusses the most visible design characteristics—length, width, tube diameter, tube shape, waterline, and floor type—and touches briefly upon how each factor affects a kayak's overall performance. Keep in mind, however, that every kayak is the sum of its parts. Despite the general rules set out below, some long kayaks spin easier than their shorter cousins. Some wide kayaks feel tippier than narrower kayaks built for the same purpose. Ultimately, you're the only one who can decide what design characteristics and overall feel suit your needs.

LENGTH AND WIDTH

Most modern kayak designers construct one-person kayaks (K-1s) with a width of 31 to 40 inches and a length between 9.5 and 12 feet. Two-person kayaks (K-2s) are often longer than their K-1 counterparts.

All other things being equal, shorter kayaks spin faster and fit easier through tight boulder gardens. Longer kayaks, on the other hand, often track better and support more weight. Narrower kayaks are usually better for smaller paddlers, but wider kayaks provide more stability.

TUBE DIAMETER

Tubes provide buoyancy and deflect water. If they're too small, waves will roll into the cockpit faster than the water bails through the floor, or the tubes will submerge in hydraulics and make the kayak tippier. On the other hand, large tubes can be difficult to reach over with a paddle. Accordingly, all manufacturers match their tube sizes to the overall shape and design of their kayaks. This usually results in a tube diameter of 10 to 12.5 inches.

TUBE SHAPE

Most kayak tubes start thick in the middle, then taper and curve upward toward the bow and the stern. The taper gives inflatable kayaks their unique pointed shape designed to pierce holes and breaking waves while the upward curvature at the bow and the stern—often referred to as *kick* or *rise*—lifts the bow over waves and holes, prevents diving in steep drops, and provides a drier ride through rapids. Stern rise

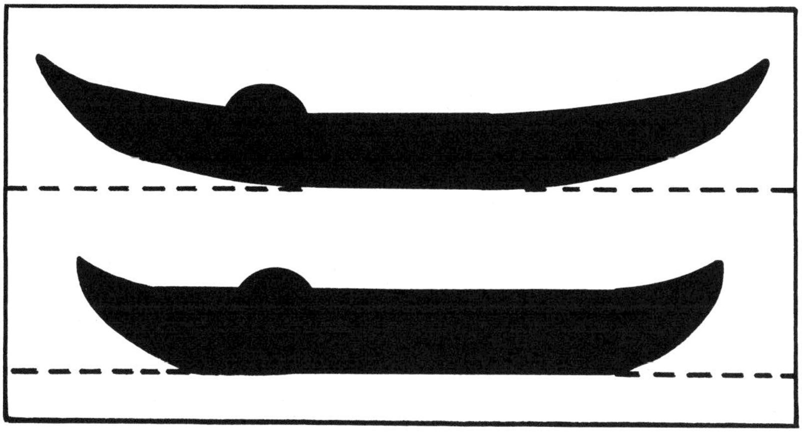

Kayaks with plenty of rocker (top) spin well and speed away from the base of waterfalls, but they can be slower and harder to paddle in a straight line. Kayaks with very little rocker (bottom) are easy to paddle straight, but can be harder to turn.

also makes back-ferrying (discussed later) easier by letting the stern slide over the water instead of trying to push it aside.

Tapering and lifting the tubes at the bow and stern also give inflatable kayak hulls a banana-like curvature known as rocker. Boats with a lot of rocker tend to spin well and speed away from the base of falls. They can also be slower and more difficult to paddle in a straight line. Boats with minimal rocker track well, but are harder to turn.

Building the right amount of kick and rocker into a kayak is tricky. For example, too much bow rise creates a bulldozer effect and allows the kayak to flex, both of which can cause the kayak to run slower and stall in strong hydraulics. Manufacturers incorporate these characteristics into their designs, and offer kayaks with good compromises that work best in a variety of rapids.

WATERLINE

Waterline measures the length of the kayak that is actually in the water. The waterline of an empty kayak is governed by its length, rocker, and bow and stern kicks. Once you're sitting in your kayak, the added weight will cause it to sink deeper into the river's surface, extending the waterline toward the bow and the stern.

Kayaks with shorter waterlines often spin faster but can be more difficult to paddle in a straight line. The inverse is also true: A longer waterline helps the kayak track straight, but hampers its ability to turn.

FLOOR TYPE

Floor design can have a profound effect on a kayak's handling characteristics. *Standard-floor kayaks* capture water in the passenger compartment like a giant bathtub, rendering the kayak heavy and unwieldy once it gets waterlogged. To keep the standard-floor kayak light and maneuverable, the water must be bailed out manually. If there isn't a pool or eddy close by to pull into and bail out your kayak, the extra water could become a real hazard. But on gentle rivers, standard-floor kayaks work just fine.

Self-bailing kayaks, with their incredible water-shedding capabilities, perform well in almost any type of whitewater. On small, technical streams the self-bailing kayak remains light and nimble. On large-volume rivers the self-bailer's quick reactions let you turn quickly into oncoming waves and deftly ferry around big holes or pourovers.

Two-Person Inflatable Kayaks (K-2s)

A two-person inflatable kayak— often called a *K-2*— is a beefed-up version of a one-person kayak. These craft are usually 1 to 3 feet longer than one-person kayaks, often have bigger tubes to support the extra weight of the second paddler, and may have a second thwart or seat.

The K-2 can be a versatile craft. While the extra space is designed to accommodate a second paddler, it is equally suited to carrying gear. In fact, many solo kayakers swear by K-2s for overnight travel.

A two-person kayak (K-2) on California's Kern River.
(Photo by Robert Laufer; courtesy of Rapid Shooters, Coloma, CA)

Other Types of Craft

CATYAKS

Just a couple of pontoons held together by a frame, the CatYak (named after its rafting cousin—the *cataraft*) is distinctly different from other types of inflatable kayak.

CatYaks with small steel frames have no bulky floor to carry around and can be easier to store or pack into remote canyons. The lack of a large, solid floor also cuts down on drag on shallow rivers, and lets the tubes pierce all but the most stubborn hydraulics. If the CatYak ever *does* find itself wrestling a sticky hole, the river will pour through the open tubes, making it harder to flip the boat.

CatYaks with wider plastic or fiberglass frames combine many of the characteristics of steel-framed CatYaks while increasing cargo-carrying capabilities. Although they are usually more difficult to pack around (due to their increased bulk), they are ideal for all types of river running. In fact, some fans of fiberglass-framed CatYaks have even taken the boats down Class V rivers with incredible success.

The flip side of all this added stability can be a small loss in buoyancy. Without a floor to provide added lift, all the weight of the frame, paddler, and gear rests solely on the tubes. The dual-tube design can also make the CatYak a tougher craft to turn and spin (the single center pivot point of a traditional kayak is now scattered out along the middle of two tubes). Finally, some paddlers using open-bottom frames find it a bit unnerving to watch rocks and water passing within inches of their butts. Still, a growing legion of delighted paddlers are becoming CatYak converts.

INFLATABLE CANOES

Inflatable canoes differ little from many inflatable kayaks. They can be paddled sitting down or kneeling while using a typical kayak paddle. However, inflatable canoes can also accommodate the kneeling or sitting positions used by most canoers. While incorporating many of the same design characteristics found in inflatable kayaks, inflatable canoes often have slightly larger tubes and lash points for installing seats or saddles.

SIT-ON-TOPS

Sit-on-tops are the latest craze to hit the river-running market. Stiffer than inflatable kayaks but more forgiving

A CatYak in action. (Equipment courtesy of So-Cat, Bend, OR)

Inflatable canoes are specially designed to accommodate the kneeling or sitting positions used by canoers.
(Photo courtesy of SOAR Inflatables, St. Louis, MO)

than hardshell kayaks, sit-on-tops combine the stiff plastic hulls of hardshell kayaks with the open cockpits of inflatable kayaks. In fact, anyone who has paddled an inflatable kayak will find a lot of familiar features in sit-on-tops, like thigh straps and self-bailing floors.

Sit-on-top owners will be delighted to know that the rest of this book applies equally well to their craft as to inflatables. The only difference is that you don't have to blow up a sit-on-top at the beginning of the day, roll it up at the end of the day, or worry about deflated tubes. Beyond that, you paddle sit-on-tops using the same techniques described in future chapters!

Sit-on-top kayaks combine the stiff plastic hulls of hardshell kayaks with the open cockpits of inflatable kayaks.
(Photo by Jill Radel, courtesy of Ocean Kayak, Inc., Ferndale, WA)

Purchasing an Inflatable Kayak

Buying a new kayak can be a big investment, especially if you're going to purchase a top-of-the-line model. Although there are kayaks for almost any budget, price shouldn't be your biggest concern. You should consider the type of rivers you'll be running, the amount of abuse you inflict upon your equipment, and the amount of gear you'll be carrying. Since you may buy and use only one kayak, your ideal kayak will be a compromise that gives you as many desired features as you can get.

Don't be afraid to ask for advice from your local retailer, or the various kayak manufacturers. Most kayak dealers are very proud of their products and are very informative. Since they want you to be happy, they'll frequently go out of their way to help you select the kayak that is right for you.

Before purchasing your next inflatable kayak, consider each of these factors:

1. How tall are you and how much do you weigh?
2. Will you be running Class III rapids? Class V rapids?
3. Will you paddle deep, large-volume rivers, or steep, rocky streams?
4. Do you want a sleek, high-performance kayak, or a more stable, forgiving kayak?
5. Will you be running day trips? Overnight trips?
6. How much gear do you intend to carry?
7. How many days will you use the kayak this year?
8. What is your budget?
9. What warranties will you get with the kayak?
10. What is the dealer's/manufacturer's reputation?
11. Do you intend to use the kayak commercially?
12. Where can you go for major repairs?
13. How will you transport or store your kayak?

USED KAYAKS

Used kayaks can be a great way to break into the whitewater game. Since properly maintained equipment lasts for many years, you're likely to find quality kayaking gear available at reasonable prices.

When looking for a used kayak, spend enough time to adequately "kick the tires." Ask a lot of questions like "How old is this kayak? What rivers have you used it on? Does it hold air?" Next, inflate the kayak and listen for air leaks. Inspect the material for any fading or discoloration that might indicate too much exposure to damaging ultraviolet rays. Check the seams to see if they're intact, and see how carefully any patches have been applied. You should also make sure that the valves open and close smoothly. To check the integrity of the baffles (if there are any), inflate one chamber at a time. Finally, the true measure of a kayak's prior use and care is its floor. Examine the floor in good lighting to see if the material's outer coating is worn away from the base cloth. Expect to find some wear, but if large patches of cloth are showing through, chances are the kayak has seen some heavy use.

Keep in mind that used equipment is bound to have some damage—patched tubes, cracked foam, and marred floors. But with some time and effort, many kayaks can be reconditioned inexpensively and used for many more years.

Paddles

PADDLE TYPES

There are scores of quality kayak paddles available on the market today. By and large, most paddles designed for hardshell kayaking will work equally well for inflatable kayaking. However, the larger dimensions of inflatable kayaks demand a slightly longer paddle for maximum efficiency.

Quality kayaking paddles can have *flat* or *curved blades*, *feathered* or *nonfeathered blades*, and *oval* or *round shafts*.

Curved blades—more commonly known as *spoon blades*—enter the water easier, improve your bite on the water, and make paddling easier than flat blades.

Feathered blades—blades that are offset, or turned 30 to 90 degrees from each other—help make the paddle more wind resistant and increase the biomechanical efficiency of each stroke. Feathered paddles come in *right-* or *left-hand-control* models to match the angle of the blades to your control hand. In a right-hand-control model—which is the most popular type of paddle—your right hand remains stationary on the shaft and determines the angle of the blades. When you take a stroke on your left side, your right hand rotates the shaft through your left hand so that the left blade can bite the water. In a left-hand-control model, your left hand rotates the shaft.

Oval shafts make all of this easier by letting you home in on your blade angle by feel alone, even when you can't see your blades.

SELECTING A PADDLE

Everybody has a different idea about the perfect paddle. Some paddlers like fiberglass, others like wood. Some like their blades feathered at 90 degrees, others opt for 30-degree offsets. Still, one of the most important steps you'll take in selecting a paddle will be to determine your optimum paddle length.

Ideal paddle length takes into account your height,

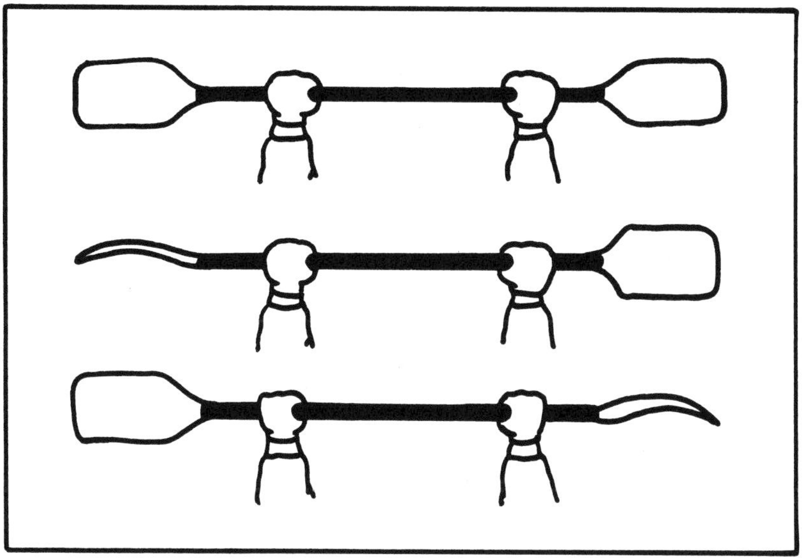

The top paddle has nonfeathered (parallel) blades while the bottom two paddles have feathered (offset) blades. The bottom two paddles also have spoon (curved) blades. Finally, the middle paddle is a left-hand-control model while the bottom paddle is a right-hand-control model.

arm length, kayak size, and paddling style. Most inflatable kayakers use paddles ranging from 200 to 240 centimeters (6.5 to 8 feet) in length. If you are quite tall, have a large kayak, or seek extra support from your paddle, opt for a paddle in the upper half of that range. Shorter paddles, on the other hand, fit smaller paddlers better. Shorter paddles are also lighter, faster, and fit into tight spaces on narrow rivers.

Don't skimp on quality when purchasing a kayak paddle! Some inexpensive paddles seem like a good deal when you buy them, but they are easy to break or bend and tend to make paddling more fatiguing.

Essential Riverwear

The first layer of protection between you and the river environment is your personal gear: helmets, lifejackets, and clothing. Carefully designed and selected riverwear not only improves the quality of your river experience, it makes inflatable kayaking safer. Wetsuits, drysuits, lifejackets, and helmets protect kayakers from the debilitating effects of hypothermia, keep them afloat in powerful currents, and protect them from injury amid rock-strewn channels.

HELMETS

Helmets are *de rigueur* for kayakers on whitewater rivers. Helmets consist of a sturdy outer shell, a shock-absorbing liner, and a chin harness designed to keep the helmet on your head. A properly shaped and fitted helmet covers the entire head—including the top, temples, and ears—but remains unobtrusive to the wearer. Some helmets even have face guards to protect against facial injuries caused by rocks, flailing paddles, or collisions with other paddlers.

When selecting a helmet, check out its liner. You may prefer foam padding rather than a suspension type of shock-absorbing system, but either works well. Make sure that the helmet fits your head comfortably: The chin strap should hold the helmet securely in place so

Wear a quality, properly fitted helmet whenever you paddle whitewater.
(Equipment courtesy of Alder Creek Kayak Supply, Portland, OR)

that the helmet won't ride up and expose your forehead or slide down and block your vision.

LIFEJACKETS

Lifejackets—also called *personal flotation devices* or *PFDs*—must be worn by kayakers on any river. They increase your buoyancy, furnish some extra insulation on cold days, and even provide some welcome body armor in the event of a swim.

When choosing or purchasing lifejackets, you must consider two important factors: *flotation* and *fit*.

The main goal of a lifejacket is to keep your mouth and chin above water long enough to let you breathe. Lifejackets accomplish this according to some fairly basic principles. An average person is surprisingly buoyant, weighing only 10 to 12 pounds when immersed in water (less if you're thin, more if you're heavy). So, anything that attaches to your body and provides more upward lift than your body's sinking weight will increase your buoyancy.

To figure out how much flotation *you'll* need on your next river trip, evaluate your own abilities and the river's difficulty. Ask yourself what type of water you will be paddling; how much you weigh and your body type; the clothing you intend to wear underneath the lifejacket (a wetsuit can add 6 to 8 pounds of buoyancy, and an air-filled drysuit can add more); whether you are likely to swim this river; and whether you're a strong swimmer.

If you're a weak swimmer or about to paddle a difficult river, a lifejacket with maximum flotation may increase your safety during a swim. On the other hand, a bulky lifejacket may interfere with your ability to paddle or swim. Also, high-flotation lifejackets might make it tougher to escape holes or reversals. Strong swimmers on gentle rivers may be able to get away with slim, low-flotation lifejackets.

A properly fitted lifejacket is comfortable enough to wear all day and doesn't interfere with paddling or swimming. It will cinch snugly around your torso and won't ride up over your face or head in rapids. Many lifejackets achieve a customized fit through the use of different sizes (from extra-small child sizes to extra-large adult sizes), flexible contoured foam panels, and buckled cinch straps.

To make sure you're getting the best fit possible, try on a few lifejackets. Put on one that has ties or straps that tighten at the waist and cinch down the straps until they're comfortably tight. Now, have a friend yank on the lifejacket's shoulders. If the lifejacket fits properly, it will budge only slightly while remaining comfortable. Keep in mind that you'll be adding bulky layers of riverwear when you're out kayaking, so make sure there's enough space under the jacket to accommodate your clothing.

Since there are so many factors in choosing a lifejacket, ask your dealer to help you in selecting one, or get a couple of different lifejackets so that you'll be ready for anything.

CLOTHING

Novice kayakers are frequently astonished when they first discover how cold many rivers are. Whether fueled by snowmelt, rainfall, or dam releases, the water temperature in many popular rivers is cold enough to require some form of outerwear, even on the warmest days.

When choosing riverwear, select garments that are comfortable, flexible, and provide sufficient insulation to ward off the onset of hypothermia. Shorts or bathing suits may be enough when the river is forgiving and the air is warm, but this is often the exception to the rule. To determine your clothing requirements, consider river and air temperatures, the type of river you'll be kayaking, and your expected level of activity.

Wetsuits

Wetsuits made of body-hugging neoprene have been a favored form of insulation for many years. A *farmer john* style wetsuit—which leaves the arms and shoulders uncovered—provides the first layer of insulation, with pile sweaters and paddle jackets or dry tops making up the outer layers.

The wetsuit works by shielding unprotected skin from direct splashes, and trapping a thin film of water between the suit and your skin during swims. Once water fills the suit, it is warmed by your skin and insulated from the river by the suit itself. Wetsuits also provide some extra flotation and padding—nice to have if you're swimming a boulder-strewn river.

When selecting a wetsuit, do not get the same type of suit worn by scuba divers. A kayaker's higher activity

Lifejackets range from bulky, high-flotation jackets (left) to slim, low-flotation jackets (right).

level and increased range of motion demand a thinner wetsuit. A thickness of ⅛ inch (2 to 3 millimeters) provides both warmth and flexibility. Also check for proper fit. A properly fitted farmer john wetsuit will follow the contours of your body without being too tight.

Wetsuits (left), paddle jackets (center), and drysuits (right) help keep you warm.

Paddling Jackets and Dry Tops

Paddling jackets and dry tops are high-tech rain jackets similar in design to the upper half of a drysuit (described below). Worn alone or over wetsuits and fleece liners, they prevent chilling blasts of cold water from creeping down your torso.

The main difference between paddling jackets and dry tops is in their ability to shed water. The more affordable paddling jackets combine loose layers of waterproof cloth with water-resistant neoprene or Lycra closures at the neck and wrist. They aren't waterproof, but they come close. Dry tops have waterproof latex closures at the neck and wrist that keep the water out even when you're getting splashed. Both paddling jackets and dry tops are effective when you're sitting up in the kayak, but let water in through the waist opening when you're swimming.

Drysuits

Drysuits differ dramatically from wetsuits in both appearance and function. Instead of trapping water near the skin, the drysuit keeps water off your body by enclosing it in a loose-fitting layer of waterproof fabric. The suit has a large waterproof zipper or flap closure that allows easy entry and exit, and is made totally waterproof with tight-fitting latex gaskets at the neck, wrist, and ankle openings.

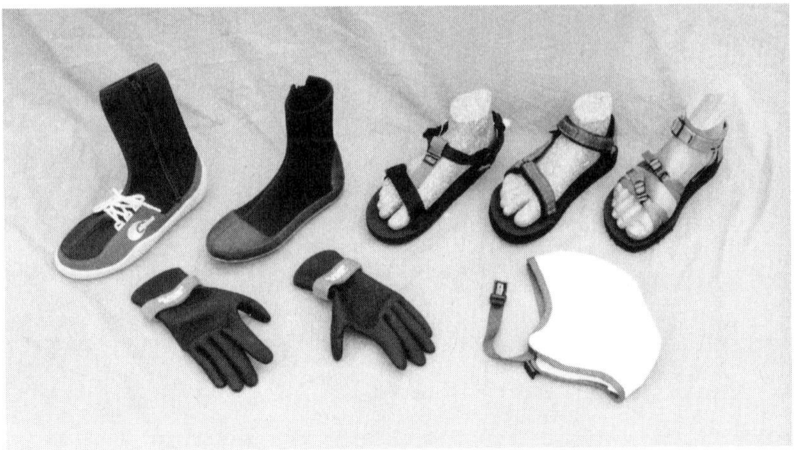

Accessories: A selection of neoprene booties, specially designed river sandals, neoprene gloves, and a helmet liner. (Equipment courtesy of Cascade Outfitters, Springfield, OR)

Though drysuits lack the insulating qualities of wetsuits, they are baggy enough to fit over inner layers of clothing. As with other outdoor sports, the best way to choose clothing that will keep you warm is to follow the *layering* concept. The innermost clothing layer should wick sweat away from your skin, and the next layers should be warm and absorbent. Since the drysuit will seal in body moisture, it is important to choose synthetic materials like nylon or polypropylene fleece for your inner clothes.

Other Clothing Accessories

Booties, gloves, pogies, and insulating caps vastly improve the quality of your kayaking experience on cold rivers. Thick neoprene booties with semirigid soles keep feet warm and provide decent traction during slippery portages. In warmer climates, specially designed river sandals (with extra straps to hold them securely on your feet) work great. Waterproof caps help retain an enormous amount of body heat by providing another layer of insulation over your head.

Your hands can be kept comfortably warm with neoprene gloves or pogies. Pogies attach directly to the paddle shaft, forming a water-resistant cocoon. Your bare hand slips into the pogie and grabs the paddle shaft without any barrier to affect your feel for the shaft.

3

SADDLE UP

ASSEMBLING YOUR GEAR

A fully outfitted kayak looks sleek sitting in the water, but it's just flotsam until somebody starts paddling it. This chapter bridges the gap between selecting equipment and learning to paddle. It teaches you how to properly inflate, balance, and adjust the kayak and contains all the information you'll need to customize your inflatable kayak to match your size, weight, and paddling style.

Before reading this chapter, take a look at your own equipment. Chances are that it will perform best when it's assembled as the manufacturer intended. Now, let's discuss the nuances of assembling your kayak.

Assembling Your Kayak

PUMPS

Pumps specially suited to kayaking range from powerful 110-volt AC electric blowers to affordable hand and foot pumps. The big AC blowers are wonderful time-savers. But unless you're inflating your kayak near an electrical outlet or generator, you'll probably use one of the more common battery-powered DC air pumps. Twelve-volt pumps attach to a car's battery and put out about 1.5 to 2.5 pounds per square inch in air pressure. These pumps are used to give the kayak its full shape, then a manual hand or foot pump is used to *top off* the kayak with the final bit of extra air pressure. Topping off the kayak with a manual pump increases the life span of your electric pump, and will make your kayak much stiffer on the river.

Manual pumps can be hand- or foot-powered and come in a variety of sizes. Hand pumps with large, wide-diameter barrels let you pump up kayaks fast, while smaller hand pumps are easy to carry in your kayak. (Don't be deceived by size—some small pumps blow out air on both the up and down strokes of the handle, making inflation fast and easy.) Any kayak pump should have a durable hose and a nozzle sized to fit your kayak's valves perfectly. Also, some pumps work in reverse and can actually suck air out of a kayak. This handy deflation feature helps get the last bit of air out of your kayak before you put it in storage.

A FEW WORDS OF CAUTION

Before you blow up your kayak, keep three things in mind: (1) If your kayak has a removable floor or seat, determine whether it should be installed before inflating the kayak. (2) Determine your kayak's recommended air pressure rating (usually 2 to 3 pounds per square inch). (3) Always blow up the tubes slowly and evenly.

A variety of manual and electric pumps.

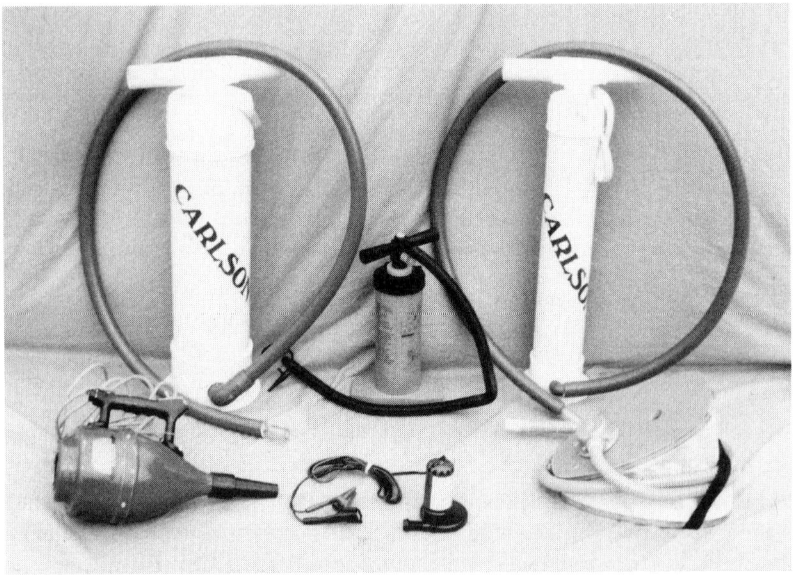

INSTALLING FLOORS AND SEATS

Many foam floors—and some air floors—must be installed before you blow up your kayak. These floors generally rest on top of the kayak's fabric floor, and slide underneath the seat or thwart.

Before installing the floor, clean any dirt or debris from both the kayak and the floor so it doesn't damage the fabric later on. Next, slide or push the floor into place. Sometimes this is easier if you splash water on the floor so it doesn't stick to the kayak. Once the floor is in place, check the alignment of the floor and the drain holes to make sure the floor doesn't cover the holes.

If your kayak also has a removable seat or thwart, it may be easier to install it now rather than after the kayak is inflated. Put the seat in the position you think will best suit you and follow the manufacturer's recommendations for securing it.

Once the floor and the seat are in place, you're ready to inflate the rest of the kayak.

INFLATING THE KAYAK

To properly inflate your kayak, first put just enough air in each chamber to give the kayak its normal shape. Then top off the kayak by adding air evenly to each chamber until the kayak is fully inflated. By adding air evenly around the kayak you'll avoid overpressurizing—and possibly damaging—any delicate baffles that might be built into your kayak. Although too much air can damage your kayak, too little air makes it sluggish and nonresponsive. Only the *proper* amount of air can keep the kayak performing at its best.

When you think you're done inflating your kayak, look at the tubes. Smooth-surfaced, identically sized tubes will tell you that you've blown up your kayak correctly, while creases

The folded foam floor and rolled-up tubes shown in the bottom left portion of this photograph are easy to assemble into a ready-to-paddle kayak.

and folds mean that the chambers aren't properly inflated. Figuring out if your kayak is properly inflated takes a little bit of experience, and can be done with an air gauge or by feel. A kayak is usually fully inflated when a struck fist bounces firmly off the tubes.

It's easy to carry light kayaks on your shoulder. You can also carry them over your head by resting the tubes on both shoulders.

Carrying Your Kayak

The most common way to carry your kayak is to rest one tube on your shoulder with the cockpit facing your body. The kayak will usually balance best if your shoulder is just in front of the seat. You can also carry your kayak on both shoulders with your head inside the cockpit, or have a friend hold the bow while you hold the stern.

Whatever method you use to get your kayak to the river, don't drag it on the ground!

Climb Aboard

ENTERING YOUR KAYAK

The easiest place to enter your kayak is in a foot or two of water. In the shallows, you can simply walk alongside your kayak and sit down in the cockpit as if you were sitting on a chair. Once aboard, you can swing your legs into the bow, nestle your lower back against the seat or thwart, and see how the kayak feels. If the water is too deep for you to wade alongside your kayak, pull it up against the shore, squat down, and plop yourself into the cockpit from the bank.

Whatever you do, don't climb aboard in an inch or two of water and scrape the river bottom on the way out to deeper water. Unless you have a durable kayak, this technique is a surefire way to wear out the floor quickly.

HOW TO SIT IN AN INFLATABLE KAYAK

Sit in the cockpit with your legs straight out in front of you and rock your upper body left and right. Not very stable, are you? Now, bend your knees, slide your heels toward you a few inches, and spread your knees comfortably apart. Now you're in a more balanced, stable position—the perfect position for kayaking.

Bending your knees and spreading your knees apart accomplishes three things. First, it unlocks your hips, letting your upper body float independently of your lower body. Second, it increases your contact with the kayak: The outside of your thighs and lower legs press against the tubes, your heels press down on the floor, and your lower back presses firmly against the seat or thwart. Finally, bending your knees moves your legs upward, where they can be secured by thigh straps. All of these factors ultimately improve your balance, flexibility, and control.

Customizing the Cockpit

TRIM

Once you're in the water, look forward and sit upright. If the bow or the stern sinks farther in the water than the opposite end, now's the time to adjust the *trim*—or weight bias—of the kayak. A kayak that is trim is perfectly balanced over its center point, or just slightly sternward. This helps the kayak perform at its best.

If your kayak has an adjustable seat or thwart, move it forward or backward until you find a comfortable position that keeps the bow and the stern equidistant above the water. (If your kayak has a permanently mounted thwart, do the same thing by adjusting the air pressure.) Once you're under way, you can affect the boat's trim yourself by leaning forward or backward whenever conditions demand it.

Sitting upright with your knees bent and spread apart improves your balance, flexibility, and control.

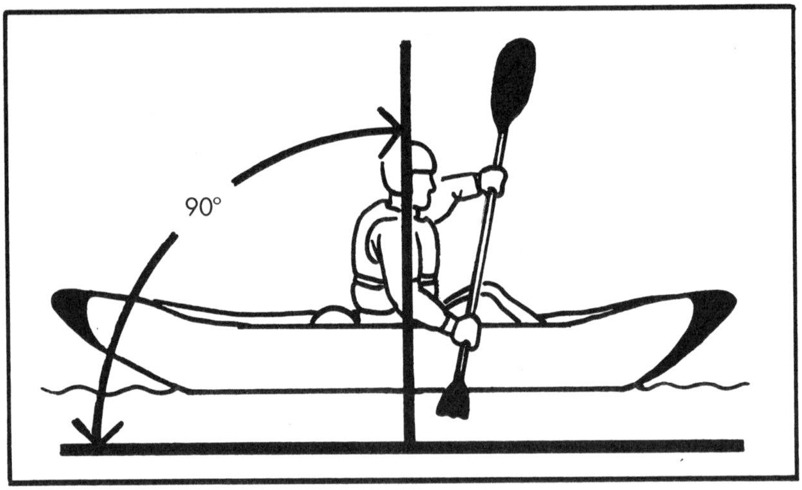

FOOT CUPS AND FOOTBRACES

Footbraces on sliding tracks can be adjusted to your leg length by sliding the braces forward or backward until they press against the balls of both feet. Remember that you still want to sit in the upright, bent-legged position that you just learned above.

Foot cups usually have to be custom-cut into foam floors before they're of much use. To find the perfect position for the foot cups, put on all of your usual riverwear, get out on the river, and sit down in the cockpit. Once again, sit upright and make sure that your kayak is level and trim. Now, look at the heels of both feet. You can cut small wells in the surface of the foam floor at the point where your heels touch the foam. (Beware: Some manufacturers want to do this for you and will void their warranties if you do it on your own!)

Both footbraces and foot cups help fuse you with your kayak. They give your feet something to press against, which helps push your back into your seat and your thighs against the tubes. Footbraces and foot cups give you a better grip on your kayak, let you transfer more power to your boat, and improve your control in whitewater.

THIGH STRAPS

Adjustable thigh straps should be tight enough to hold your legs in place, but loose enough to allow a quick exit if trouble arises. For most inflatable kayakers, this

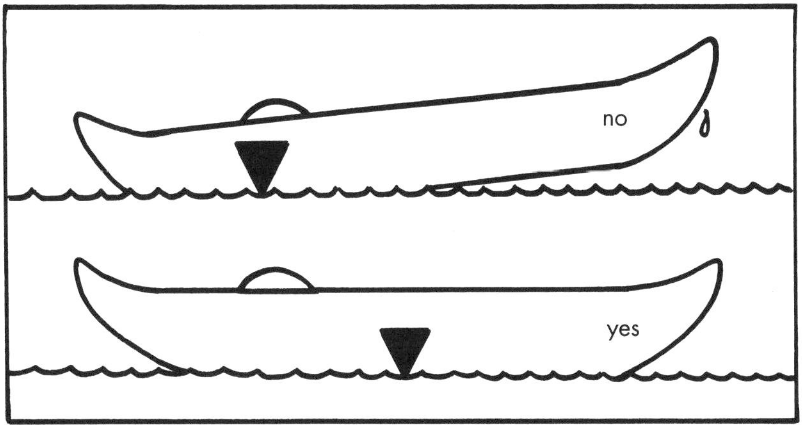

A kayak is trim when it is balanced over its centerpoint.

KNEELING

Not everybody sits in an inflatable kayak the way traditional kayakers do. In New Zealand and some parts of Europe and North America, kneeling is the preferred method of paddling. Kneelers praise their ability to see farther downriver, reach farther over the tubes, and use more of their torsos to execute powerful strokes.

means that the straps wrap around the inside of the inner thighs and the upper shins somewhere just below your knees. If the strap rests too low on your shins, or too close to your groin, the chance of getting stuck in the straps increases to dangerous levels!

Whether sitting or kneeling, the principles of fusing yourself with your kayak are the same: You want to have maximum contact with your kayak while being able to exit quickly in an emergency. Thigh straps can again be used to hold you in place, but kneeling demands a slightly different setup.

Some kneelers use thigh straps that anchor between their knees, extend over the top of their thighs, and

Some kayakers prefer to kneel rather than sit.

anchor on the side tubes or floor. (This is the same configuration used in many whitewater canoes.) When properly adjusted, the straps won't slide down over your knees or slide up into the crease between your thighs and hips. Toe blocks—which rest behind your toes and let you push yourself into the thigh straps—complete the system, and a quick-release system gives you a way out if you flip or wrap.

Other kneelers rely on customized cross-tubes or braces for outfitting their boats. In some craft, the tubes are built such that the thighs and toes rest against the tubes the same way they do with straps and toe blocks.

Stowing Gear

Your first trip in an inflatable kayak will be easiest if you leave all excess gear on the bank. The lighter your boat, the more maneuverable you'll be. However, you'll often want to carry a throw bag, first aid kit, or spare paddle with you. Learning how to properly store everything from cameras to lunch bags will help keep your kayak performing at its best.

There are three keys to stowing extra gear: Keep it away from your legs and feet, store it low in the kayak, and balance the weight fore and aft. Most kayakers strap gear to the floor in the stern. This works great if it doesn't unbalance your kayak because it keeps gear away from your body. But no matter what you do, use the shortest straps possible and don't let excess lines flop around the cockpit. Put the heaviest items close to the bottom of the kayak, with lighter items on top. If you store anything in the bow, make sure there's no way your feet can slide into the gear and become entangled. Finally, recheck your kayak's trim after you have stored your gear. It may be necessary to adjust the seat or the thwart a bit to get your kayak balanced again.

You never have to inflate sit-on-top kayaks! (Photo by Jill Radel, courtesy of Ocean Kayak, Inc., Ferndale, WA)

4

RIVER MORPHOLOGY

THE DYNAMICS OF RUNNING WATER

To the ordinary landlubber, whitewater rapids are a primal source of fascination. Flowing like unbridled liquid avalanches, rapids are breathtaking in their beauty and awe-inspiring in their power. But to an experienced river runner, rapids are predictable and orderly. Obstacles, constrictions, and changes in volume and gradient have definite and reliable effects on the river's surface. The seasoned paddler understands these effects intimately and can anticipate how currents and rapids will affect an inflatable kayak.

In this chapter we will disassemble and examine rivers. Rather than looking at the big river picture, we'll dissect rapids into tangible components, like pieces of a puzzle. Then, once we've gained an understanding of how the pieces work and fit together, we'll reassemble the puzzle and form complete rapids much like the ones you'll see on your next river trip.

A Look Beneath the Surface

WATER MECHANICS

Ask the average river runner how water moves and in what state, and he or she is likely to respond, "It moves

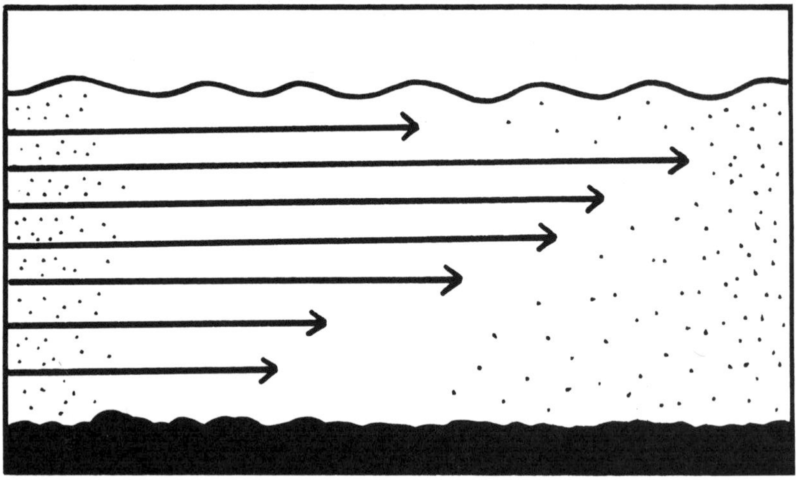

In this example of laminar currents, the longer arrows represent faster currents and appear just below the surface. The currents near the riverbed are slowed by friction.

downstream in West Virginia." Well, yeah, that's a correct response. But ask a hydrologist about water movements, and he'll mention three very different states: *laminar, turbulent,* and *chaotic.* Each state describes a different pattern of currents and appears at different places within the river system.

For many kayakers, *laminar flow* is the most comfortable type of current to experience, for it is the safest and most predictable. Laminar flows show up on smooth, straight riverbeds where, if we were to slice the river from bank to bank, we would find some distinct patterns. As the accompanying diagrams show, rivers have multiple sheets of water, each moving at a different speed. The small circles and long arrows represent the fastest-moving sheets and are located near the center of the river below the surface. Large circles and short arrows represent slower sheets, their downstream progress hampered by friction from the riverbed, banks, or air. Between each sheet there's a zone of mild shearing, better described as an interface between two laminar sheets moving quite independently and at different speeds.

To *feel* the differences between laminar sheets, let your kayak glide freely across the river surface. If you plant your paddle deep in the river, you will feel a forward tug. That tug is caused by subsurface laminar sheets moving forward faster than the sheets on the surface. If you've ever fallen out of your kayak in a big, powerful river, you may have experienced a *tunnel effect,* as if you were trapped inside a giant horizontal tube that wouldn't let you go. That is because the core of the river (just below the surface) is an independent laminar sheet totally separated from its surrounding sheets. Once you are in the tunnel, the shear zones hold you inside until your lifejacket finally propels you back toward the surface.

Turbulent flows arise wherever obstacles obstruct the current. An obstruction forces too much water into too little space, which in turn forces one laminar sheet into another. When this happens, the laminar sheets begin to break up, leaving smaller ribbons of current that seek their way independently through the neighboring currents.

In another example of laminar currents, the smaller circles represent the faster flows.

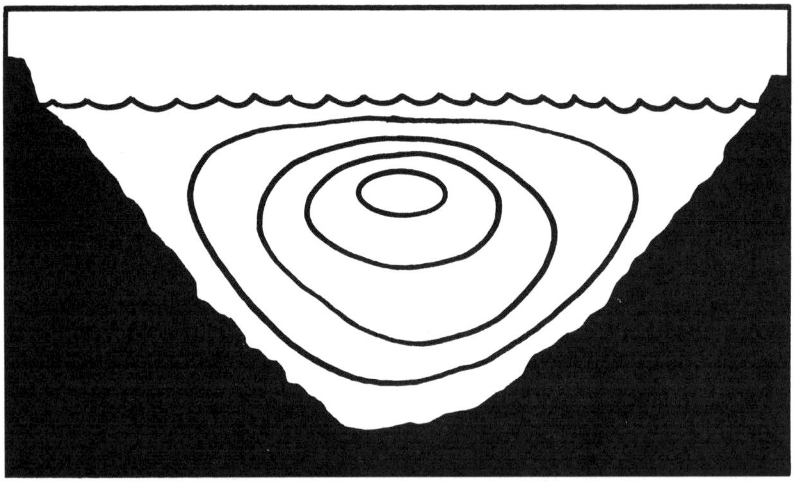

Kayakers should look for turbulence at places like chutes, where the independent ribbons slip free and create ripples or waves on the river surface. In another example, turbulence appears in eddies. Here, an obstacle compresses the laminar sheets together as they slip around the obstacle. Then the turbulent zone appears behind the rock where the laminar sheets break up. The zone of turbulence (the eddy) is separated from the passing laminar sheets (the main current) by an abrupt boundary kayakers call an *eddy line.*

As the main current slips past an obstacle, the straight lines (laminar currents) begin to shear off and rotate behind the obstacle (turbulent currents). In this case, the result is an eddy.

At the extreme end of water behavior patterns—just as with many kayakers' behavior patterns—there is *chaos*. Simply put, chaos is an utter state of confusion. The river's normal flow lines disintegrate and bounce around randomly. Interestingly, all of this commotion cancels itself out, leaving little real movement at all. Probably the best example of chaos is the ordinary hole (discussed in detail later in this chapter): At the base of a steep slide (like at the back of a rock or ledge) too little water tries to fill too large a space, and settles on trying to be everywhere at once . . . chaos. Though the water explodes randomly throughout the hole, the hole itself ends up being stationary.

Within any river, other universal patterns emerge. *Helical currents* flow outward from the bank along the surface until they collide with the main current. There they spiral downstream, dive, and work their way back toward the bank under the surface.

If you have ever swum a river before, you may have noticed that the last few feet to the shore seemed harder to swim than anywhere else. That's because the helical currents were pushing you away from the bank, out toward the center of the river.

In the main current you'll find *horizontal* and *vertical meanders*. In horizontal meanders, the main current weaves back and forth across the river trying to make one complete trip from one bank to the other and back again in a distance equal to 11 times the channel width.

Helical currents flow away from the bank on the surface, meet the main current, then dive. Next, the water works its way back to the bank, then rises along the shore to repeat the cycle.

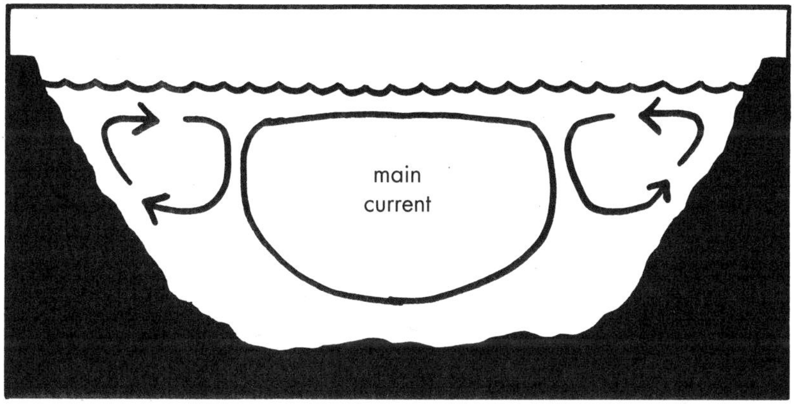

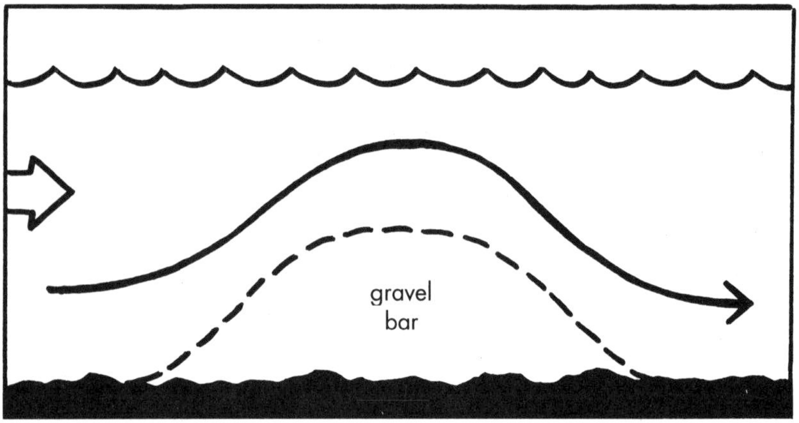

Vertical meanders rise and descend as the current flows downstream. Eventually, this action creates alternating shallow gravel bars and deep pools.

In vertical meanders, the main current climbs from deep pools to shallow riffles and back again at a downstream distance of 3 to 7 times the channel width.

Since meanders can be confusing, a couple of examples are in order. Let's start off with horizontal meanders. First, pick a bend in the river. Next, measure the river's width. Finally, multiply the river's width by 11. Now, if you proceed downstream that distance, you would theoretically find another bend in the river where the current completes a horizontal meander. For vertical meanders, measure the distance across the river at a pool, multiply by 3 to 7, float that distance downstream, and—*voilà*—another pool. (Now, before you go try out these experiments, I've got to add a caveat: Currents don't always get their way. Banks are constantly eroding and rerouting the main channel. So it's a constant battle between the hydrodynamics of water and the impediments of new boulders.)

So, what does all of this scientific mumbo jumbo mean for river runners? Well, each of these well-defined properties influences the shape and feel of rivers in ways that kayakers can see and understand. For example, the river's desire to follow its meander route causes it to lean against any bank that gets in its way. As the river continues to lean on that bank, the water's erosive power gradually carves out a new bend. Next, something different happens. Since water travels only in a linear course, the current piles up on the outside of the bend where it has to travel faster than the water on the inside of the bend to reach the same point downstream. At the same time, the outer flow hits the bank, dives toward the bottom, and creeps along the bottom toward the slower currents at the inside of the bend.

The net effect of all this activity is that the fast-moving water on the outside of the bend keeps acquiring erosive power, continues to gnaw at the outer bank, and slowly pulls part of the bank into the current itself. At the same time, the slow water along the inside of the bend loses its ability to support the eroded particulates and deposits them on shallow bars.

Horizontal meanders work back and forth across the river, continually pressing against the outside bank. Left to its own accord, the meander will erode the outside bank until the riverbed takes on the same shape as the meander.

If the process continues, deeply undercut cliffs, exposed roots, and overhanging trees begin to appear along the outside of the bend, while the inside bend becomes increasingly shallow and waterless.

River Characteristics

Outwardly rivers display a broad range of emotions—at times calm and soothing, at other times angry and riotous. But inwardly, rivers are lazy by nature. Water can be compared to a train running along a track. It just keeps rolling in the same direction unless something comes along and knocks it off course. Water, just like trains, follows a path of least resistance as it is pulled downhill by its natural engine, gravity. So, then, why do rivers and rapids look so different from one another?

There is much more to whitewater rivers than water's natural tendency to follow a course of least resistance. Obstacles clutter river channels, riverbeds descend at different rates, and water levels fluctuate with seasonal rains, snowmelt, or droughts. In the end, three factors have a profound effect on the intensity and character of whitewater rivers: *volume, gradient,* and *changes in river structure.*

VOLUME

River volume is measured in cubic units per second. In the United States, the foot is used for the cubic unit, and the correct term is *cubic feet per second,* or *cfs.* In metric countries, the meter is used in place of the foot, so river volumes are measured in *cubic meters per second,* or *cms.* Simply stated, cfs and cms measure the amount of water that passes a specific point each second. However, the proper formula is the river's width, times its depth, times the current's velocity. For example, a river 20 feet wide by 10 feet deep, with a current flowing 5 miles per hour, has a flow of 1,000 cubic feet per second (10 x 20 x 5 mph = 1,000 cfs). Using this basic formula, you can see that the addition of more water—say from a recent rain or a tributary—to the same 10-by-20-foot river increases the speed of the current dramatically. For example, double the flow of the river, making it 2,000 cfs instead of 1,000 cfs. Since the river's depth and width haven't changed, the additional water must move *twice as fast* to make the formula work: instead of 5 miles per hour, the velocity jumps to 10 miles per hour (20 x 10 x 10 mph = 2,000 cfs).

Changes in volume or river velocity have some important effects that kayakers need to understand. Since water is *heavy*—weighing 8.33 pounds per gallon, or 62.4 pounds per cubic foot—the addition of a few cfs or an increase in river velocity causes a big change in the amount of force that water exerts on a kayak or a swimmer.

Let's look at this by going back to the cubic foot of water. Instead of using just 1 cubic foot of water, slice a long rod of water out of the river 1 foot wide by 1 foot high. Now, make that rod the same length as the river's flow in cfs. For example, if the river is flowing at 1,000 cfs, make the rod 1 square foot wide by 1,000 feet long. The weight of that long pillar of water flowing past a designated point in the river doesn't have a force of just 62.4 pounds; it is backed by the force of 1,000 cubes of water, or *62,400 pounds!* Fortunately, the fluid properties of water let much of that force slide around a kayak, rock, or body unnoticed. However, a kayak held in place against the main current—for example, during a wrap—can prove just how powerful and heavy the river really is. The wrapped kayak is held tight by thousands of pounds of pressure, making it very difficult to remove.

Up until now, we've assumed that rivers move downstream at a constant rate of speed. However, as you will soon discover, rivers flow upstream in places and at differing speeds within the same section of river. In an eddy, reverse currents can flow upstream toward an obstacle just as fast as the main current flows downstream. When the two currents slide by each other, powerful *rotational* or *twisting* forces are created. Kayakers caught on the interface between the currents have to fight the current's desire to spin their kayak wildly. Rotational forces are also found where fast and slow currents meet. As the faster currents pass the slower currents, friction pulls pieces of both currents free and causes them to rotate. The interface between the two currents is not as dramatic as those found in eddies, but is still enough to spin your kayak around unless you fight to keep it straight.

MORE ON VELOCITY

A change in velocity—whether from an increase in gradient, a narrowing of the river, or an increase in flow—changes the river's force dramatically. It works like this: For every doubling of the current's velocity, the force exerted by the water quadruples. This added force can exert itself on anything in the water's path, or can be used to support debris suspended in the river's current. (That is why flooded rivers can lift and displace giant boulders or transport giant logs like overgrown corks.)

RIVER SIZE

Without even looking at a river up close, kayakers can get some idea how *big* a river is by looking at its average flow. In a very general sense, rivers can be categorized as small, medium, or large. Small rivers can range from a few hundred cfs up to about 1,000 cfs, medium-sized rivers from 1,000 to 6,000 cfs, and some large rivers can exceed 100,000 cfs! Still, this type of description is pretty subjective. One kayaker's *small* may be another kayaker's *big* depending on the point of view. Also, rivers grow and shrink in size and power with seasonal water fluctuations or dam releases.

GAUGES

Many governmental agencies monitor river flows. In turn, kayakers can obtain water level information by contacting whichever agency monitors the rivers they plan to run. If you're not quite sure which agency to call, check out the guidebooks at your local paddle shop—many books list the phone numbers to call for each river they describe.

One problem I've run into with gauges is that many agencies monitor water levels on a *gauge-height* basis. Rather than simply announcing the flow in cfs or cms, the recording will give you a gauge height in feet or meters. All this information tells you is how high a river has climbed up an oversized ruler placed in the river at a set location. To use this information you'll have to know the river intimately or else ask someone to correlate the gauge height with river flow. Again, many of the guidebooks explain how to do this. If that doesn't work, the agencies themselves usually maintain a correlation table.

FLOW VERSUS DIFFICULTY

Trying to correlate changes in water volume with the river's difficulty rating is nearly impossible. On most rivers, rapids become more difficult as water levels rise, although rapids disappear beneath gentle blankets of swift water on other rivers. Nonetheless, kayakers should remember that larger volumes and faster currents bolster the river's power and can turn gentle rivers into powerful hazards.

GRADIENT

In North America, gradient is described in *feet per mile* (fpm) or *meters per kilometer* (mpk). Both ratings

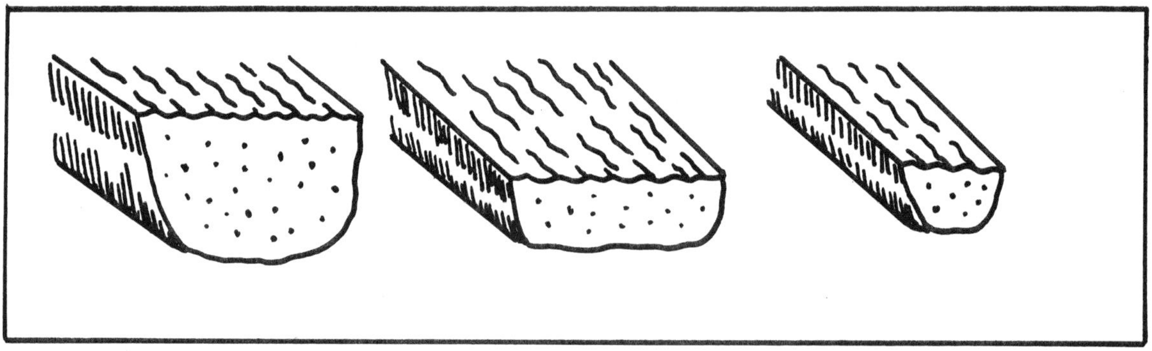

This diagram shows three cross sections of one river at different places. The section on the left is broad, deep, and slow. The center section is the same width, but shallower, forcing the current to move faster. Finally, the section on the right is both shallow and narrow—that water must flow the fastest.

measure a river's average descent over a given distance.

To figure out a river's gradient you will first need to know three things: the elevation at the put-in, the elevation at the take-out, and the distance between the two points. Here's an example of how these numbers work: If the put-in is at an elevation of 3,000 feet and the take-out is at 1,200 feet, the river drops 1,800 feet in that section. Now, if the section to be kayaked is 36 miles long, the river drops 50 feet per mile (1,800 ÷ 36 = 50). Here's the formula: (put-in elevation take-out elevation) miles = gradient.

Rapids appear where the gradient of one section of river exceeds the river's average gradient, and pools form where the gradient dips below the overall average. So if a river descends evenly over its entire length, the rapids might be long and constant. But if the river alternates between pools and drops, the rapids might be short but intense. The most severe example of a pool-drop river would be one that descends very little in its placid stretches, then plunges violently over giant waterfalls.

As with the other descriptive factors, gradient gives you some clues about the character of a river. Most whitewater rivers have an average gradient of 10 to 100 feet per mile. However, it is becoming quite common to see kayakers boating rivers with gradients upward of 200 feet per mile. Still, one rule of thumb should be kept in mind, especially when exploring new rivers: The steeper the river, the more difficult the whitewater.

Surface Features

River structures are seldom uniform. Riverbeds descend more steeply in some places than in others, cliffs narrow and confine channels, and obstacles clutter and obstruct the main current. Each of these structural changes has profound effects on the river, some of which we have already discussed: If the same amount of water is forced into a smaller space (e.g., between two cliffs), its velocity will increase dramatically; if the main current descends down a steep slide, the gentle laminar currents will gradually give way to turbulence or chaos; and if the river travels around a bend, the currents along the outer banks will move faster than those found along the inside of the bend.

Since kayakers like to spend most of their time above the river's surface (after all, a majority of kayakers rate their whitewater success in terms of avoiding submarine adventures and close encounters with aquatic creatures), it is the surface effects of changes in river structure that we are most interested in. So let's step away from the river, scramble to a point high upon the bank, and start looking at the river's surface features.

Let's begin with a calm, straight river—one that flows freely over an unobstructed channel. Then let's make some changes. As obstacles enter the current, rapids begin to appear. Here you'll find chutes, waves, holes, and eddies . . . the things river runners call *fun*—at least if they're not too large or too dangerous.

TONGUES

At the top of many rapids, the main current enters a slick, smooth-surfaced ramp called a *tongue*. Tongues are typically V-shaped, with the tip of the V pointing downstream. These *downstream tongues* form between rocks, cliffs, or shallows, and point out the deepest, least-obstructed channel. There may be just one large tongue, or there may be many tongues of different sizes. When there's more than one tongue—as when there are large boulders or islands dividing the river into many channels—the safest and deepest tongue will usually be either the largest tongue or the one that begins dropping soonest. (The reason for this is that channels that wait longer before they begin to drop lose water to deeper channels. So by the time the smaller channel reaches the base of a rapid, it may consist of boulder fans barely wet enough to float a kayak.)

The second type of V is the *upstream V*, which has the tip of the V pointing upstream. Upstream Vs are shockwaves created by obstacles that pierce or lurk just beneath the surface. Unlike tongues, the upstream V is a warning sign—a signal to kayakers to steer clear or else risk damaging their boats on the partially submerged obstacle.

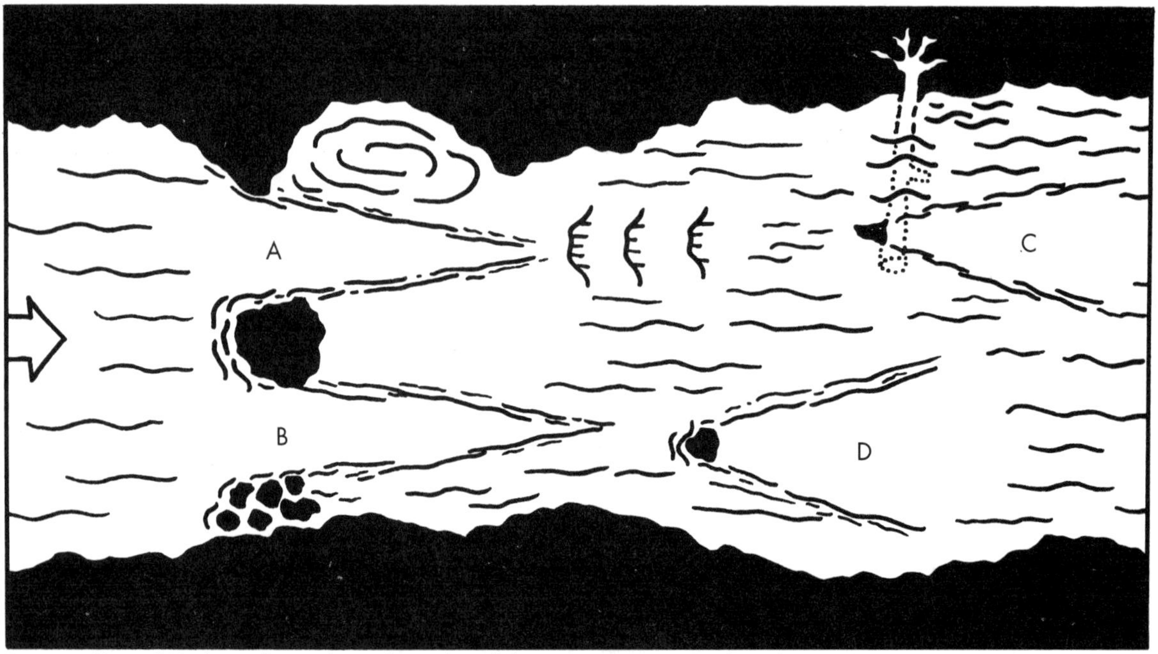

Tongues (A and B) show deep, clear channels, while upstream Vs (C and D) show subsurface hazards. Kayakers should stay on the tongues and avoid the upstream Vs.

STANDING WAVES

Standing waves are one of the most fascinating and entertaining of all river features. From the small erratic riffles of your local creek to the giant haystacks of large-volume rivers, standing waves provide kayakers with the ultimate aquatic roller coaster ride.

No discussion of river waves would be complete without some comparison to *ocean waves*. Although ocean and river waves may look remarkably similar, there are some distinct differences. First, river waves are stationary and remain at the same location as the forces or obstacles that form them. Ocean waves, on the other hand, travel toward shore, where they dissipate or crash as they roll up the beach. Second, water travels through river waves, releasing its energy as it goes, while the water inside ocean waves hardly moves at all. Instead, the water inside an ocean wave transfers its energy as the wave rolls toward the beach.

WHAT FORMS A STANDING WAVE?

Many things form waves: subsurface boulders, changes in gradient, converging currents. But most standing waves are created from a change in water speed. Since water can't be compressed like air, it moves faster when it is confined by narrow streambeds or obstacles. In fact, water gains speed whenever it: (1) is squeezed *horizontally* between banks or boulders, (2) is compressed *vertically* over rocks or river bottom, or (3) falls down a steeper section of riverbed. Standing waves are associated with all three changes in water velocity.

The most common standing waves are those that form at the bottom of downward-sloping riverbeds. Here, the potential energy stored in fast, downward-moving water dissipates gradually when it hits the bottom of the slope. In the most basic example of a sloping riverbed, there are no obstacles to interfere with the formation of standing waves. As the river reaches the end of the slope, a series of waves—a *wave train*—forms, with each wave lining up perpendicular to the main current. The first wave in the train is usually the largest, and each successive wave diminishes in size. (*Tail waves*—another name used to describe standing waves—are wave trains that begin at the base of a rapid.)

Standing waves also appear after cliffs, shallow gravel bars, boulder piles, or other obstacles force a broad river into a narrow channel. Since the river has less space to occupy, it is forced to travel faster. The moment the channel reopens, the energy stored in the fast-moving water dissipates in the form of standing waves.

Submarine boulders or ledges can also form standing waves. The current picks up energy as it travels faster over the top of the obstacle, then releases it downstream in a series of waves. A hump or cushion—not a standing wave—forms above the obstacle, followed by standing waves downstream. Since waves formed by rocks and boulders frequently stand alone, their solitary presence foretells the obstacle beneath the surface.

Still another cause of standing waves is converging currents. *Convergence waves* often form where two

Standing waves form when the current slows down at the base of a sloping riverbed.

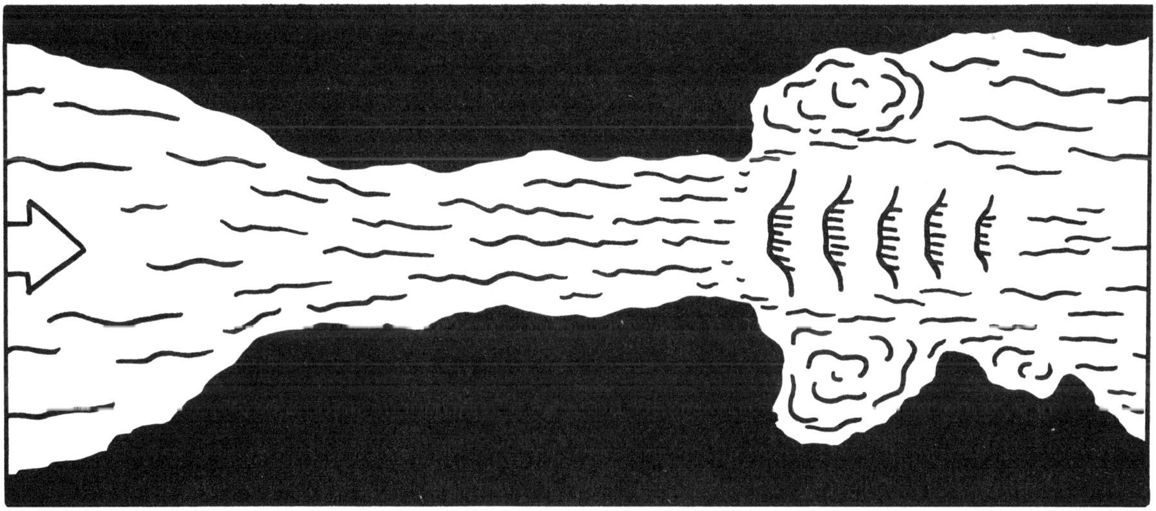

Standing waves form where the fast current of a chute meets the slower-moving water below.

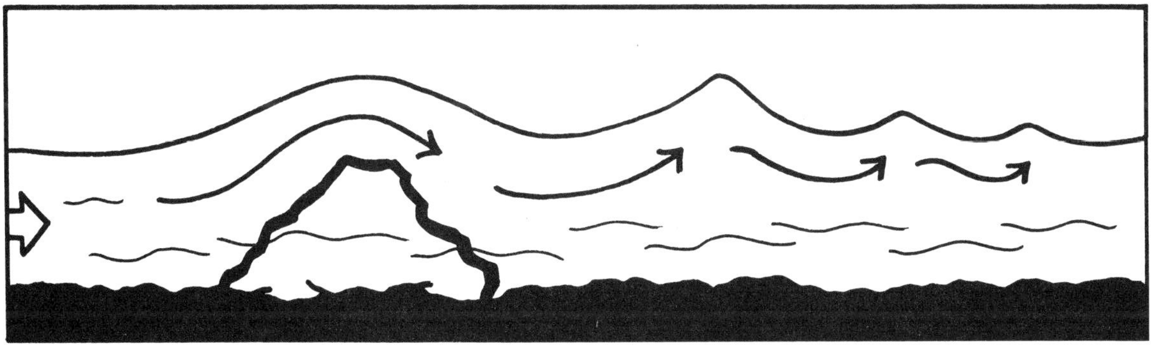

Standing wave forming after a boulder.

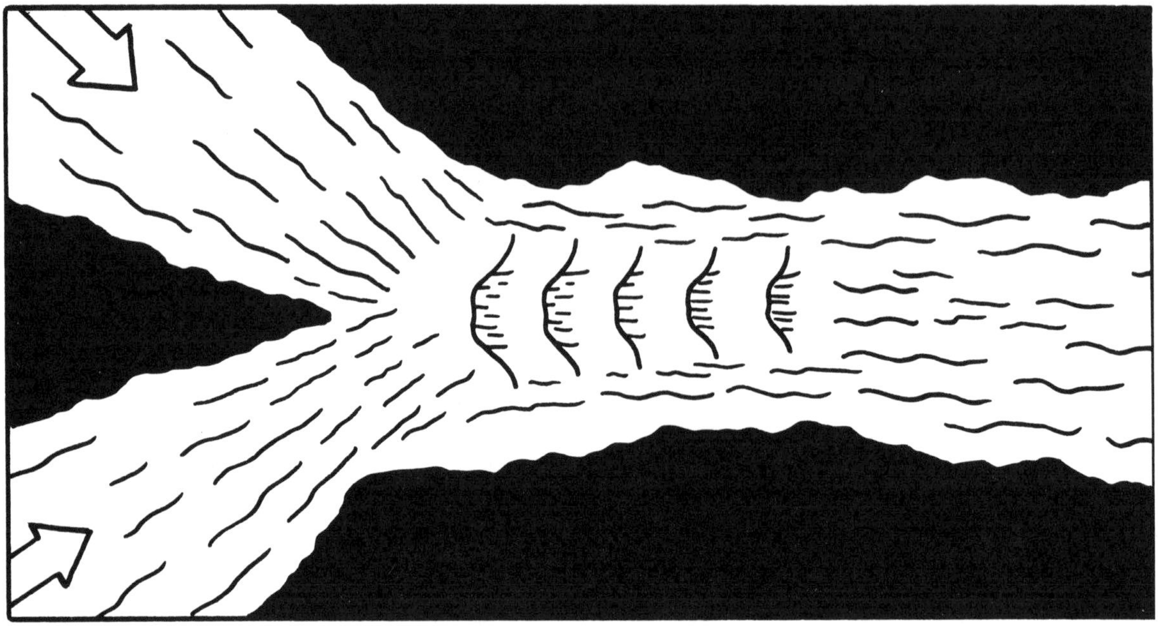

Convergence waves forming where two currents meet.

channels meet, or where a tributary spills its current into the mainstream. Water piles up and gathers energy at the convergence, then releases the excess energy gradually in the form of standing waves. If the cause of the convergence is a deflection of the main current back upon itself by cliffs or steep banks, the waves that bounce off the cliffs are sometimes called *reflection waves*.

DIAGONAL WAVES

When a submerged ledge or boulder cuts diagonally across the main channel, surface waves won't line up perpendicular to the main current. Instead, the first wave or two below the ledge will lunge upward at an angle to the main current, forming *diagonal* or *lateral* waves. Diagonal waves also appear wherever submerged boulders, converging currents, and constricted channels deflect waves at an angle to the main current. No matter what forms the diagonal waves, the waves following the first few diagonal waves realign themselves with the main current just as any other standing wave does.

HAYSTACKS

Haystacks are the mountain peaks of the riverscape. Although they look like towering, peaked standing waves, they're actually formed from converging standing waves, each contributing its energy to force the haystack higher than its surroundings. With all of this energy packed into one wall of water, haystacks are rarely stable—they tend to dance around on the river's surface and surge randomly.

BREAKING WAVES AND STOPPERS

When a wave becomes too large to support its own weight and shape, it starts spilling the highest water down the wave's upstream face. Whether they're called *curlers, curling waves, breaking waves,* or *reversals,* these waves can be very powerful. If enough water is falling down the upstream face, it can carry sufficient force to stop and flip your kayak—hence the name *stopper.*

PILLOWS

When the current collides with an obstacle, some of the current flows vertically on the obstacle's upstream side and forms a mound of water called a *cushion* or *pillow.* These mounds stand higher than the surrounding river and disclose the presence of boulders and other obstacles. As pillows grow, they eventually become too large to support their own weight. When that happens, the

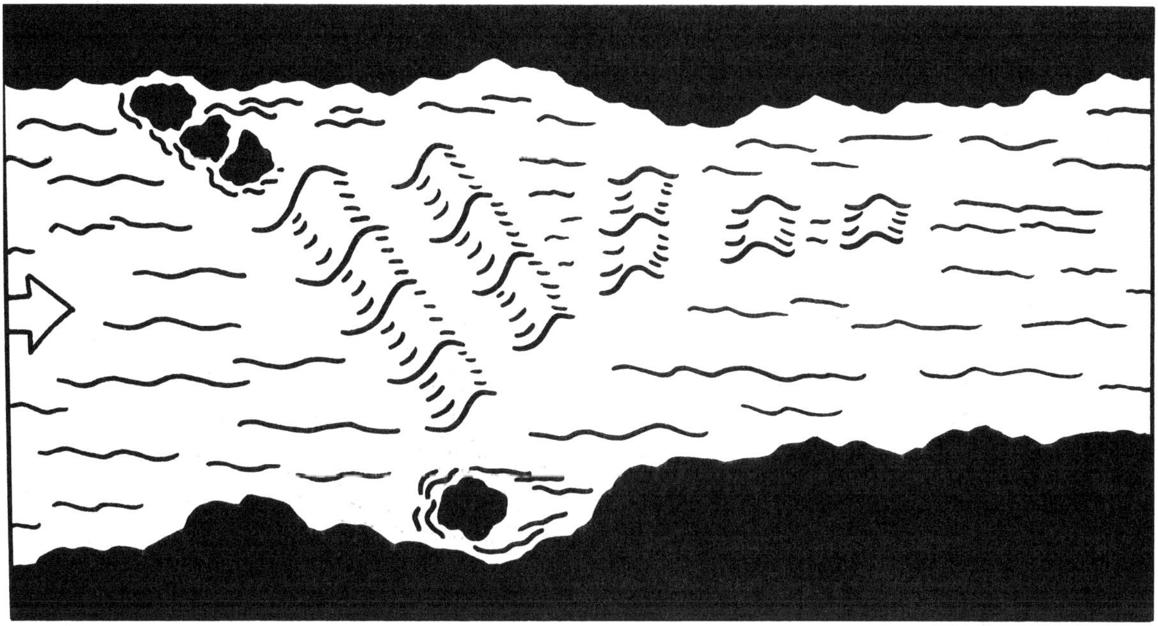

Diagonal waves forming after a submerged diagonal ledge. After the first couple of waves, the tail waves realign themselves perpendicular with the current.

highest water spills down the upstream face, creating a hydraulic much like a breaking wave.

A pillow—or, rather, the lack of a pillow—also reveals a major river hazard: *undercuts*. To spot an undercut from your kayak, watch the river. Whenever the current collides with an obstacle without forming a pillow, beware! It is a certain indication that the obstacle is undercut and that the current is diving under the obstacle—just where you don't want to be! Since powerful currents can carry kayaks and swimmers beneath undercut ledges, banks, and boulders, undercuts are to be treated as some of the biggest hazards to be found on whitewater rivers.

When a standing wave becomes too large to support its own weight, the crest spills down the wave's upstream face and forms a breaking wave. This kayaker is passing just to the right of a breaking wave.

ROOSTER TAILS

Rooster tails are pillows gone berserk. Like pillows, rooster

Pillows form where the current collides with the upstream side of an obstacle. The current rises upward on the obstacle, forming a cushion, then settles back down as it slips around the side of the obstacle.

tails form when a fast current piles into the upstream side of a rock or boulder. However, rather than building smoothly upon the shoulder of the rock, the rock slices through the current and deflects water into the air, creating an aerial fountain in the shape of a rooster's tail.

There are two types: *upstream* and *downstream rooster tails.* Upstream-angled rooster tails form when the rock is tilted upstream, and are identified by the fan of water deflecting through the air in an upstream direction. Downstream rooster tails are caused by downstream-tilted rocks and fan water through the air in a downstream direction.

Kayakers should avoid any kind of rooster tail since the exposed rock and fast-moving currents can combine to tear or wrap the kayak in an instant.

Kayakers should steer clear of undercuts, like the large slab rock shown at the bottom of this photograph.

BOILS

Boils are upwellings in the river current caused by things like underwater boulders, undercut ledges, and converging currents. They cause the river surface to roll and surge like a giant boiling pot of water.

HOLES

When water pours over a rock or ledge, the water plunges down a *falls* toward the riverbed, then flows downstream along the bottom of the river. A deep cavity appears in the river surface just downstream of the falls. In an effort to fill this cavity, the river grabs surface water from downstream and pours it in a reverse direction back into the cavity. (This zone of upstream currents is called the *backwash.*) Viewed from the side, the hole's currents rotate like a wheel, with the surface rolling upstream and the bottom rolling downstream. This rotating liquid vortex goes by many names, including *hole, reversal, souse hole,* and *stopper.*

Holes, like waves, come in all shapes and sizes. Large

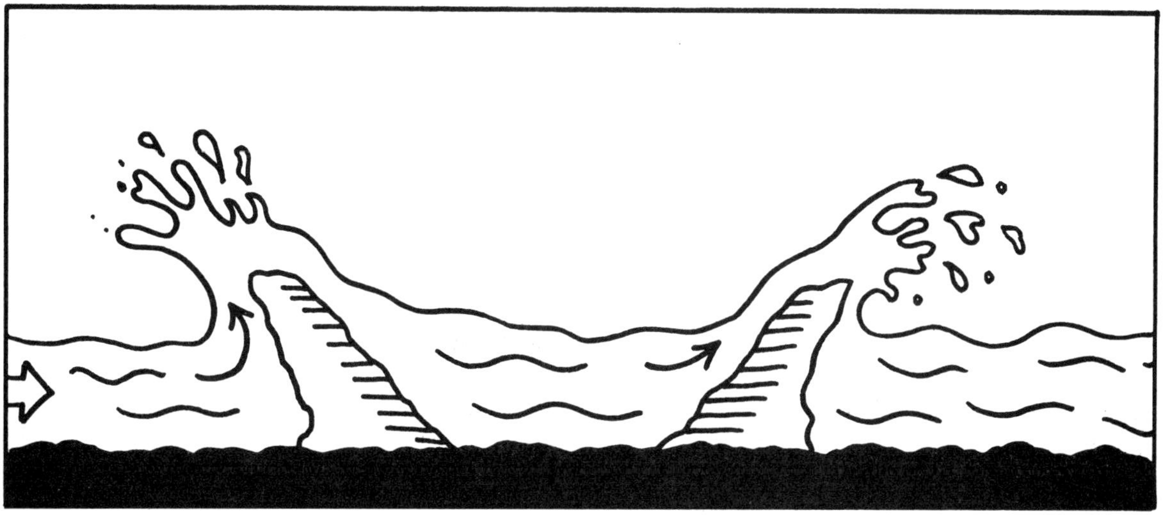

The upstream rooster tail (left) and the downstream rooster tail (right) pose serious hazards to kayakers and should be avoided.

holes—sometimes called *keepers*—can hold and flip a kayak with ease; small holes can be crashed or avoided. Getting to know the difference between friendly and unfriendly holes is one of the most important skills any kayaker can have. Fortunately, there are five factors that reveal the intensity of a hole: (1) the *height, angle,* and *volume* of the falls, (2) the *shape* of the hole, (3) the *width* of the hole, (4) the hole's *depth,* and (5) the *length of the backwash.* These factors mix and match in countless ways, but understanding how they work together will reveal a lot about a particular hole. Let's start by looking at the falls.

A hole: The water falling over the ledge escapes downstream along the riverbed, while the water at the surface flows upstream to fill in the cavity. If the hole is large enough, kayaks and swimmers can actually get caught in this vortex.

Water plunges downward at the upstream side of a hole. Generally, the steeper and taller this *falls,* the more severe the hole. In vertical falls—often called *pourovers*—water plummets toward the bottom of the river and can create a deep hole with a small pocket of violently opposing currents, especially if the pourover is more than a few feet high. Sloping falls, on the other hand, can create long zones of backwash—a perilous hazard for kayakers.

Falls with a lot of water usually create stronger holes than low-volume falls do. In a tight, constricted channel, the whole river might plunge over a sharp ledge. This can create a nearly impenetrable hole that can easily trap and hold kayakers. On the other hand, a small boulder in the middle of a broad stream might create only a small hole—one barely noticeable or just big enough to splash your crew. In any case, the addition of more water to the falls generally makes for a more powerful hole.

There are four different shapes that can describe almost any hole: *smiling, frowning, horizontal,* and *diagonal.* Each shape describes the hole's appearance from an imaginary perspective upstream. In a smiling hole, the middle of the hole is the farthest upstream, while the hole's outer edges curl downstream and away from you. This lets some of the current—and anything floating on it—escape laterally out of the hole. Because of this, smiling holes are the safest holes to run. If the outer edges curl back at you, the hole is frowning. Frowning holes focus much of the current's energy toward the middle of the hole, creating a powerful magnet for anything stuck in its grasp. For kayakers, this can spell disaster. Large frowning holes can make lateral escapes nearly impossible, and can hold kayaks and swimmers indefinitely.

Horizontal holes show up in two places: at the base of an artificial dam and at the base of riverwide ledges. If the volume of water flowing over the ledge is even all the way across the river, the resulting hole forms a foreboding bank-to-bank obstacle for kayakers. Like frowning holes, these types of holes can be powerful and dangerous, making escape very difficult.

The final type of hole—a diagonal hole—appears wherever an obstacle or ledge cuts across the channel at an angle to the current. Diagonal holes have one side farther upstream than the other and contain a current that slides downstream across the face of the hole. If a kayak moves to the downstream end of the hole, it will eventually slip free of the hole and back into the main current—hopefully upright.

Hole width and *hole depth* are the next factors that indicate the strength and danger of any hole. Hole width is measured perpendicularly across the current. Wide holes are much more difficult to exit than are narrow holes and should usually be avoided. Hole depth describes how far beneath the surface the recirculating current extends and is determined by the speed and volume of the falls. In deep holes, the falls forces water all the way down to the riverbed. From there, the current climbs back toward the surface and repeats the cycle without letting much water escape. On large-volume rivers, a kayaker trapped in a hole's grasp could be in real trouble. Not only can the downward current behind the rock slam swimmers against the river bottom, there is only a narrow zone of escape

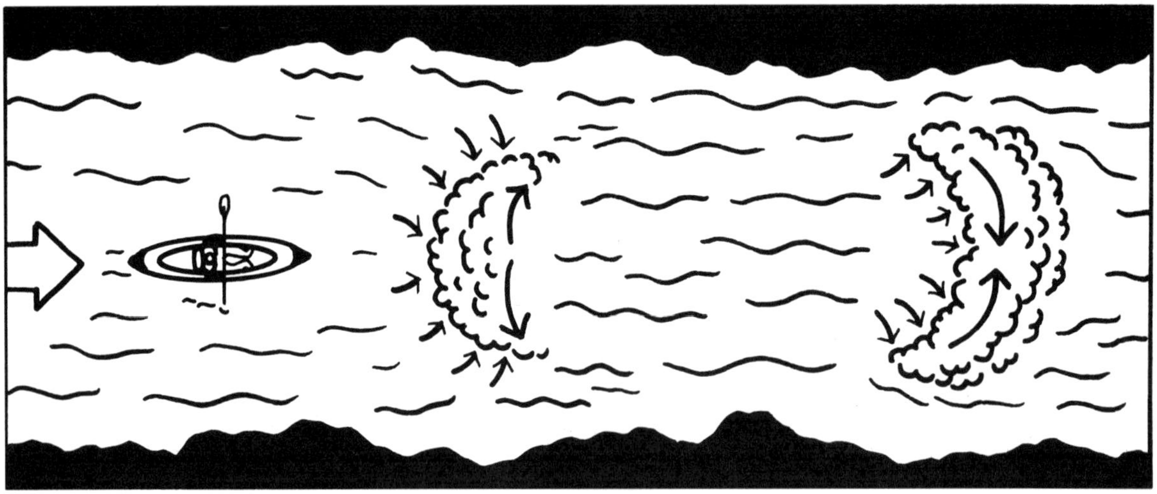

A smiling hole (left) and a frowning hole (right). The surface current in the smiling hole kicks outward and provides an escape route for kayaks, but the frowning hole's surface current kicks inward, creating a powerful trap.

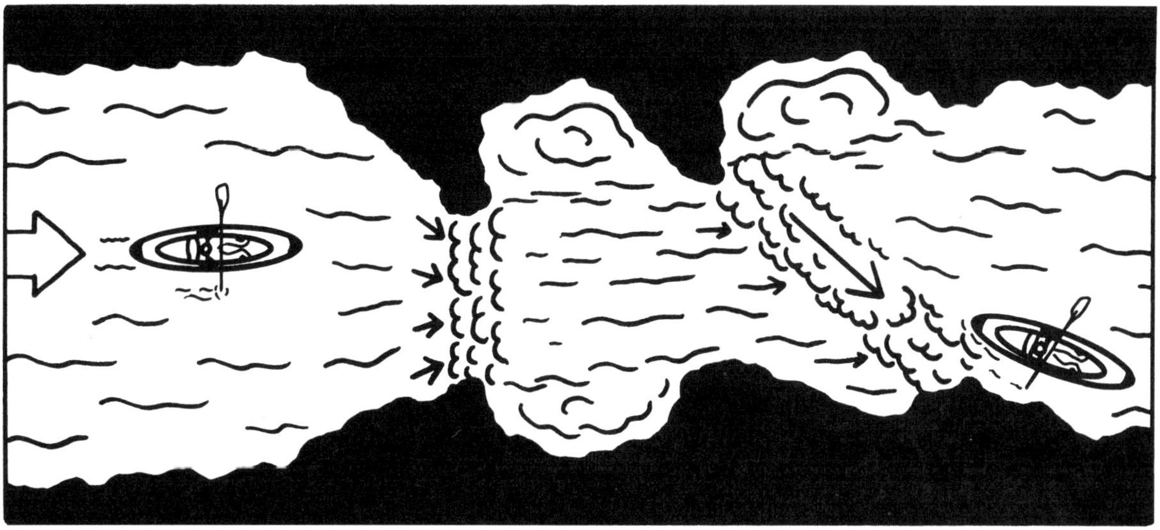

A riverwide horizontal hole (left) and a diagonal hole (right). The horizontal hole has no escape route and can trap a kayak. The diagonal hole, on the other hand, has a surface current that kicks from the top of the diagram to the bottom. A kayak caught in the diagonal hole will eventually wash up on the right (lower) bank.

directly on the bottom of the river.

Shallower holes don't extend all the way to the bottom of the river and are usually much safer for kayakers, all other factors being equal. Since the hole's rotating currents reach only partway to the riverbed, swimmers can easily swim out from under the upstream currents by utilizing the free-flowing downstream current.

BACKWASH

The term *backwash* describes the zone of upstream current that forms downstream of a hole. In some holes, an object floating on the surface 20 or more feet downstream of the falls can travel back upstream on the backwash, only to find itself caught in the swirling maelstrom yet another time. Kayakers can follow an easy rule of thumb: The longer the backwash, the more difficult and dangerous the hole.

SPOTTING HOLES

Holes can appear anywhere a ledge or boulder lurks beneath the surface. But since the river plunges over the obstacles, the hole itself might be hard to see from upstream. Still, there are signposts that reveal the hole's presence to observant kayakers. In a rapid, look for the calm, smooth hump that forms as the water stays level when passing over a submerged rock. If you can see beyond the hump, look slightly downstream for the foamy backwash. Gradually you will get better at spotting holes, and eventually you'll be able to discern fun, runnable holes from hazardous holes just by looking at them from upstream.

LOWHEAD DAMS AND WEIRS

Lowhead dams and weirs include a variety of artificial structures. Many lowhead dams were originally designed to divert water into grain mills or irrigation networks. Now they are built for such purposes as flood control and power generation.

Fabricated from cement, asphalt, rebar, and riprap, most lowhead dams are installed straight across the river channel, with walls rising out of either end of the dam. As the water drops over the top of the dam, it slides down a smooth face and spills onto a flat or angled apron. Then, as the water plummets into the pool below the dam, the currents form *incredibly dangerous* holes.

Holes below lowhead dams can extend all the way across the river, are very straight, display a lot of power, and have a long zone of backwash. Any one of these

In this shallow hole, the downward current extends only partway to the river bottom and allows easy escape under the backwash. In deep holes—especially those in which the falls plunges all the way to the riverbed—escape is much more difficult.

To spot holes from upstream, look for a smooth hump in the river's surface or for the backwash that forms at the base of the hole. Both can be seen in this photograph.

Lowhead dams and weirs contain killer holes with powerful backwashes. Don't run them!

factors could create a very dangerous hole in its own right. But when combined, they form one of the most hazardous obstacles known to whitewater enthusiasts. In fact, a great number of river-related fatalities are due to lowhead dams. For kayakers, I've got only two words of advice: Steer clear! Even runnable-looking lowhead dams contain dangerous currents, and many contain nasty piles of submerged rebar, trapped logs, and construction debris.

When you're on the river, watch for artificial structures and smooth, riverwide horizon lines. These signs can tell you that a dam is coming up and that it is time to pull to the bank!

WATERFALLS

When holes get too big for their britches, we call them waterfalls. To me, waterfalls include pourovers, slides, or any type of drop that's high and steep enough to make me think twice before I kayak it. In many ways, waterfalls are no different than holes. Each waterfall has a downward-plunging current and a zone of backwash and can be any of a number of shapes or sizes. Accordingly, everything we just learned about holes applies to waterfalls.

Waterfalls can be detected from upstream by their distinctive horizon lines. When you first start kayaking, keep a keen eye downstream. If the river seems to disappear suddenly without going around a bend, pull over and walk downstream. It may be simply that the gradient has increased, or it could be that the river is about to plunge over a waterfall. As you start to discern the differences between rapids and falls, things like nearby trees, large boulders, or even the sound of the water will give you clues as to whether the river is about to pour over a dangerous waterfall.

EDDIES

I've waited until the end of this chapter to discuss eddies for two reasons: First, eddies combine almost everything mentioned so far about currents and river

Poised at the lip of a big, vertical waterfall.

features. They have oppositional currents, appear behind obstacles, and contain both laminar and turbulent currents. Second, eddies are the most important hydraulic formations for kayakers to know and understand. They provide gentle parking zones for loading and unloading kayaks, safe havens for scouting or resting before the next drop, and can even make cross-river maneuvers easier.

Eddies are found behind any obstacle that deflects the main current—boulders, bank protrusions, even bridge abutments and logs. No matter what the obstacle is, it has the same effect: When the main current collides with the upstream face of the obstacle, it works its way around the obstacle and accelerates. This leaves a depressed zone of low pressure behind the obstacle. Water from downstream actually flows *upstream* toward the obstacle to fill the gap, creating a pocket of current moving in the opposite direction to the main current.

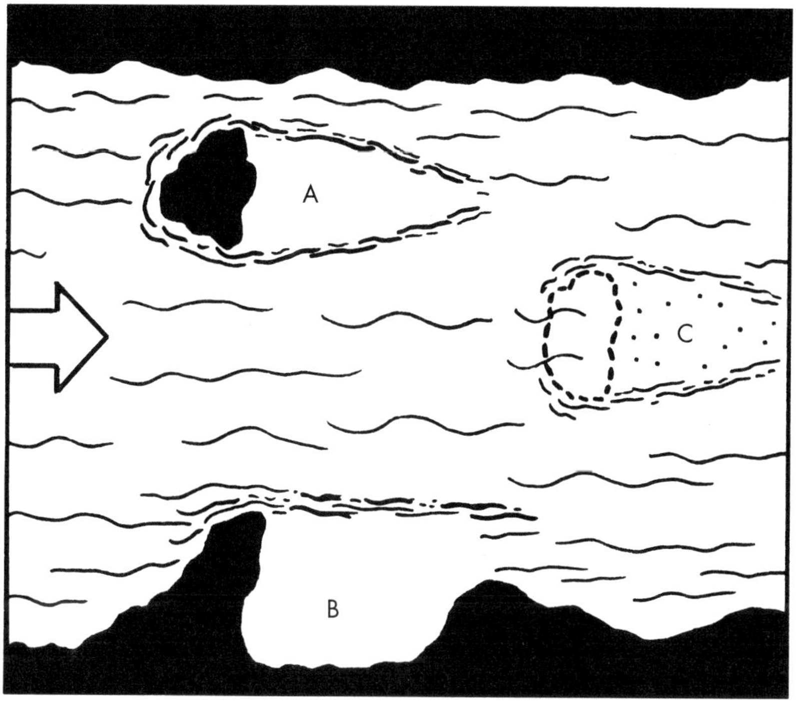

Solid green eddies form behind an exposed midstream boulder (A) and a peninsula (B). An aerated white eddy forms behind a partially submerged boulder (C).

A feature called an *eddy line* marks the narrow divide between the oppositional currents of the eddy and the main current. Here, the currents of the eddy and the main channel mix and swirl. On powerful, large-volume rivers, the eddy and the main current might rise to two different levels, causing the currents of the eddy and the main channel to wrestle violently along the transition zone. When there is a visible wall of water blocking the entrance to or the exit from the eddy, kayakers call the eddy line an *eddy fence*.

Two factors affect the intensity of an eddy: (1) the size and shape of the obstacle, and (2) the velocity of the current. If the obstacle has chiseled, well-defined edges, it will sever swift currents sharply from the eddy, creating a crisp eddy line and stable eddies. On the other hand, rounded obstacles and slow currents allow the currents to mix, weakening the eddy and melting the eddy lines. Shallow obstacles can create eddies even if they don't pierce the river's surface. As the river slides over the top of the obstacle, it loses its momentum and swirls in an aerated pocket. The foamy eddy that is formed behind the obstacle is called a *white eddy*, and the more solid eddies are called *green eddies*. The last type of eddy contains powerful, vertical boiling currents. For lack of a better term, call these *boiling eddies*.

The Big Picture

The thing that makes kayaking so exciting is that no two rapids are alike. The river features we've discussed in this chapter not only vary in size and intensity from river to river, they mix and match in myriad combinations. Some rivers might contain a long series of gentle waves interspersed with calm pools, others might display steep boulder gardens punctuated by steep holes, and still others might have giant haystacks bordered by vicious eddy fences.

As you move from one river to another, the same

distinctive hydraulics will be found again and again, and their distinguishing characteristics will become comfortable and familiar. You'll soon associate solitary waves or pillows with submarine boulders, strange water fountains with surface-piercing rocks, and smooth humps of water or foaming backwash with holes. Eventually, each feature will direct you to safer channels or forewarn you that any attempt at running some rapids is at your own risk.

Rating the Rapids

Kayakers use two universal systems to classify the difficulty and intensity of rapids. The most popular system in the world is the *International Scale of River Difficulty*, which grades rapids on a scale of I to VI. In the southwestern United States, another system, known as the *Deseret Scale* or *Grand Canyon System,* is sometimes used. This system rates rapids on a scale of 1 to 10. Unfortunately, neither system is perfect. Rapids change constantly, and are affected by water level fluctuations and shifts in the riverbed. Kayakers might rate rapids differently depending on their attitudes or skill levels. Also, the pursuit of more difficult whitewater has resulted in a downgrading of many rapids. Rapids once considered Class VI (extreme) have been downscaled to Class V after many successful descents. So river classifications are little more than a starting point for finding out about any river. You should gather as much additional information about rapids as you can.

THE AWA RIVER RATING SCALE

The American Whitewater Affiliation has published the leading version of the International Scale of River Difficulty. Here it is:

This is the American version of a rating system used to compare river difficulty throughout the world. This system is not exact; rivers do not always fit easily into one category, and regional or individual interpretations may cause misunderstandings. It is no substitute for a guidebook or accurate first-hand descriptions of a run.

Paddlers attempting difficult runs in an unfamiliar area should act cautiously until they get a feel for the way the scale is interpreted locally. River difficulty may change each year due to fluctuations in water level, downed trees, geological disturbances, or bad weather. Stay alert for unexpected problems!

As river difficulty increases, the danger to swimming paddlers becomes more severe. As rapids become longer and more continuous, the challenge increases. There is a difference between running an occasional Class IV rapid and dealing with an entire river of this category. Allow an extra margin of safety between skills and river ratings when the water is cold or if the river itself is remote and inaccessible.

Class I: Easy. *Fast moving water with riffles and small waves. Few obstructions, all obvious and easily missed with little training. Risk to swimmers is slight; self-rescue is easy.*

Class II: Novice. *Straightforward rapids with wide, clear channels which are evident without scouting. Occasional maneuvering may be required, but rocks and medium-sized waves are easily missed by trained paddlers. Swimmers are seldom injured and group assistance, while helpful, is seldom needed.*

Class III: Intermediate. *Rapids with moderate, irregular waves which may be difficult to avoid and which can swamp an open canoe. Complex maneuvers in fast current and good boat control in tight passages or around ledges are often required; large waves or strainers may be present but are easily avoided. Strong eddies and powerful current effects can be found, particularly on large-volume rivers. Scouting is advisable for inexperienced parties. Injuries while swimming are rare; self-rescue is usually easy, but group assistance may be required to avoid long swims.*

Class IV: Advanced. *Intense, powerful but predictable rapids requiring precise boat handling in turbulent water. Depending on the character of the river, it may feature large, unavoidable waves and holes or constricted passages demanding fast maneuvers under pressure. A fast, reliable eddy turn may be needed to initiate maneuvers, scout rapids, or rest. Rapids may require "must" moves above dangerous hazards. Scouting is necessary the first time down. Risk of injury to swimmers is moderate to high, and water conditions may make self-rescue difficult. Group assistance for rescue is often essential but requires practiced skills.*

Class V: Expert. *Extremely long, obstructed, or very violent rapids which expose a paddler to above average endangerment. Drops may contain large, unavoidable waves and holes, or steep, congested chutes with complex, demanding routes. Rapids may continue for long distances between pools,* *demanding a high level of fitness. What eddies exist may be small, turbulent, or difficult to reach. At the high end of the scale, several of these factors may be combined. Scouting is mandatory but often difficult. Swims are dangerous, and rescue is difficult even for experts. Proper equipment, extensive experience, and practiced rescue skills are essential for survival.*

Class VI: Extreme. *One grade more difficult than Class V. These runs often exemplify the extremes of difficulty, unpredictability and danger. The consequences of errors are very severe and rescue may be impossible. For teams of experts only, at favorable water levels, after close personal inspection and taking all precautions. This class does* ***not*** *represent drops thought to be unrunnable, but may include rapids which are only occasionally run.*

The Rating Game

The International Scale of River Difficulty's six generic categories work well when making basic comparisons between rivers or rapids, but kayakers have had to fine-tune the descriptions to keep up with the vast spectrum of rapids being run today.

With the addition of mathematical signs and decimals, the International Scale explodes into a long list of highly descriptive ratings with smaller increments between classifications. With plus and minus signs, a rapid that spans a gray area between the International Scale's Class III and IV ratings can be rated Class III + (slightly harder than Class III) or Class IV– (slightly easier than Class IV). By the time all the potential ratings are tallied, the International Scale's six classifications multiply into 15 classifications (Class I–, VI–, and VI+ are rarely used).

At the upper end of the whitewater scale, a decimal system has emerged that helps distinguish one Class V rapid from another. Similar to the numerical system used by climbers, the Class V rating system classifies rapids Class V.1 (easy Class V) to V.10 (extremely difficult). This system keeps the occasional Class V kayakers

A Class II rapid.

from getting into something above their skill levels.

Remember that any rating system is subjective and that as time goes by, kayakers will keep getting better. What was rated Class V ten years ago may be rated Class IV today, and today's Class IVs may be the Class IIIs of the next decade. Rely on your own skills and judgment, and don't let anyone—or any system—tell you what you can or can't do!

Class V.1 or V.10? You be the judge.

5

PROPULSION BASICS

DIFFERENT STROKES TO MOVE YOUR BOAT

Paddling an inflatable kayak through whitewater embraces two very distinct activities acting in harmony: reading rapids and executing the proper set of maneuvers. Watching a skilled paddler run a difficult rapid reveals both the simplicity of individual strokes and the complexity of combined whitewater maneuvers.

In this chapter we'll explore the basic techniques for paddling your kayak through rapids: power strokes, turning strokes, and braces. From the fundamentals of the forward stroke to the intricacies of the duffek stroke, this chapter will provide your first glimpse of the techniques you'll need to paddle whitewater successfully. It is your opportunity to put your hands on the wheel and feel what it is like to drive a kayak on the river.

Why Paddle?

As terrestrial beings, humans long ago adapted to their environment by learning to crawl, walk, and run. Rivers provide a unique escape from these mundane modes of travel. Relax on the land, and you just become part of the scenery. The world becomes static. Float along in your kayak, and you become one with the river—part of a process in which rain and snow follow a descending route back to the ocean. Paddling lets you tune your descent and adapt to the river. It allows you to adjust to currents, change your position on the river's surface, and travel faster or slower. Ultimately, paddling will even increase your stability and—when done properly—keep you out of trouble.

How Paddling Works

The first person to figure out how paddling works was the renowned physicist Isaac Newton (the same guy who discovered gravity). Even though Newton wasn't a river runner, he understood a basic law of physics—one known as *Newton's third law of motion*.

Newton's third law of motion is simple: For every action, there is an equal and opposite reaction. Kayakers supply the *action* every time they take a paddle stroke. This applies force from their bodies to the water. The kayak *reacts* by moving in the opposite direction to the force of the stroke. For example, when you pull back on a forward stroke, your kayak moves forward. Push forward on a backstroke, and your kayak moves backward.

The best way to put Newton to work for you is to imagine planting your paddle in a block of cement.

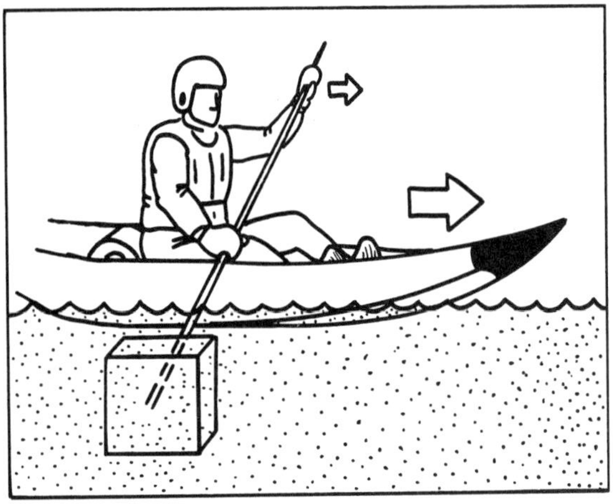

When forward-paddling, pretend your blade is frozen in a block of cement. Always pull your body toward the paddle, not vice versa.

Every time you plant your blade in the river during a power stroke, the paddle freezes in the cement. When you pull on the paddle, your boat slides on the surface to the paddle, not vice versa. If you use your body to pull your boat to the paddle in power and turning strokes, your strokes will become powerful and efficient.

Once you grasp the basics of Newton's third law of motion, you will discover that you can change the amount of force you apply to the water by changing the angle of your paddle blades. Turn the blade perpendicular to the current and you'll feel a lot of force. Turn the blade parallel with the current, and you'll feel very little force. This *feel* is what will eventually make paddling easier.

Body Talk

There's much more to paddling than sticking your paddle in the river and moving it around. Every stroke you take is only as good as the foundation you laid for that stroke. This foundation consists of many factors, including posture, balance, leans, and paddle control. So, let's take a look at a few more items before we start paddling.

PADDLING POSTURE

Some inflatable kayaks are the whitewater equivalent of a lounge chair. They're comfortable, cozy, and just beg you to lie back and relax. That's fine if you're floating gentle rivers. However, serious whitewater calls for a more upright paddling posture.

Sitting upright in your kayak will increase your paddling power, increase your flexibility, extend your range of motion, and improve your balance. It allows you to *rotate your torso* during each stroke and to use the big, strong trunk muscles to propel the paddle. While your arm muscles may tire out quickly after some intense paddling, your torso muscles can keep providing power to your paddle stroke after stroke.

Sitting upright and rotating your torso also keeps your chest and shoulders facing your hands. This, in turn, reduces the chance of shoulder injuries by keeping your arms in front of your body.

LEVERAGE AND RELAXATION

It sounds paradoxical, but you can simultaneously be a powerful and a relaxed paddler. The key to powerful strokes is *leverage*, not strength. Fully extend your arms and use that torso. At the same time, *relax*. You don't have to tense every muscle in your body to stroke effectively, just the ones that are moving your paddle. Also, relaxing between strokes will save energy for when you need it.

BALANCING AND LEANING

Most inflatable kayaks are quite stable. However, good balance and an effective lean will help keep you upright and paddling long after lazy paddlers flip.

Balancing blends the upright and relaxed posture discussed above with the bobbing motion of your kayak. If you relax your stomach muscles, your upper body floats independently of your lower body. This lets the boat dance beneath you while your upper body remains steady. *Leaning,* on the other hand, helps you maximize your reach with some strokes, and counteracts the tipping forces associated with hydraulics and obstacles. In some cases—as when you're broadsiding a hole or boulder—leaning will even help prevent flips and wraps.

If your kayak is outfitted with thigh straps, your lower body does most of the leaning—not your upper body! You can lean the kayak to the right by lifting up your left knee and pushing down on your right hip and buttocks. Do just the opposite to lean to the left. If your kayak is strapless, the most effective way to lean may be to lean your upper body over the tube opposite your raised knee.

No matter which technique you use, the best direction to lean is usually downstream. That keeps the river from pushing your upstream tube underwater and flipping you over. The big exception to this rule is in eddies. In eddies the water is flowing upstream, so you have to lean upstream to accomplish the same thing.

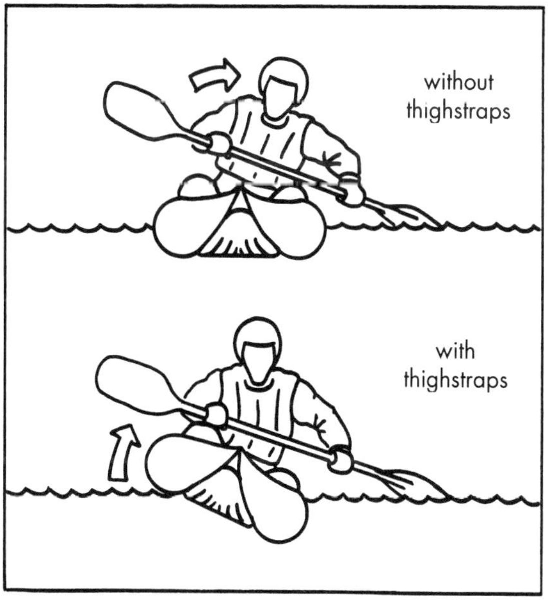

If your kayak lacks thigh straps, you have to shift your upper body over a tube to lean. Thigh straps let you lean your kayak while keeping your upper body tall and balanced.

Holding Your Paddle

In Chapter 2 we discussed a variety of paddle designs. There are feathered and nonfeathered paddles, flat and spoon blades, oval and round shafts. Now it's time to learn how these features work.

POWER FACES

Let's start off by looking at the blades. Curved (spoon) blades enter and bite the water better than flat blades, but they can be a little confusing to use. The concave side of the blade is called the *power face.* The opposite side of the blade is called the *nonpower face* or *back face.*

When you start forward-paddling, the power face will face the stern and press against the water. If the paddle is nonfeathered, finding both power faces will be easy. But if you're using a feathered paddle, the offset blades will pose a bit of a quandary: How do you get both blades to work the same way?

CONTROL HAND

The key to paddle control lies right in the palm of your hand. Your *control hand,* that is. Your control hand always maintains a solid grip on the shaft and rotates the shaft within the other hand (the noncontrol

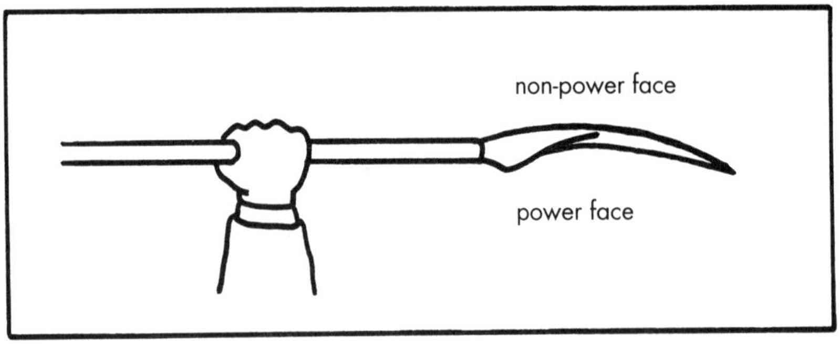

The power face and nonpower face of a paddle blade.

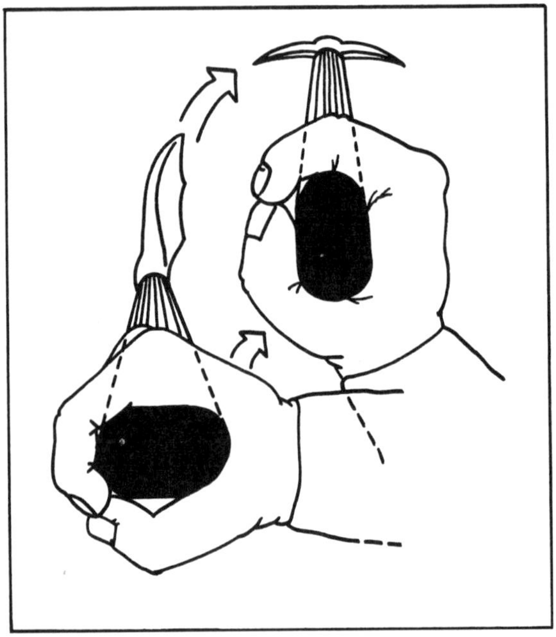

In a right-hand-control paddle, cocking your right wrist back rotates the shaft and sets the left blade up for a stroke.

hand). If you're using a right-hand-control paddle (the most common paddle), your right hand grips the paddle so that the top of your hand, wrist, and forearm are at a 90-degree angle to the blade. Your right wrist stays that way when you stroke with the right blade, but cocks outward to set the left blade for a left-side stroke.

Don't worry if this wrist movement feels funny at first; it will soon become second nature. If you have a paddle with an *oval shaft,* the shaft will nestle snugly in your control hand and impart a feel that your brain will become used to. (If you don't have an oval shaft, you can customize your round shaft. Tape a thin dowel or spread Shoo Goo, Aqua Seal, or fiberglass putty in a long strip under the palm of your control hand.) Even if you're a slow learner, resist the urge to rotate the shaft partially with both hands! You'll have a more difficult time learning advanced paddling strokes, and you'll never have quite the same feel for the water.

HAND PLACEMENT

Hand placement is the last step in learning to hold your paddle. It ensures that you'll transfer plenty of power through your paddle while maintaining your reach and control.

To find your proper hand placement, rest the paddle on your head parallel with the ground. Then hold the paddle so your elbows are bent at 90 degrees. Make sure that your hands are equidistant from both blades, then slide both hands inward an inch or so. Using this as your starting point, you can widen or narrow your grip slightly to suit your paddling style. Keep in mind, however, that big variations in your hand placement may reduce your power, control, or reach!

The Basic Paddling Strokes

Now that you have figured your paddle out, it's time to learn *how* to paddle. Amazingly, there are an infinite number of ways to move your paddle through the water. Fortunately, we can sort every stroke imaginable into just a few categories: *power strokes, turning strokes,* and *braces.*

Power strokes—like the forward stroke and the backstroke—move your boat forward and backward. Turning strokes—such as sweeps or duffek strokes—spin your boat while moving it across the water. Finally, braces help keep you upright when you use your paddle for support and stability.

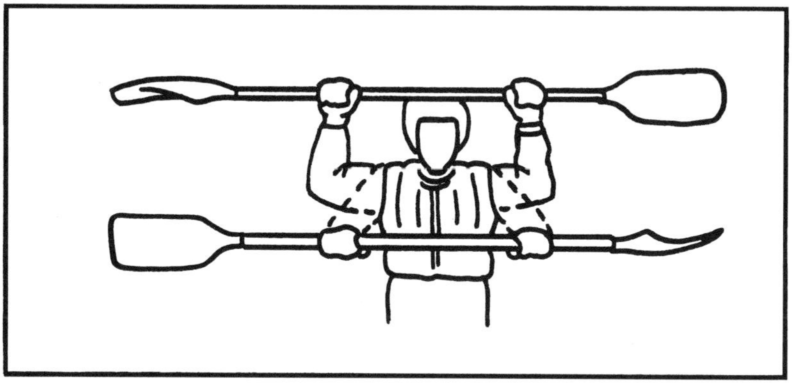

To find your optimum hand position, first hold the paddle on your head with your elbows bent at 90 degrees then slide both hands inward an inch or so. You can later slide your hands inward or outward.

Power Strokes

FORWARD STROKE

The *forward stroke* can be as simple or as complex as you want to make it. In the most basic forward stroke, all you have to do is plant one blade near the bow with the power face facing the stern, then pull back on the shaft to drive the kayak forward. Paddlers who thrive on simplicity can get away with this technique on gentle rivers without any problems. However, you'll become a much better kayaker if you spend a few more minutes reading about the forward stroke, then practicing your paddling techniques on the river.

The forward stroke has four phases, each of which blend into one fluid stroke: *reach*, *plant (catch)*, *power*, and *recovery*. Let's start with a forward stroke on the right side of your kayak and see how these phases work:

1. Reach

Extend your right arm and rotate your right shoulder forward. This *winds up* your torso, extends your reach, and gets you ready for the plant.

2. Plant

Plant the blade near the bow, keeping the shaft vertical and the blade submerged up to the throat.

3. Power

Drive your left hand (the upper hand) forward between forehead and shoulder level and pull your right hand (the lower hand) toward your right hip. Instead of using big arm motions to do this, think of your upper shoulder as the engine driving your upper hand forward and your torso as the engine pulling the lower hand back. As you move through the power phase, the paddle should come straight back alongside the tubes. Finish with the lower hand near your hip.

4. Recovery

Start the recovery phase by lifting your lower hand and slicing the blade out of the water just behind your hip. Notice how your left arm is extended and your left shoulder is rotated forward. That's the perfect position for starting a forward stroke on your left side.

STRAIGHT AND CLEAN

Your first forward strokes are as likely to spin your kayak as to drive it forward. That happens to everybody—even top paddlers. However, the best kayakers know how to anticipate and counteract spins before they happen.

There can be many reasons why your kayak spins when you're forward-paddling, but three common forward-paddling mistakes show up repeatedly: letting your hands cross your body's centerline, sweeping your paddle outward, and paddling harder on one side than the other. If *your* kayak is turning with each forward stroke, you might be making one of these mistakes. Read on.

Imagine that there is a line that goes straight through your spine and sternum. With each forward stroke, your upper hand punches *forward* along this line, not across your chest. If either hand crosses this line, it may cause your paddle to stray from the side of the

Rotate your shoulder forward during the reach phase of a forward stroke to wind up your torso and extend your reach.

The forward stroke begins with the reach. Here, the paddler's right arm and shoulder are rotated forward. This winds up the paddler's torso, extends his reach, and gets him ready to plant his paddle.

A split second before the catch (plant). Note that the blade is being planted near the bow and that the opposite blade remains high.

During the power phase, the paddler drives his left hand forward between forehead and shoulder level while pulling his right hand toward his hip. Instead of using big arm motions to do this, he has used his upper shoulder to drive his upper hand forward, and has used the unwinding of his torso to pull the lower hand back.

The recovery phase begins by slicing the paddle out of the water just behind the hip.

The paddler is now set up to begin a forward stroke on the opposite side.

kayak, which can cause you to turn.

If your hands are crossing your centerline, your paddle may be too short or you may need to concentrate harder on your upper-hand movement. The cure may be to find a longer paddle or to spend more time practicing your techniques until you have the motions correct.

The path your blade traces through the water can also affect your kayak's movements. Again, the best way to execute the forward stroke is to pull the blade straight back along the tube. A wide, sweeping arc, on the other hand, will cause the kayak to turn. If you're finding yourself sweeping rather than pulling your paddle straight, you can often correct the problem by holding the shaft more vertically during the power phase of the stroke.

To keep your kayak moving straight, apply the same amount of force to both blades when stroking.

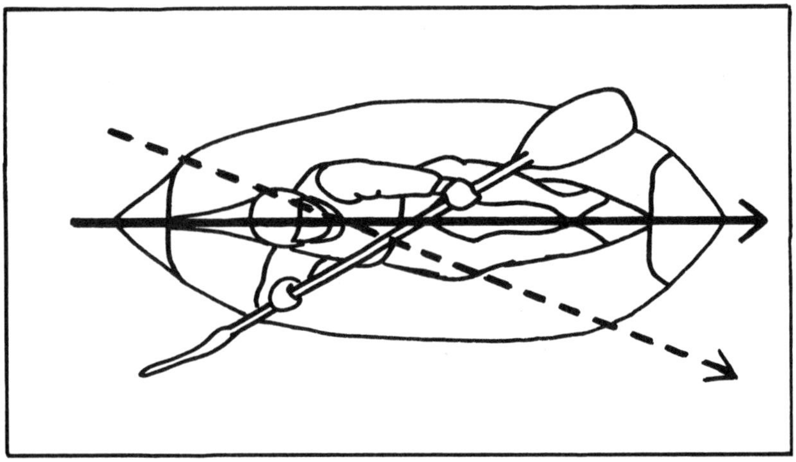

During forward strokes, don't let your hands cross an imaginary centerline passing through your spine and sternum. Note how the centerline shifts as you wind up your torso.

Once you work the basic kinks out of your forward stroke, begin to concentrate on a smooth stroke from start to finish. Make the end of one stroke the beginning of the next. You don't need to lean forward and backward to execute each stroke; the winding and unwinding of your torso will provide reach and power. As you put all of this together, you'll be on your way to smooth, efficient paddling!

THE BACKSTROKE

The *backstroke* is similar to a forward stroke—in reverse. It moves your kayak backward, which can buy you some extra time before paddling over a drop and can make some maneuvers easier to execute.

To start a backstroke, plant one blade just behind your hip (your lower hand will be near your hip) with the power face facing the stern. Then push the blade toward the bow while pulling your upper hand toward your shoulder. Your lower arm will end up stretched forward, with your upper arm ending near your shoulder.

To keep your backstrokes smooth and powerful, remember the basics you learned in forward paddling. Wind and unwind your torso during each stroke, keep the paddle vertical, and don't let your hands cross your centerline. Also, look over just one shoulder—not over both—if you need to see behind you. That will keep you from getting disoriented each time you swivel your head.

Turning Strokes

THE PIVOT POINT

Finding your kayak's *pivot point*—the balance point around which your kayak spins—is the first step in learning how to turn your kayak.

The pivot point is the point at which your kayak is trim from bow to stern and from tube to tube. The pivot point also sits deepest in the water, causing it to resist any kind of turn or spin. As you read about turning strokes, always use the pivot point as a reference point. The farther your turning stroke is from the pivot point, the more effective your turns will be.

FORWARD SWEEP

The *forward sweep* is the most basic of all turning strokes. It turns your boat while moving forward and can be used to get you back on a straight path after you have veered off course.

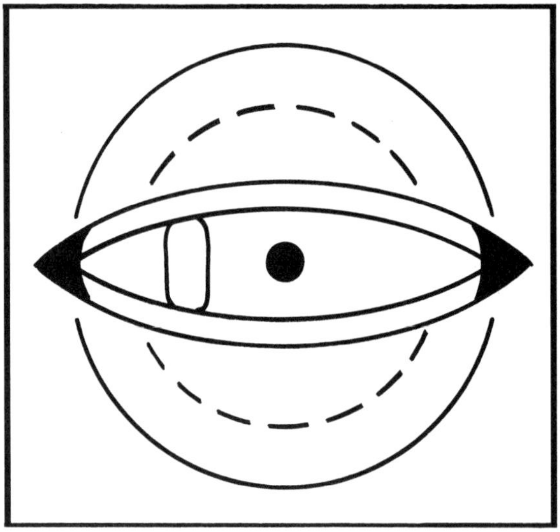

Turning strokes become more powerful when they are executed farther away from the pivot point.

Plant the blade just behind your hip to begin a backstroke. . . .

Then push the blade toward the bow while pulling your upper hand toward your shoulder. Your lower arm will end up stretched forward, and your upper arm will end near your shoulder.

In the forward sweep, the blade traces a wide arcing path from the bow to the stern. It works by pushing the bow away from the paddle during the first half of the stroke and pulling the stern toward the blade during the last half of the stroke.

To execute the forward sweep, you must keep your hands low and the shaft nearly horizontal (the shaft was almost vertical in the forward stroke). It also helps to wind up your torso. This gives you plenty of reach, flexibility, and power without forcing you to lean forward.

To execute a forward sweep stroke, first wind up your torso by extending your right arm, rotating your right shoulder forward, and planting the right blade near the bow. Your left hand starts out close to your chest.

To execute a right-side forward sweep, first wind up your torso by extending your right arm, rotating your right shoulder forward, and planting the right blade near the bow. Your left hand starts out close to your chest. During the power phase, unwind your torso by sweeping the right blade 180 degrees from the bow to the stern with your right arm fully extended. At the same time, push your left arm diagonally across the front of your body while keeping your chest and shoulders almost parallel with the shaft. Finish the stroke with the right blade near the stern, both arms nearly straight, and your right shoulder rotated back.

During the power phase of the forward sweep, unwind your torso by sweeping the right blade 180 degrees from the bow to the stern with your right arm fully extended. At the same time, push your left arm diagonally across the front of your body while keeping your chest and shoulders almost parallel with the shaft. Finish the stroke with the right blade near the stern, both arms nearly straight, and your right shoulder rotated back.

THE CLEAN SWEEP

There are many subtleties that will make your forward sweep stronger and more efficient. First, make sure that you sink the entire blade (without drowning it) and keep the blade (not the shaft) vertical throughout the stroke.

Next, fully extend the paddle—reach out! If your sweep arm is bent, your turn will be compromised. One trick to improving your stroke is to watch the blade. Soon, the sweeping path will become second nature and you'll be able to look at more important things—like the river!

Finally, use your torso to provide power to the stroke and don't lean backward—especially toward the end of the stroke. Keeping your shoulders and chest parallel with the shaft while sitting upright will make sure this happens and will ward off shoulder injuries.

BACK SWEEP

The *back sweep*—also called a *reverse sweep*—retraces the path of the forward sweep, but in reverse. (Look at the photo sequence of the forward sweep on page 56 and perform the stroke in reverse.) During your first back sweeps, look back at the paddle blade as you plant it behind you near the stern. Once again, wind up your torso, keep your sweep arm straight, and unwind during the stroke. Remember to keep your hands low and to sit upright.

RUDDERING

By planting the paddle blade vertically in the water near the stern and leaving it there, you can use it the same way a sailor uses a rudder.

Keep both hands low and on the same side of the boat (just as they were at the end of the forward sweep). Then pull the paddle toward the stern to turn the boat one way (this is called a *stern draw*) or push it away from the stern (just like the start of the back sweep) to turn the boat the other way.

THE DRAW STROKE

The *draw stroke* is used to move your kayak sideways across the water toward the paddle blade. It isn't the most efficient stroke—it pits the whole side of the boat against the force of the river—but it is very useful in eddies, steep chutes, or narrow slots when a quick lateral adjustment is needed.

To start a draw stroke, plant one blade at a right angle to your kayak, even with your hip, with the power face toward your kayak. Hold the shaft vertical by placing your top arm across your forehead and lining both hands atop each other on one side of the kayak. (This is a whole lot easier if you turn your torso to face your paddle!) Then execute the draw by pulling the blade in toward your kayak. Before the blade reaches the tube, twist your wrists inward to slice the

Ruddering can be used to keep a precise angle to the current.

The proper position for a draw stroke.

blade away from the kayak or out of the water. (If the blade hits the side of the kayak, it might pull under the kayak and pop out of your hands!)

DRAW VARIATIONS

Once you master the basic draw, you can vary it to create dozens of new strokes. If you reach out diagonally toward the bow, instead of sideways, you will have a *bow draw*. The bow draw moves your kayak sideways and forward at the same time. A diagonal draw that starts near the stern is called a *stern draw*. Like rudder strokes, stern draws are great for adjusting your angle on the river or for keeping your kayak straight.

There are still many variations beyond bow and stern draws. If you lower your top hand, you will have the basic position for a *"low" high brace* (discussed on page 63). If you twist the blade and plant it near the bow, you will be on your way to executing your first *duffek stroke* (see page 59). Experiment with your draws, and see how each new angle moves your kayak.

SCULLING DRAW

The *sculling*—or *feathering*—*draw* lets you move your kayak sideways for longer periods of time. The trick is getting used to slicing your paddle blade back and forth with the correct blade angles while simultaneously pulling on the shaft. This takes a bit of finesse, but will ultimately improve your boat control.

Start the sculling draw by planting the blade slightly closer to the tube than you would with an ordinary draw stroke. Next, twist the blade so that one edge angles out from the tube 20 to 30 degrees. Whichever edge is facing outward will become the *leading edge*. Slice the paddle a couple of feet in the direction of the leading edge while pulling on the shaft. The blade will want to travel away from your boat, but your pulling motion will pull the kayak in the same direction that your paddle is traveling. At the end of the first slice,

In a sculling draw, you keep moving sideways by slicing your paddle back and forth and pulling your kayak toward your paddle.

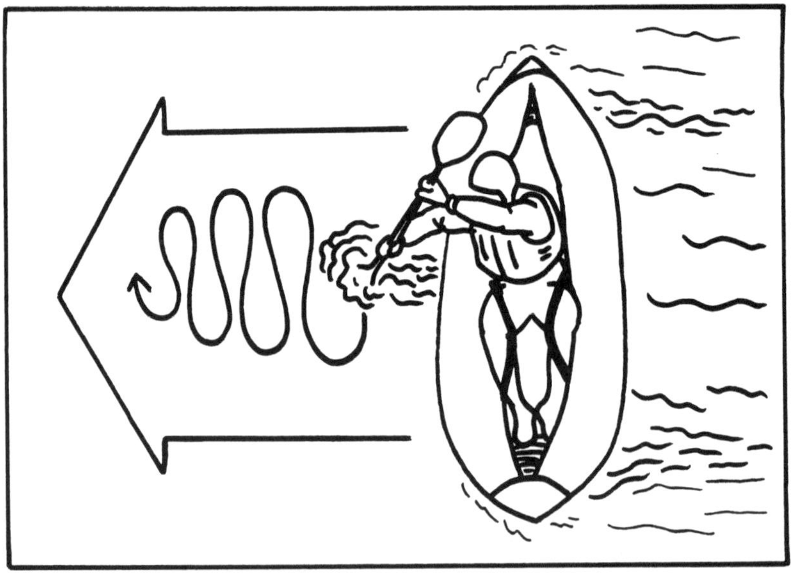

twist your wrists to reverse the blade angle, then slice it in the opposite direction. Keep changing the blade angle and the direction while slicing the blade back and forth to keep the sculling draw going.

THE DUFFEK STROKE

The *duffek stroke*—named after Czech paddler Milo Duffek—is a curious blend of some techniques you have already learned. It may be more challenging to learn than other strokes, but it will let you turn faster and smoother than you ever dreamed possible.

Before practicing the duffek stroke, keep two new points in mind: First, your paddle blade always stays to your front or side in the duffek stroke—never behind you. Second, your upper arm position always stays low—usually across your forehead, chin, or neck. Letting your upper arm rise above your head invites shoulder dislocations.

There are two ways to do a duffek stroke. Let's learn the *static duffek* first. Plant the blade as if you were doing a draw stroke, but plant it near the bow and turn the leading edge of the blade *outward* at a 45-degree

The duffek stroke is similar to a draw executed near the bow, but provides a great way to make fast, powerful turns.

angle (this is called an *open* blade angle). Your lower arm will be fully extended, your upper forearm horizontal across your forehead, and your upper wrist turned outward. As in the draw, both hands will be on one side of the kayak. Your kayak will turn toward the side where you planted your blade.

Practice planting the paddle in the static duffek position a couple of times with your kayak stationary. Once you learn what the plant feels like, begin paddling forward. Then plant the paddle again as just described and watch your kayak spin slowly around your paddle. If you have done this correctly, you'll feel like a kid grabbing and spinning around a pole. Essentially, you're doing the same thing you did when ruddering near the stern, except that now you're doing a *bow rudder.*

Once you have the static duffek down, you can experiment with blade angles and boat speeds. The more open your blade angle, the faster your turn, and vice versa. Once you're quite comfortable with the static duffek, you're ready for the next step—the *dynamic duffek.*

The dynamic duffek starts as a draw stroke by your side, then travels diagonally toward the bow. If you froze the stroke midway, it would look like a static duffek or a bow draw, but the dynamic duffek calls for more paddle movement. You simultaneously slice and pull the blade toward the bow with a slightly open blade angle (just like the starting position for the static duffek). As the blade travels diagonally toward the bow, the bow turns toward the blade. Again, you can experiment with different blade angles and boat speeds to adjust your turns.

DOCTORING YOUR DUFFEKS

Duffek strokes take time and practice to perfect. When practicing, look at your paddle shaft. If it isn't vertical, reach farther across your forehead with your upper arm. Next, check out your blade angle. If you don't open your blade angle enough, the blade will slam into the side of the boat and throw you off balance. On the other hand, if you turn your blade out 90 degrees from your boat, it will just act as a brake instead of a rudder.

Practice your duffek strokes slowly at first, setting a 45-degree blade angle each time. As your confidence and ability grow, you can modify your blade angles and add speed to your turns.

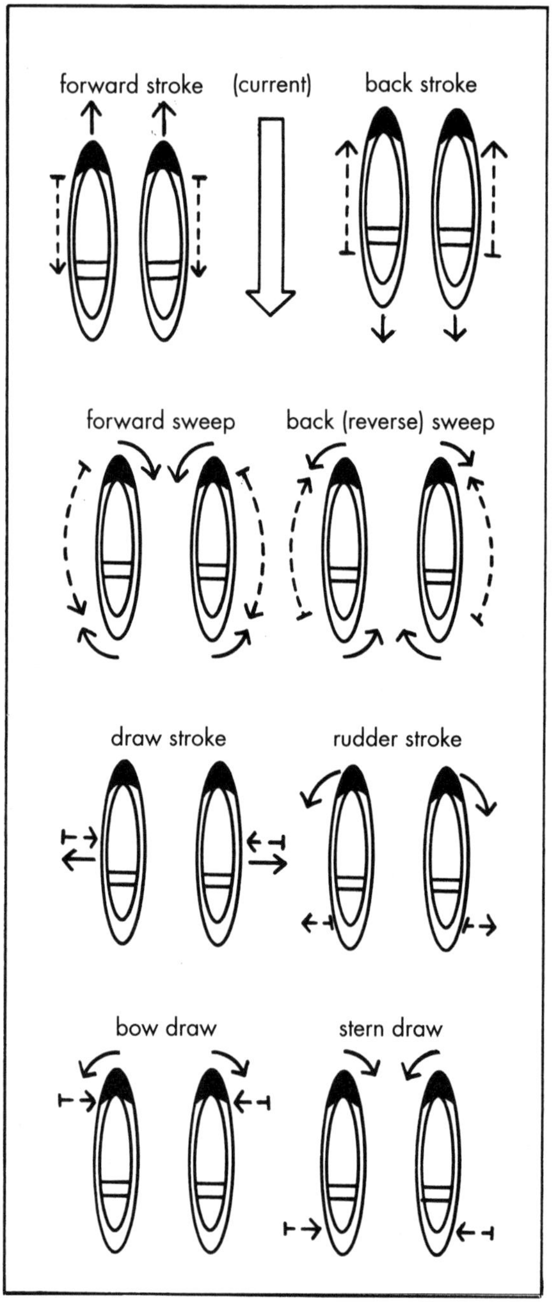

Wondering how to execute a particular stroke? Look for it here.

DON'T STOP THERE

If you are overwhelmed by the long list of power and turning strokes, relax! Simply look at the illustrations for every stroke and use them as a handy reference for

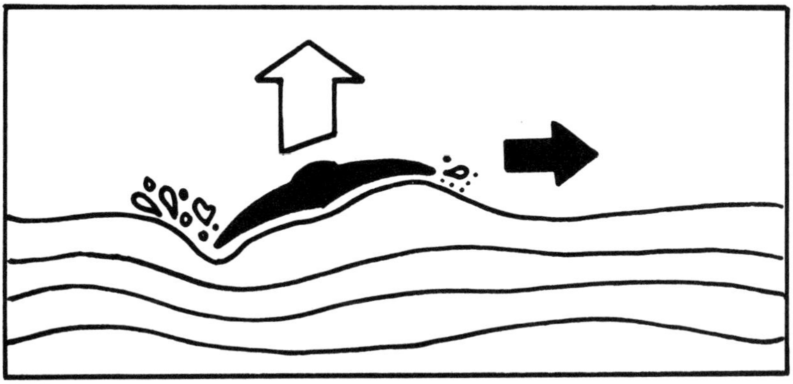

The key to every brace is to keep your blade at a climbing angle. This keeps the blade at or near the surface and provides a lot of upward lift.

cataloging your strokes. Soon you'll be able to match names to the paths your blades follow every time you take a stroke.

Braces

Once you start paddling whitewater, you'll become addicted to the feeling of water in your face. Your first big surprise will come when your face ends up in the water. Flipping or falling overboard happens to everybody sooner or later, but there are techniques that will lower your chances of getting dunked. These techniques are called *braces* or *recovery strokes.* They turn your paddle into a sort of outrigger and provide support when the river threatens to upset your kayak.

BLADE ANGLES

As we start to discuss braces, think of your paddle blades as water skis. When they're sitting still, they sink easily and can't hold you up. But when they're moving, they'll plane along the water's surface and offer incredible support. As long as the forward edge of the ski or paddle blade is kept at a climbing angle, you'll get lift.

The easiest way to experience this concept is to walk out into some waist-deep water and skim one blade across the surface while pressing down on the shaft. Remember to keep the leading edge at a climbing angle to keep the blade skimming. As your technique improves, lean harder on the shaft or experiment with starting with the blade beneath the surface. It's amazing how much pressure your paddle can take before the blade begins to sink.

You can do the same thing in your kayak by setting the blade at a climbing angle while doing a forward sweep stroke. Tip your kayak slightly to one side, then sweep your blade on that same side while pushing down. Provided you keep the blade at a climbing angle, you'll get some forward movement and a lot of support from your paddle.

Once you learn the feel of climbing angles and how to keep your blade at the surface, you'll have learned the basics for low braces, high braces, and sweep braces.

HIP AND KNEE MOVEMENT

Your hips and knees complement your paddle in every brace. They help increase the mechanical

Your hips and knees complement your paddle when bracing. To help level your kayak, lift the hip and knee nearest the bracing blade while driving the opposite hip and knee downward. At the same time, press down on the bracing blade.

advantage on the paddle blade and bring your kayak back to a balanced position. You can restore your balance by lifting the hip and knee on the side you're flipping toward and driving the opposite hip and knee downward. (This motion is easiest with thigh straps.)

At the same time that you're rocking your hips, you have to resist the urge to pull your head and shoulders away from your bracing hand. Keep the shoulder nearest the bracing blade over your bracing hand to maximize your downward push on the paddle. In a high brace or a sweeping brace, discussed below, you essentially lean toward your bracing blade to maximize your leverage. Once the brace starts working, you can slide your body back over your kayak and regain your balance. Though all of this will feel a bit disconcerting at first, plenty of practice in a warm, shallow eddy will build up the confidence you'll need for big brace strokes later on.

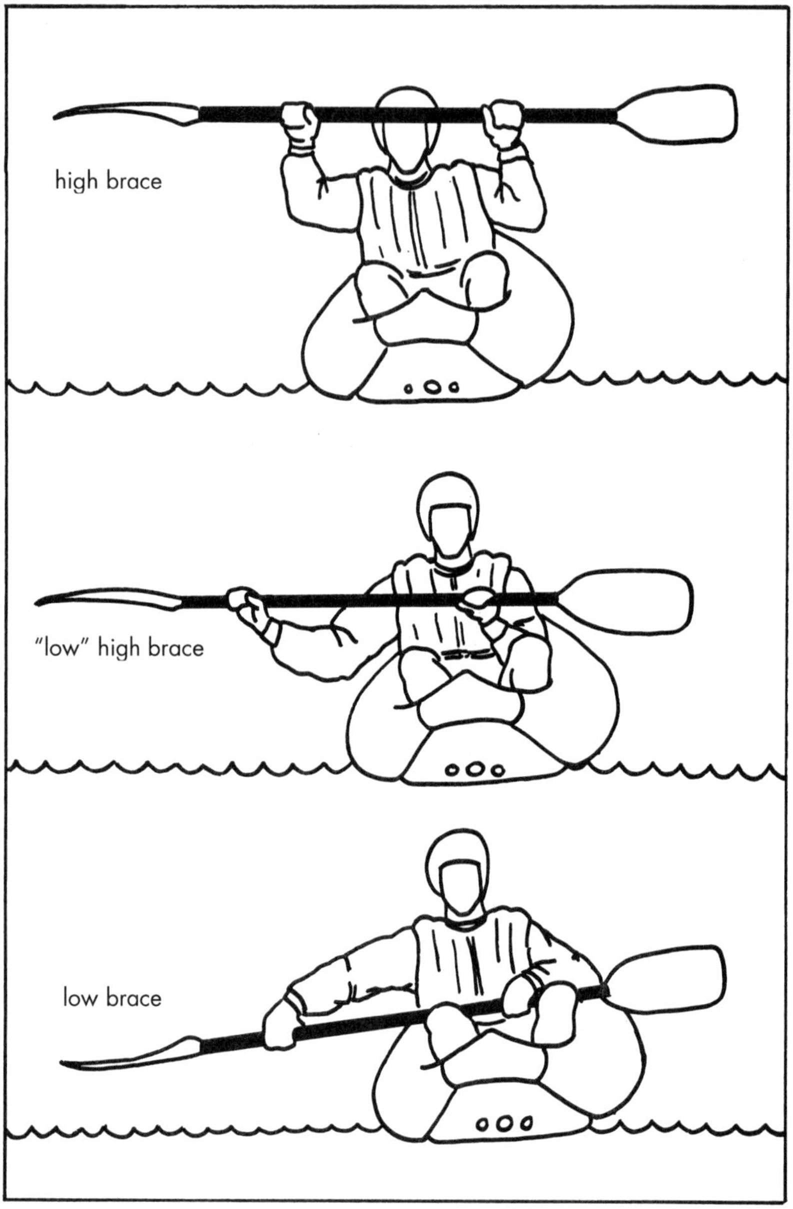

The proper position for a high brace (top), "low" high brace (middle), and low brace (bottom).

LOW BRACE

The *low brace* is a very stable brace that can be used for surfing holes, practicing eddy turns, or maintaining your stability in rapids.

The low brace position starts with your paddle just above your tubes and your forearms fairly level. From this position, you can *slap* the nonpower face of the blade on the water and move it on the surface for stability (remember to keep the leading edge of the blade climbing toward the surface). At the same time that you slap the water, pull the hip nearest the bracing blade up while forcing your shoulder down over the bracing hand. If your kayak has thigh straps, you can pull up on the knee nearest the bracing blade while forcing the opposite knee downward.

HIGH BRACE

The *high brace* is a powerful recovery stroke. It can be used in rapids, in holes—anywhere that you need to keep from flipping.

A powerful high brace comes in handy in big hydraulics. (Photo by Mark Lisk/Lisk Studios, Boise, ID; courtesy of AIRE, Inc., Boise, ID)

The high brace position places the paddle higher than the low brace position and puts the power face down on the water. You can find this position by first resting the paddle across the tubes in front of you, then flexing your elbows to bring the paddle to your chest. Then extend the paddle out to one side of your kayak and rotate your control wrist back to turn the power face toward the river's surface.

Once again, you brace by slapping or pushing down on the water with your paddle, moving your paddle to keep it on the surface, and lifting the hip and knee near the side you're bracing on.

To maximize the power of the high brace, keep your upper hand lower than your chin. Keeping your high brace *low* helps put the blade flat on the water. The "low" high brace—when combined with keeping your paddle in front of you—also helps prevent shoulder injuries.

SWEEPING BRACE

The *sweeping brace* (also called a *sculling brace*) is bracing's equivalent of the sculling draw. It works by constantly changing the blade angle and by sweeping the blade back and forth.

To execute a sweeping brace, set one blade on the water in either the low or high brace position. Angle the blade so that the leading edge is climbing, then sweep the blade in that direction. After sliding the blade a foot or two, reverse the blade angle and sweep the blade in the opposite direction. Keep practicing this motion, sweeping the blade back and forth, until you can press down on the shaft while keeping the blade on the water's surface. The better you become at this, the longer you can keep yourself from flipping over.

Two-Person Techniques

Paddling a two-person inflatable kayak—also called a *K-2*—adds a new dimension to river running. The magical dance of synchronized paddles and the power of coordinated maneuvers can be exhilarating when shared by competent paddlers. On the other hand, inexperienced paddlers often waddle downriver with

You can lean your kayak for a long time using a sweeping or sculling brace.

all the grace and poise of a one-legged duck.

Effective K-2ing takes a team effort. Although forward-paddling or back-paddling comes naturally to most teams, it takes a new line of thinking to turn or to move laterally. This section will get you thinking about most of the basic paddling maneuvers you'll use when K-2ing.

Notice I used the phrase *paddling maneuvers* and not *paddle strokes*. That's because the strokes you just learned work equally well whether you're paddling solo or tandem. It's the *combination* of each paddler's strokes that determines how your K-2 will move.

The easiest way to describe K-2 maneuvers is by illustration. Look at the accompanying diagram showing K-2 maneuvers, practice each one with your partner, and be patient. The keys to a successful K-2 team are communication and experience. Talk about your

A well-tuned K-2 team. *(Photo by Robert Laufer; courtesy of Rapid Shooters, Coloma, CA)*

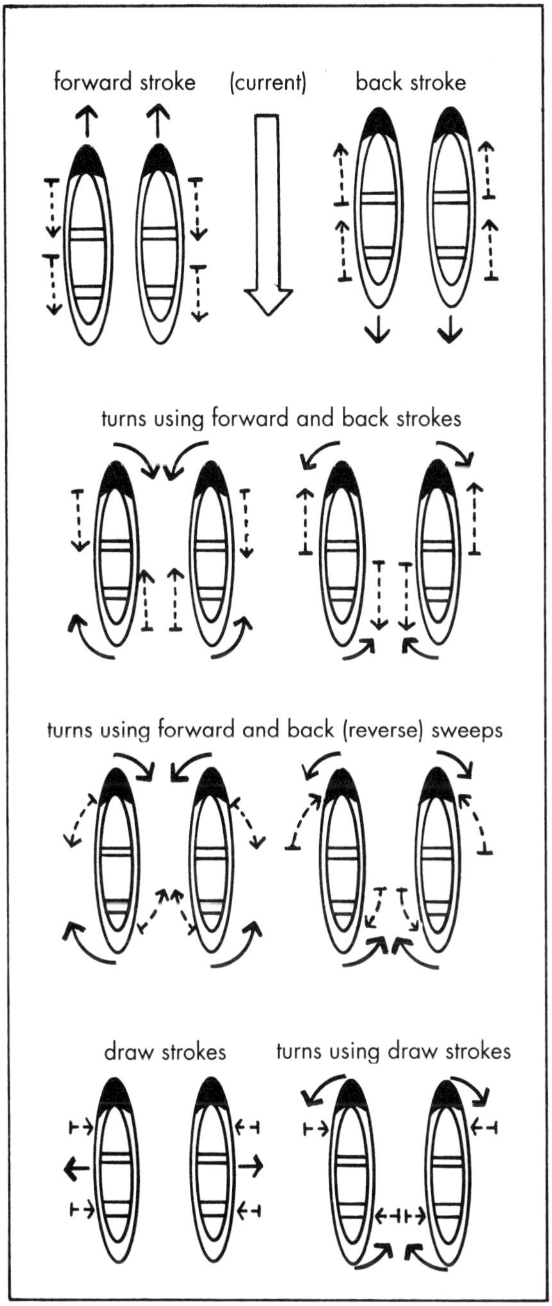

K-2 maneuvers.

next move and plan your route before you're in a rapid. Also, pay attention to your partner's paddle and mimic his or her strokes. As the two of you improve as a team, experience will outweigh communication and a sixth sense will replace needless chatter.

When you're paddling in a K-2 team, keep in mind that your kayak is bigger, bulkier, and heavier than you're used to as a solo kayaker. It will take longer to change direction, spin, or cross eddy lines. Anticipate each move and become more decisive with your maneuvers. By thinking fast, paddling hard, and practicing a lot, you'll be well on your way to becoming a powerful K-2 team!

6

WHITEWATER

RUNNING THE RAPIDS

Heraclitus once said, "You cannot step twice into the same river, for other waters are continually flowing on." Few words capture river running's mystique as eloquently as those. With each bend in the channel, rivers reveal new facets of their personalities—sometimes tranquil, sometimes tumultuous. Even the personalities of individual rapids transform as water levels rise and fall, or as streambeds erode and shift. Although rapids shift freely from one mood to another, the skills and techniques needed to read and run them remain constant.

By now you've learned the strokes that kayakers use to harness a kayak's capabilities. It's time to combine those strokes into definite maneuvers, to expand your knowledge of river features, and to learn the fundamental techniques necessary to run rapids. This is your next big step toward becoming a whitewater kayaker!

Heading Downriver

READING THE RIVER

To novice kayakers, unfamiliar with the distinctive components of rapids, whitewater rivers exemplify

Go with the flow!

nature in chaos, liquid furies. But to the seasoned river runner, rapids share common features, each one a road sign to routes of safe passage. *Reading rivers* is the art of interpreting those road signs, recognizing the pitfalls of ill-chosen routes, and envisioning the maneuvers that will be necessary to float rapids safely.

BASIC CONCEPTS

While reading the rest of this chapter, keep three important concepts in mind: First, think of paddling as a means of changing your kayak's speed and direction in relation to the *current,* not in relation to solid obstacles such as rocks or cliffs. Second, always have a *contingency plan* in case you miss a stroke, spin off a wave, or bounce off a rock. Finally, remember that whitewater is ever changing and that your ability to *adapt* is more important than learning the names or categories of techniques. If you keep these mental footnotes handy, the following techniques will make more sense and your boating success will increase.

LEANING REVISITED

As you move downriver and into bigger rapids, you'll find yourself spending more time turning your kayak to the current. To overcome the unstable feeling that generally goes along with being sideways, you must learn to lean correctly. Most of the time, the correct lean will be obvious: Lean downstream in the main current and upstream in eddies. If you don't do this, the effect will be very much like having a rug pulled out from underneath you: Your boat will roll upside down into the current.

The correct lean will also be critical when paddling amid rocks, logs, or holes. Always lean *toward* these obstacles to avoid flips and wraps.

Kayak Maneuvers

Amazingly, every type of maneuver known to inflatable kayakers falls within one of five categories:

Lean toward rocks and boulders to avoid being pinned.

(1) maneuvers that keep you *parallel* with the current, (2) *ferries,* (3) *turns and spins,* (4) *sideslips,* and (5) *eddy turns and peel-outs.* Each of these maneuvers either moves the kayak in a new direction or rotates the kayak around its pivot point.

As you begin to learn about these maneuvers, think of how they'll work on moving currents, and visualize the two components that make up each one: your kayak's *momentum* and its *angle* in relation to the current. Some maneuvers—like ferries and eddy turns—rely heavily on current to drive the kayak across the river's surface. Other maneuvers—such as turns and sideslips—have to overcome currents to be effective. The same current that assists one maneuver may hinder another.

River Directions

As you read through this chapter, you will see references like *river left* and *river right.* Rivers have descriptive directions, just as maps are labeled north, south, east, and west. When describing river directions, four terms are used: (1) *upstream* is where the current is coming from, (2) *downstream* is where the current is flowing to, (3) *river left* is to your left as you face downstream, and (4) *river right* is to your right as you face downstream. These terms will help you understand the movement of the kayaks in the accompanying diagrams and will make your descriptions of rapids understandable to fellow river runners.

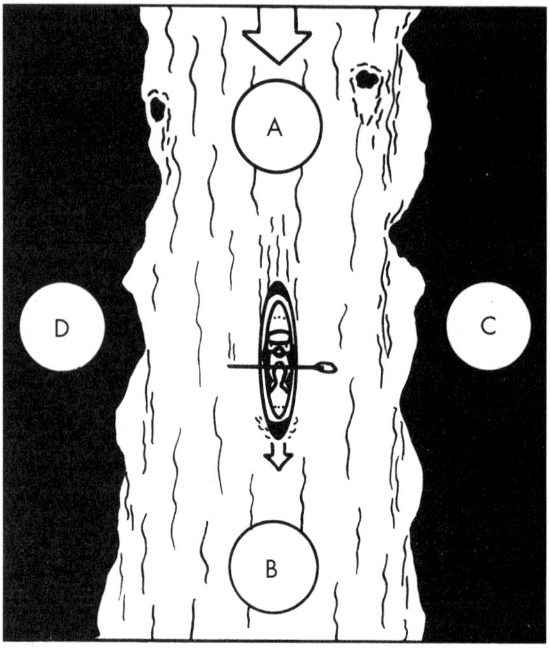

River directions: The river is flowing from the top of the diagram to the bottom. A is upstream; B is downstream; C is river left; and D is river right.

Staying Parallel with the Current

One of the fundamental techniques all kayakers learn is how to keep the kayak parallel with the current. This not only helps when it comes time to slow your kayak down, it continually expands your understanding of river currents and provides a starting point for many other river-running techniques.

STARTING EASY

Since rivers rarely flow in a straight line, keeping your kayak parallel with the current can be trickier than it sounds. There are bends to contend with, eddies and

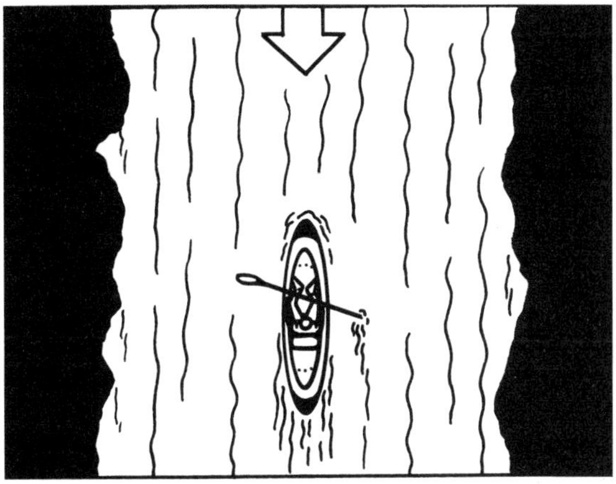

Staying parallel with the current.

slack water that try to spin your kayak, and obstacles that interfere with your strokes. Still, you can first practice these techniques on a straight, obstacle-free section of river where it will be easier to work on basic river-running techniques.

To slow your kayak on a straight section of river, point your bow upstream and use subtle adjustment strokes (gentle turning strokes) to line up the kayak's long axis with the current. At the same time, slow your kayak using forward strokes. The more you practice this, the easier it becomes. Once you're comfortable slowing your descent while facing upstream, point your bow downstream and backstroke against the current.

CHANGING CURRENTS

The current's velocity often changes when a swift, deep channel collides with the slow waters of a shallow shoals. As the kayak crosses the interface between faster and slower currents, the slower current drags on the bow at the same time that the faster currents push on the stern. If your kayak turns even slightly to the current, the river will try to twist it sideways. To avoid getting turned sideways, you must turn your kayak in the opposite direction with well-gauged turning strokes.

Eddies have the same kayak-twisting effect as changes in the current, only worse: Eddies are flowing in the opposite direction to the main current! The added force of these oppositional currents can frustrate even the best kayakers. If it becomes impossible to turn your kayak back in the direction of its original

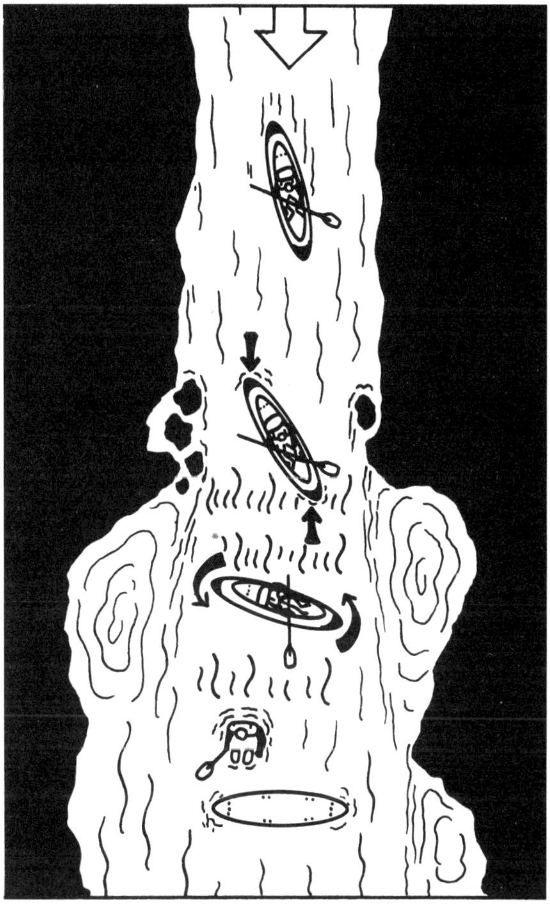

The kayak is emerging from a fast chute at a slight angle to the current. As the bow hits the slower water flowing through the waves, the fast water of the chute is still pushing on the stern. As a result, the kayak spins sideways as it goes into the waves. If the waves are big and powerful, the kayak might flip.

course, just spin it in the opposite direction with a turning stroke and realign it with the current.

Ferrying

HISTORY

Today's ferrying techniques date back to days when cable-guided ferries transported people, horses, and wagons across swift rivers. Attached to a cross-river cable by one or two strong chains, these barges could be turned at an angle to the current either by turning a

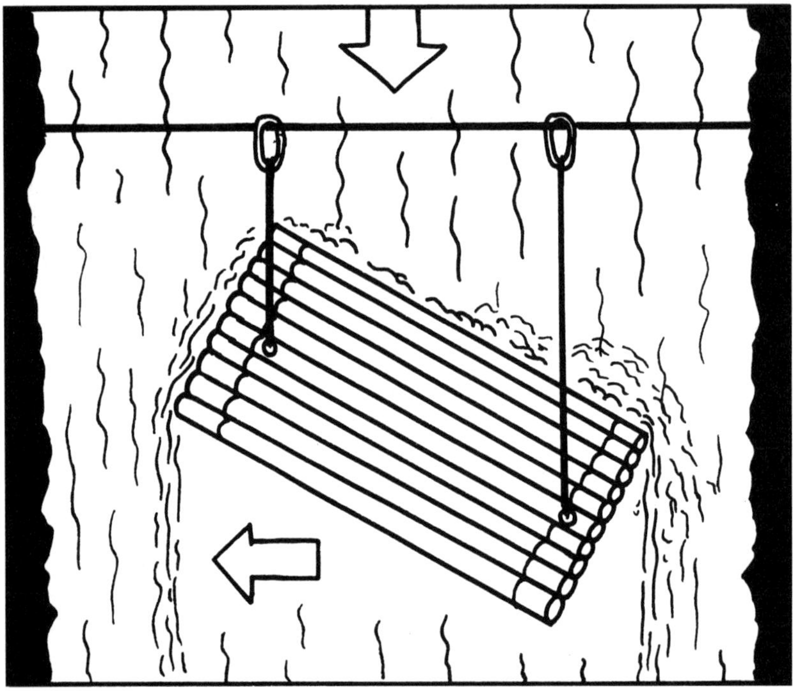

Old-time ferries relied on strong cables and river currents to move back and forth across a river. By increasing the length of one cable, currents would build up on one side of the barge and push it to the opposite bank. Kayakers use the same techniques today as the basis for ferrying.

rudder or by changing the length of one chain. Once the barge was turned at an angle, the current would build up pressure on the barge's upstream side and force it toward the opposite bank.

Kayakers push against the current with forward and back strokes instead of cables, but they use the same angles and forces to move back and forth across a river.

TECHNIQUES

There are two types of ferrying techniques: *forward-ferrying* and *back-ferrying*. To forward-ferry, point your bow upstream, align your kayak parallel with the current, and begin forward-paddling. Once you slow your descent, begin ferrying toward the left bank by turning the bow 30 to 45 degrees to *your* right (toward the *left* bank). If you continue forward-paddling while maintaining that angle, your kayak will move sideways toward river left (again, the left bank as you look downstream). To reach the right bank, angle the bow 30 to 45 degrees toward the right bank and forward-stroke again.

Back-ferrying relies on the same principles as the forward-ferry, only in reverse. To back-ferry, you point your bow downstream and use backstrokes to counteract the downstream current. Since you're not looking at the water coming at you, it often takes a little practice to get the feel of back-ferrying. But stick with it until it becomes second nature.

BETTER FERRYING

There are a few tips that will improve your ferrying techniques—especially in fast currents or swirling hydraulics. First, adjust your angle to the current. The faster the current, the less angle you'll use to maintain your position. If you turn too far sideways, a fast current will force you downstream before your ferry is complete. Second, avoid using backstrokes on your upstream side when forward-ferrying. They'll slow you down and cause you to slip downstream with the current. A stern draw on the downstream side will help you maintain your ferry angle without giving up any momentum. Finally, use the river's surface features to help your ferries. You can ferry on the upstream face of small waves to add power to your ferries. Here, gravity holds your kayak on the wave as you *surf* it across the river.

When all else fails, err on the side of pointing directly upstream. That will buy you extra time to adjust your ferry angles and ferry where you want to.

APPARENT VERSUS REAL COURSE

The first few times you try ferrying across a current, you're likely to notice that it may take a stroke or two to stop your downstream momentum and start moving across the river. Even if you execute a ferry properly, you may notice that you often *drift* or sideslip down-

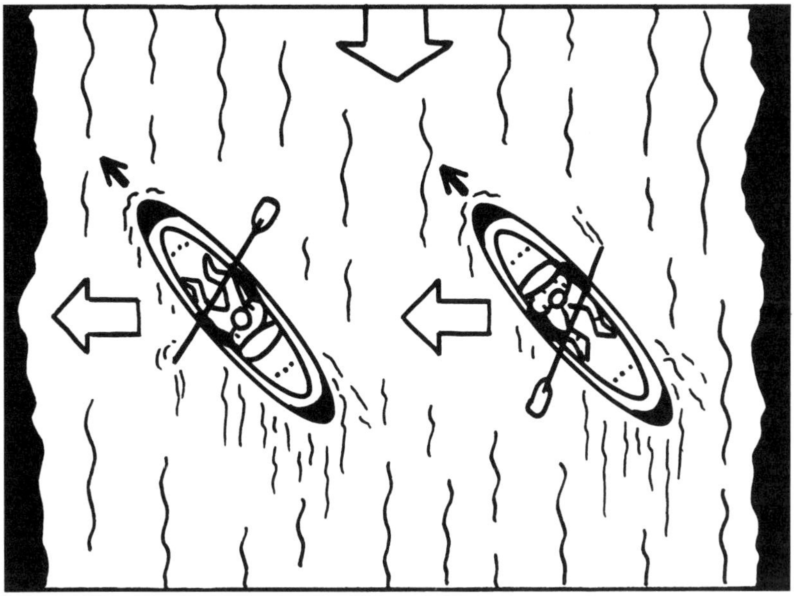

The kayak on the left is forward-ferrying. The kayak on the right is back-ferrying.

river a bit. This means that the cross-river route you *imagined* you would follow may not be the same route you *really* follow. By anticipating the difference between your *apparent* and your *real* course, you can adjust early and make the moves you desire.

FERRYING AROUND BENDS

As you already learned in Chapter 4, currents don't curve around bends, they flow along a straight line from the inside to the outside of bends. To compensate for the river's tendency to push you toward the outside of the bend, you should often enter bends from the inside corner and turn your kayak at an even greater angle to the inside bank than you would expect. (Remember, you're staying parallel with the current, not with the bank!) If the inside corner is strewn with obstacles, just remember that the outside currents will be fast and strong.

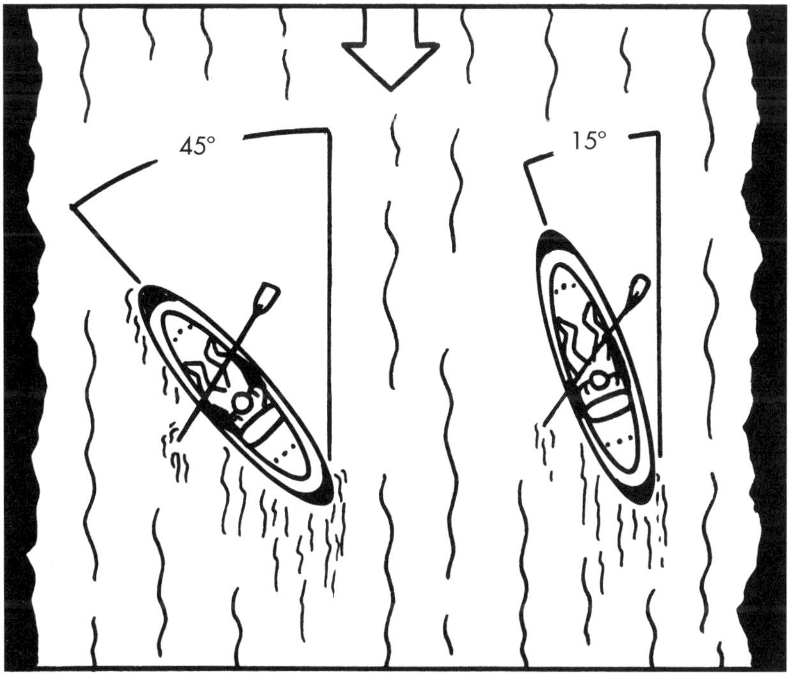

The 45-degree ferry angle (left) works well in a variety of situations. It transports you across rivers quickly, but also exposes you to the currents. Small ferry angles (right) dramatically slow your descent and work best in fast currents.

Turns and Pivots

TURNING STROKES REVISITED

Let's take a fresh look at some familiar strokes. The same sweep strokes, rudders, draws, and duffeks you learned in Chapter 5 will now help you set a ferry angle around a big boulder or aim toward a fun wave. The only difference between your flat-water and whitewater techniques will be *water movement*. Whitewater is a three-dimensional world of waves, holes, chutes, and eddies.

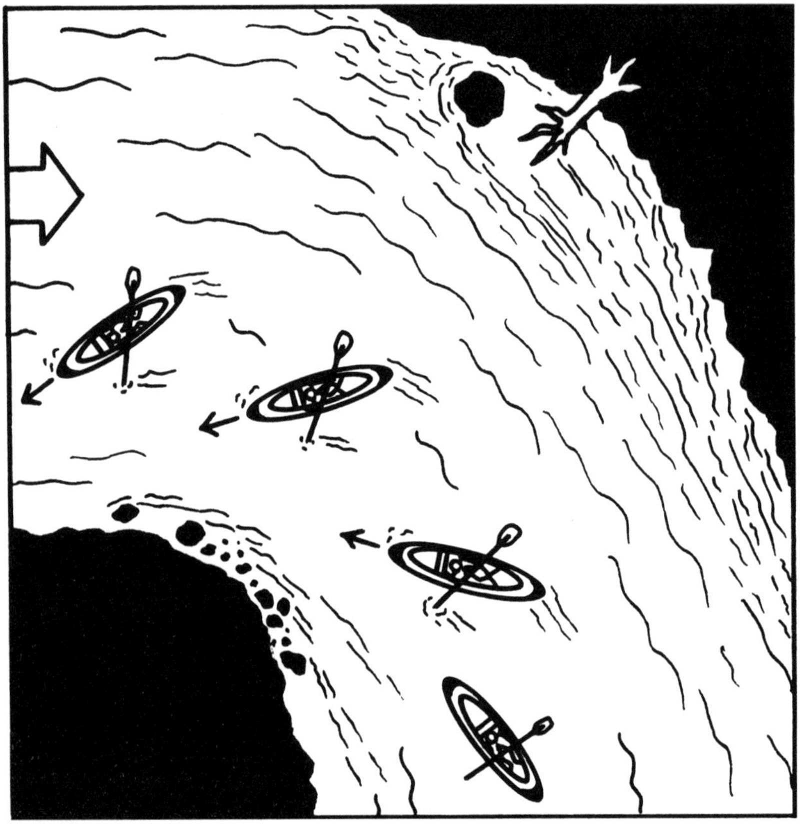

When ferrying around bends, remember to angle your kayak to the current, not to the bank. Here, the kayaker is back-ferrying toward the inside of the bend—usually the safest area to paddle. If there are obstacles on the inside of the bend, it will be easy to move toward the outside of the bend quickly.

Understanding rapids lets you anticipate the river's effect on your kayak and tailor your turns or spins to your game plan.

APPARENT COURSE REVISITED

As you just learned, downstream currents sometimes make a difference between where you *think* you're going to go and where you *actually* go. As you start your turn, your momentum can carry you downstream. As long as you anticipate the effects of the current, you can adjust to the river.

STANDING WAVES

As your kayak reaches the crest of standing waves, the bow and the stern become unweighted. For this split second, your kayak will spin easier than it does when compressed into a trough between standing waves. Experienced kayakers can execute fast turns on wave crests by anticipating the moment of weightlessness. On the other hand, a poorly timed stroke can send your kayak spinning off the crest and out of control. Accordingly, beginners are sometimes better off forward-paddling through wave trains until they become familiar with the roller coaster ride of a wave train.

Sideslips

There will be times when a well-executed turn or powerful ferry is not enough to maneuver safely through a rapid. This may be the case in a fast chute that slams into a boulder or in a hole-riddled rapid that threatens to flip you if you turn broadside.

Draw strokes can be the cure-all for some of these situations. Done correctly, the draw stroke moves you laterally across the river in a hurry.

Eddy Maneuvers

A kayak floating on the main current has a lot of inertia. It carries not only its own weight but also the force of the main current. So to stop your kayak in its tracks, it takes at least the same amount of braking force working in the opposite direction. One example of incredible braking forces are midstream boulders. If a boulder hasn't been moved for a while, chances are it isn't going to let some measly kayak push it out of the way. Other examples of braking forces are big holes or reversals. Here, the surface current is moving upstream at the same rate as the downstream current.

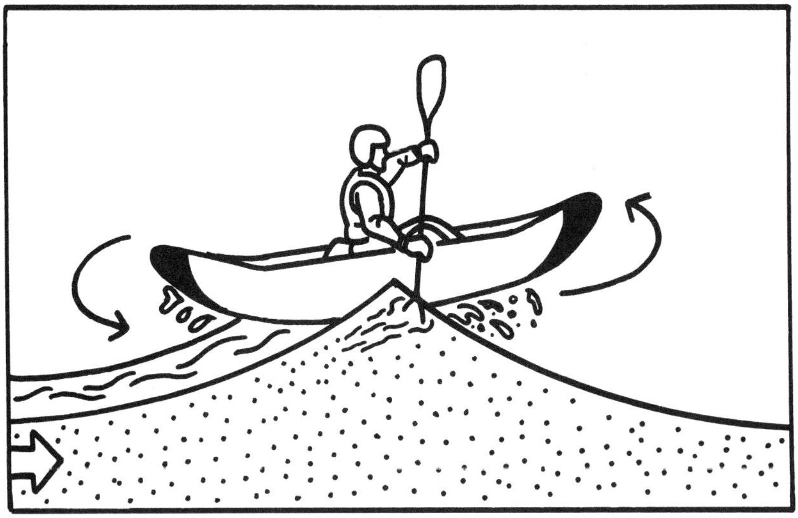

It is much easier to turn on the crest of standing waves than it is in the troughs.

A kayak hitting this surface current broadside might find its downstream progress violently arrested.

The braking forces *you're* looking for are *user-friendly*. Something that will let you stop without wrapping, flipping, swimming, or losing your composure. What you're looking for is *eddies.*

Eddies are one of the most important features on the river. Their upstream currents can provide enough braking power to gently—or powerfully—stop your kayak. A mild eddy provides a calm haven when you're weary, a parking area for boarding and exiting your kayak, and a placid platform from which rapids can be scouted. Conversely, large, tumultuous eddies

If you have to hit a hole, paddle straight through it with momentum.

Lean upstream when entering eddies (top) and downstream when exiting eddies (bottom).

can trap and flip you and can make any trip across an eddy line difficult.

LEANING

Whether entering or exiting an eddy, you'll have to contend with strange currents swirling about the eddy line. The overlapping currents found there not only slide horizontally past one another—speeding up and throwing off your maneuvers —they drive downward, building within themselves strong *capsizing forces*. On large-volume rivers, giant eddy fences can generate enough capsizing force to suck down one tube and cause you to flip.

Even on mild rivers, these capsizing forces can wreak havoc. When you exit a fast-moving eddy, your upstream tube is exposed to the main current. The main current drives against—then under—the upstream tube. As it does, it tries to drag the upstream tube under with it.

When entering or exiting eddies, kayakers can avoid flipping by leaning away from the diving currents. In other words, lean *upstream* when entering eddies and *downstream* when exiting eddies. Once a vulnerable tube has been unweighted, the river has little chance to do any harm.

If your kayak has thigh straps, lift your downstream knee and hip to maximize your upstream lean. A downstream lean, on the other hand, requires you to lift your upstream knee and hip. Strapless cockpits call for upper-body leans to make the kayak tilt.

WHERE TO ENTER EDDIES

The best way to enter an eddy is to paddle into it *high* (upstream, where the maximum current differential is located) and *deep* (directly behind the center of the obstacle). Entering high and deep brings the river's friendly forces into full effect—upstream currents that will brake your momentum and bring your descent to a halt. (If you're

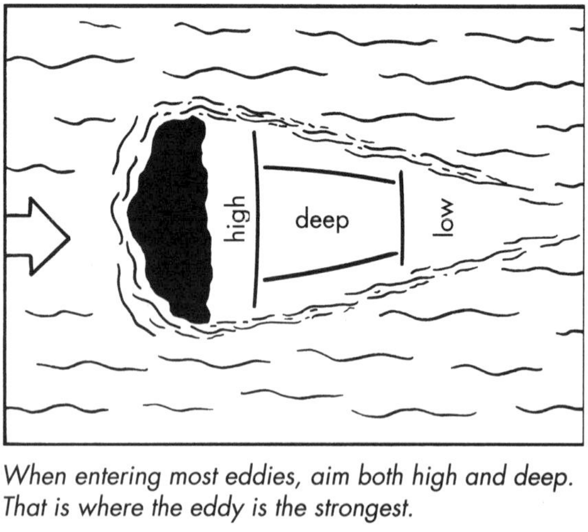

When entering most eddies, aim both high and deep. That is where the eddy is the strongest.

wondering why you shouldn't enter eddies low, here's the answer: The powerful upstream currents found higher in the eddy begin to disappear downstream. So a kayak entering an eddy low is left with nothing more than its own paddle power to stop its descent.)

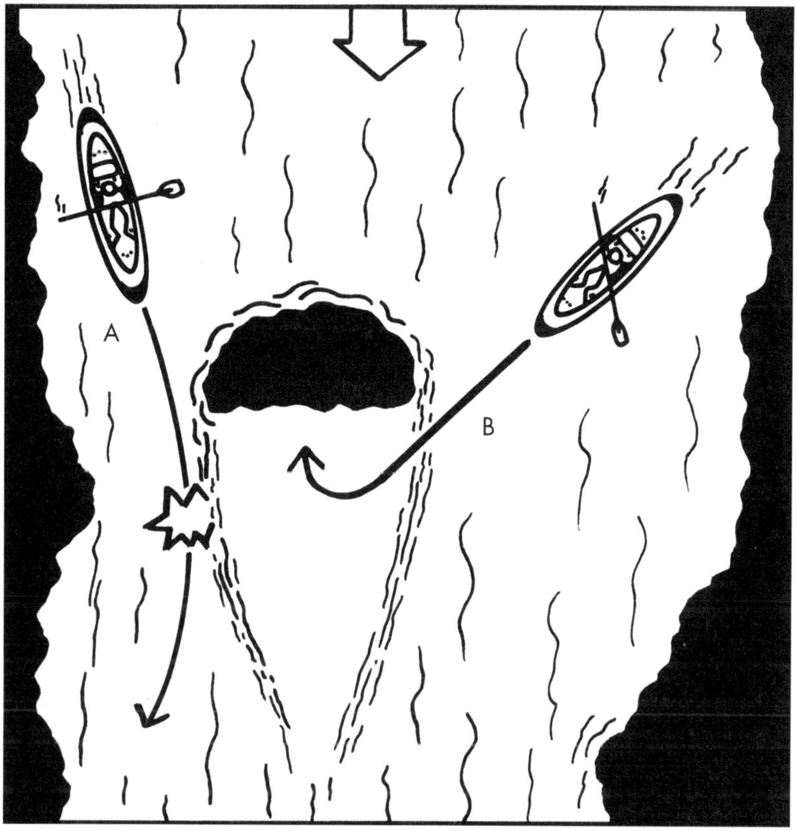

Kayak A bounced off the eddy line because it approached the eddy with too little angle. Kayak B used a better angle and entered the eddy perfectly.

SPEED AND ANGLE

There are two things to think about when entering an eddy: your *speed* and your *angle* of entry. Both concepts tie into one goal: to get across the eddy line quickly . . . upright!

The most important step in entering an eddy is establishing a good angle upstream of the obstacle. Since currents *jet* along eddy lines faster than they do either inside the eddy or out in the main current, eddy lines create hydraulic shields that deflect any kayak that approaches the eddy with too little angle. On the other hand, any kayak that approaches the same eddy line with too much angle will succumb to the main current before it has a chance to cross the eddy line. The idea is to cross the eddy line at a 45-degree angle. (Later on, as your eddy skills improve, you can tailor your angles to meet the demands of the river.)

Speed is one of those vague terms that varies in meaning from person to person and eddy to eddy. The key to entering an eddy is to get across the eddy line—fast! The slower you try to cross an eddy line, the more likely you are to flip or to miss the eddy altogether. Then again, if you enter a small midriver eddy too fast, you're likely to blow out the other side. So match your speed with the eddy's power, and choose an angle that will quickly expose your kayak to the eddy's upstream current and drag it to a halt.

Once you've made it into an eddy, look around. Are you at a standstill or are you still moving? Since an eddy has its own set of currents, it will carry you upstream toward the confluence with the main current. Since this confluence marks the most powerful transition point between the eddy's current and the main current, you'll probably prefer to relax in the calmer waters deep in the eddy. To stay in the heart of the eddy, use small correction strokes or lean against the wall or boulder that formed the eddy and hold on.

EXITING EDDIES

There are three ways to exit an eddy: (1) ferry across the eddy line, (2) *peel out*, or (3) exit downstream. Downstream exits are used only in mellow eddies with weak currents—all you have to do is paddle downstream until the eddy releases you. Ferries and peel-outs, on the other hand, take a little bit of finesse.

The paddler is initiating an eddy turn into the dark eddy at the top of the photograph. Notice that he uses one last forward stroke on his left side to obtain the proper eddy entry angle.

As the bow crosses the eddy line, the paddler begins to lean upstream and prepares to plant a duffek stroke in the eddy.

As the kayak pierces deeper into the eddy, the paddler uses a duffek stroke to pivot the kayak upstream. Notice that the paddler continues to lean upstream.

The kayak is totally in the eddy pointed upstream. Notice that the paddler continues to lean upstream slightly.

Ferrying out of an eddy: The paddler is leaving the eddy located at the bottom right of this photograph and entering the main current. He has already paddled aggressively up the eddy and is now using a slight sweep stroke to set a good ferry angle.

Ferrying out of Eddies

Ferrying out of an eddy is little different than ferrying across the main channel, except that the transition between currents tends to take novices by surprise. The moment the bow hits the main current, the kayak will try to spin downstream. To avoid spinning out, anticipate the main current, build up some upstream momentum as you paddle to the top of the eddy, and cross the eddy line pointing more upstream than usual (10 to 25 degrees to the main current). Place your last stroke on the downstream side of your kayak to compensate for the main current, and concentrate. The only way to tell what strokes you'll need next will be to watch your ferry.

The combination of momentum and a good ferry angle allows the paddler to ferry across the current without drifting downstream.

Peel-Outs

A *peel-out* is an exciting maneuver that spins your kayak downstream as you exit the eddy. To start your peel-out, accelerate up the eddy and cross the eddy line just as in the ferrying exit, but point your bow 30 to 45 degrees to the main current and lean downstream. As you cross the eddy line, continue leaning downstream and do a forward stroke, bow draw, or duffek stroke on your downstream side. The main current will pile against your upstream tube and spin you around to face downstream.

To start a peel-out, the paddler accelerates up the eddy and takes one last stroke on his left side.

The SAFE System

Now that you understand all of the basic maneuvers, just plug them into a system—one with regular routines that will simplify the way you run rivers. I call this preset game plan The SAFE System. The SAFE System is an easy way to evaluate any rapid and provides a safe and simple approach to whitewater travel. It is based on four steps:

The paddler crosses the eddy line at a 45-degree angle while leaning downstream. He is using a duffek stroke for support and to pivot his kayak downstream.

1. **Scout** rapids fully before entering them. This may be done from either bank, or if there is an eddy or slow pool, from your kayak.
2. **Analyze** the rapid and your ability to run it. Where are the obstacles? Where are the safest channels? Is there a safe line through the rapid? Which way will you swim if you fall out? Are you and your equipment capable of running the rapid safely?
3. **Formulate** a plan. Which route will you follow? What is your backup plan? What maneuvers will you have to execute? Should you portage instead? Should a rescue team be stationed along the banks?
4. **Execute** your plan. Run the rapid or carry the kayak along the bank.

SCOUT

Unless you know what is around a bend or over a horizon line or you can paddle to shore in an emergency, *scout!* Pull ashore well above the lip of a rapid and long before strong currents drag your kayak places you don't want to go.

Starting from your landing point, walk all the way to the base of a rapid or all the way around a bend so that you can see the entire section of river you'll be running. A lot of times, it may take some scrambling to reach the best vantage points, but the clear lines of sight are usually well worth the extra effort! While scouting, make mental notes of easily recognizable

As the paddler nears the end of the peel-out, the kayak is almost completely in the main current and is pointed downstream. The duffek stroke has become a forward stroke, which helps the paddler match the kayak's speed to the current.

landmarks and distinctive hydraulics—if you decide to run the rapid, you can use them as signposts to tell you where you are and where you need to turn. Remember that rapids are areas of *falling water* and that your landmarks might not be visible from upstream. Keep looking over your shoulder as you walk back to the kayak to see if your landmarks disappear. If they do, walk downstream again and pick new ones.

ANALYZE

By now you have learned about the most common hydraulics and obstacles you'll see in a typical rapid. You learned that tongues and wave trains signify safe channels, while sharp ledges, rooster tails, and under-

Scouting helps you choose safe routes through or around rapids.

cuts are hazards to be avoided. It's now time to apply your knowledge of river features—together with your knowledge of kayak maneuvers—to analyze the rapid before you.

When scouting a rapid look for two things: obstacles and safe routes. On smaller rivers the hazards will probably be solid obstacles, like rocks or logs. Large-volume rivers, on the other hand, might not have any solid obstacles that cause you concern but can have minefields of keeper holes and menacing haystacks.

To find safe routes, try walking upstream from the bottom of the rapid and play *connect the dots*. Can safe routes be connected or are they broken up by major hazards? (The more broken and twisted the route is, the harder the rapid will be.) Your goal is to discover at least one *clean line* through the rapid—one that you can maneuver without putting yourself in serious danger. If you are scouting a particularly difficult rapid, note where you can exit the current if you flip and where *not* to be if you find yourself swimming.

Once you find a runnable line through the rapid, ask whether you and your equipment are up to the demands posed by the river. If not, take a look at the bank and figure out a way to portage.

FORMULATE

If you think you *can* run this rapid, run it mentally first. Imagine each move you'll make as your kayak descends the rapid from top to bottom. Again, keep in mind the landmarks you scouted out before and correlate them with moves you'll make in the rapid. As you imagine each maneuver, think of what could go wrong and what you'll do in the event of a mishap. Finally, discuss your plan with your fellow kayakers, especially if you're paddling as part of a K-2 team. If there's any chance you'll have problems, station rescuers at key points along the bank to assist you. (More on that in Chapter 7.)

EXECUTE

The entry into the rapid is the most critical maneuver. Unless you have to punch a big hydraulic right at the top of the rapid, consider approaching the lip as slowly as possible to glean a last glimpse downstream. Remember that the rapid is going to look quite different from your new vantage point—especially if the rapid is steep—and that you'll probably have prerapid butterflies.

As you enter the rapid, relax and look around. It is amazing how many kayakers experience tunnel vision in whitewater, emerging wet and excited in the pool below but utterly unable to remember what just happened upstream. Run the rapid methodically, sticking to your main plan and adjusting it whenever the river proves to be too cunning a foe. Make each move by adjusting your kayak's momentum and its angle just as you learned earlier in this chapter, and be ready to celebrate your trip when you reach the safety of the pool downstream! If all goes well, you'll have plenty of reason to rejoice!

Honing Your Skills

As your basic skills improve, you may find yourself longing for wilder rapids or contentedly returning to the gentle rivers you have become accustomed to. No matter what your aspirations, you can vastly improve your kayaking skills by looking at the river you're on *right now* in a very different light.

Until now you have been taught to look for the safest, easiest routes through rapids. At the same time, you learned that many rapids have several runnable channels. Now it's time to shun the obvious passages and to test your skills by *using* the river to challenge yourself.

Rather than taking the cleanest line through a Class II or III rapid, look for an imaginary slalom course, using boulders, holes, or logs to mark your serpentine route. Ferry back and forth around boulders and try to connect the eddies behind rocks, stopping in each eddy as you go. Soon you will be able to paddle exactly where *you* want to go, not merely wherever the *river* carries you. With just a little practice, your skill level will skyrocket, preparing you for greater challenges to come.

7

SAFETY AND RESCUE

KEEPING YOUR HEAD AND GEAR ABOVE WATER

Today's kayakers find themselves in a unique quandary. Equipped with top-quality equipment and a wealth of intellectual know-how, modern kayakers are able to tackle rapids that would have sent previous explorers scurrying toward the riverbank in search of portage routes. Also, the techniques that took our predecessors many years to learn can now be acquired by zealous novices in just a few weeks or months.

The rush toward more exciting and difficult whitewater has carried with it greater risk and increased perils. The difference between a Class III and a Class V swim can be astounding, yet many newcomers find themselves on expert runs without even having perfected their basic strokes. Also, fundamental rescue skills—such as those necessary to retrieve a wrapped kayak or pinned swimmer—frequently elude the eager novice while he moves on to harder and harder rivers.

As in any outdoor sport, uncontrolled risk invites calamity. Accordingly, safety should be the primary concern on any river outing, whether it involves a peaceful scenic float or a heart-pounding Class V descent. In this chapter we'll learn the safety and rescue techniques experienced kayakers use to stay out of trouble.

If you're in trouble, solid safety and rescue skills will get you out of it.

A Word of Caution

Safety and rescue procedures—like rivers themselves—change from one situation to another. There may be dozens of ways to extract yourself from a predicament, but it may also take plenty of know-how to decide which techniques will work best.

This chapter will give you the tools to handle many rescue situations. Still, before you jump onto rivers that push your skills to their limit, take a course in river rescue from a certified *Rescue 3* instructor (listed in the appendix under "Safety Instruction Organizations") and read books like Charlie Walbridge and Wayne Sundmacher Sr.'s *Whitewater Rescue Manual* (Ragged Mountain Press, 1995). With proper skill, knowledge, and judgment, your river outings will be safer and more enjoyable.

Pretrip Preparedness

One of your most important pretrip considerations is to select a river that every member of your group is capable of doing. Using the weakest members of your party as the reference point, pick a river that is within your *entire* group's skill level. There are scores of outstanding guidebooks, maps, and other resources to assist you in your search for the ideal river. Be sure to research adequately the location of and distance between put-ins and take-outs, the time it will take to run the river, the classification and location of major rapids, and the recommended safe water levels. Pay particular attention to road access and shuttle information—important factors on any trip since shuttles frequently consume a lot of valuable time and daylight. Also keep in mind that any guidebook is only a reference source, and that rivers change constantly. Seek out the recommendations and advice of more experienced kayakers whose firsthand knowledge of the river exceeds that of any guidebook author.

The next step in your pretrip agenda is to survey water levels and local weather forecasts. Gentle streams can become angry, dangerous torrents at high water, and bone-chilling winds or driving rains can dampen even the liveliest spirits. A number of government agencies provide prerecorded river level readings and weather reports over the phone. Another source of information is your local whitewater shop or an outfitter located near the river.

TIME ON THE RIVER

Rivers flow—dams notwithstanding—on their own schedules. Veteran kayakers can *guesstimate* how long a trip will take by comparing the current's average velocity to the distance between the put-in and the take-out. Beginner to intermediate kayakers can avoid this kind of guesswork by simply consulting a guidebook or a knowledgeable kayaker to find out how long a particular trip usually takes.

Once on the river, kayakers can try to beat the clock by paddling faster than the river's average flow, but that expends a lot of energy and cuts down on the quality of the experience (unless, of course, you're racing). Also, rivers tend to hold time-consuming surprises for the wary and the unwary river runner alike—an unseen snag can puncture a tube and delay your take-out, or an unexpected rise in water level might increase the river's difficulty, leading to more scouting or portaging.

To make sure that you have enough time to enjoy your whitewater trip safely, *expect the unexpected* and leave enough time to handle ordinary mishaps.

PRETRIP DISCUSSION

Before leaving the put-in, take some time to gather the group and select a group leader. Discuss the day's itinerary, expected hazards, what order the group should travel in, and the signals that will be used to communicate between boats. There are a few common signals suggested in the accompanying diagram, but decide what signals your group will use and make sure everyone understands them.

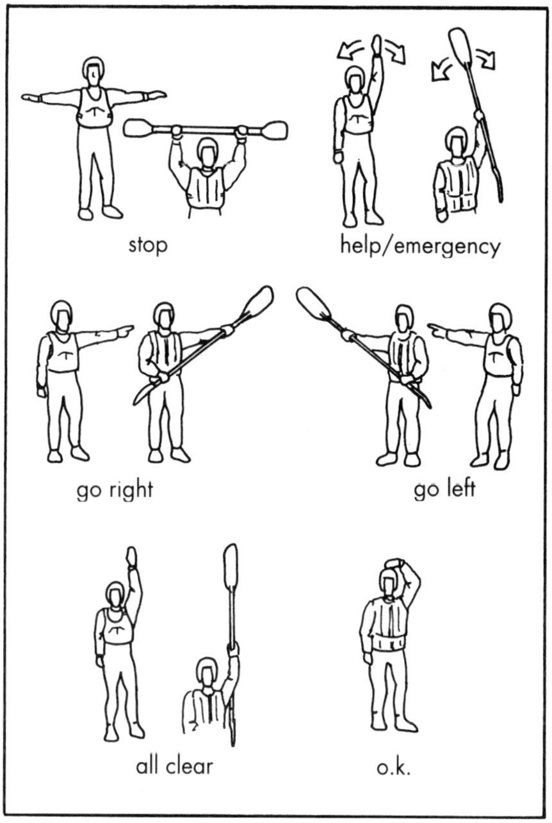

Common hand and paddle signals.

Equipment

Top-quality equipment often makes the difference between enjoyable river excursions and whitewater fiascoes. On the other hand, you don't have to dump all of your hard-earned money into the most expensive, top-of-the-line gear available. Simply utilize good-quality equipment that is specifically designed to withstand the rigors of whitewater use.

In addition to the equipment described in Chapter 2, kayakers should carry an assortment of essential safety gadgets—*carabiners, knives, whistles, prussiks, pulleys, throw bags, web slings,* and *first aid kits.* Also, whenever there's a chance of a paddle breaking on a remote river, someone should carry a *two-piece/take-apart paddle* (also

Make sure you have all of the safety gear you'll need to keep your trip safe and enjoyable.

known as a *breakdown paddle*). These paddles split in half and can be stored in the stern of your kayak until they're needed.

The downside of carrying rescue gear is that it will add weight to your kayak and make it harder to maneuver. However, if an emergency arises, its presence will bring peace of mind. Carry it along, and hope that the gear just collects water spots while you enjoy the river.

CARABINERS

Carabiners are the river runner's *multipurpose tool*: They can be used to clip in gear and attach lines to kayaks and can be substituted for pulleys in an emergency. Experienced river runners carry two or three carabiners clipped to the shoulder or waist of their lifejackets so that they'll be readily accessible when needed. (It is important to keep the carabiners tucked flat against the lifejacket with the gates *facing inward* to prevent injury or accidental clipping onto stray ropes or branches.)

KNIVES

Knives have many applications on the river. They can quickly sever a thigh strap before it puts you or a fellow kayaker in danger and can cut any other straps or lines that threaten your well-being. Quality river knives have solid sheaths of plastic or stiffened leather and can be worn on the chest or shoulder of your lifejacket for quick access. If you have a thumb-released sheath, check the thumb release frequently to make sure your knife will still be there when you need it.

WHISTLES

Whistles are real attention getters in almost any situation, and can be used to signal an emergency with three short blasts.

PRUSSIKS

A prusik is a short loop—about 4 or 5 feet long—made of 5- to 7-millimeter kernmantle rope. It can be used to tie off kayaks or to set brakes in Z-drag rescue systems (discussed later in this chapter).

When making your own prussiks, decide if you'll wear them around your waist like a belt. If you will be wearing the prussik belt fashion, measure your waist with your lifejacket and river clothes on, then double your waist measurement and add 1 foot to get the length of rope you'll need. Next, tie the ends of the rope together with a double fisherman's knot to form the loop (see the appendix). Now the prussik is ready to be worn around the waist and clipped in with a carabiner.

PULLEYS

Pulleys are handy friction-reducing tools that can be used in Z-drag rescues to increase the efficiency of the system. For river use, select sturdy aluminum-alloy pulleys designed to accommodate ½-inch (11-millimeter) rope.

THROW BAGS

Throw bags—also known as *throw ropes, rescue ropes,* and *rescue bags*—are remarkable rope-retaining tools designed to spool out rope freely when the bag is tossed to a swimmer. They simplify the rope-throwing process and make it easier for swimmers to see the rope coming—especially when the bag is filled with brightly colored, high-floating rope. When not in use, the throw bag neatly stows the rope out of harm's way.

STATIC ROPES

Wraps and entrapments are two of the biggest perils facing kayakers. While a throw rope may be strong enough to unwrap a kayak or free a stranded swimmer, there may be times when a rope with superior strength and minimum stretch is needed.

High-quality static lines have incredible tensile strength—far more than found in most throw-bag ropes. If practicable, you should store 100 feet of ½-inch (11-millimeter) static rope in your kayak. Note, however, that the static rope's bulk and weight often makes this impractical.

WEB SLINGS

Web slings—made of 1- or 2-inch-wide nylon webbing—can be used as anchors in Z-drag systems, rappel

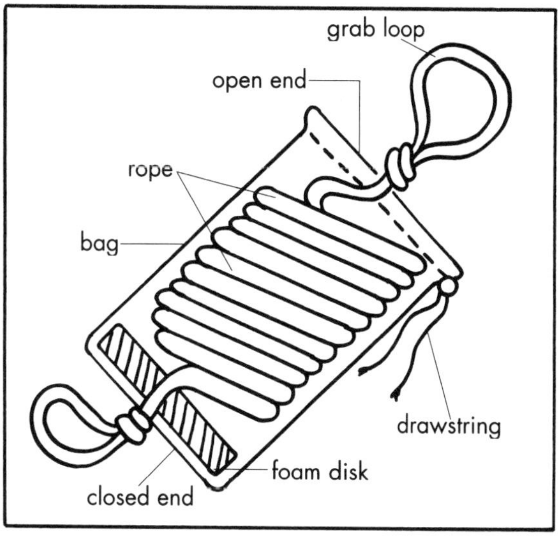

Anatomy of a throw bag.

anchors, and makeshift harnesses for vertical extrications. By carrying a few slings of varying lengths (10 to 20 feet long) in your rescue kit, you'll be prepared to set up anchors in most any type of canyon environment.

FIRST AID KITS

A first aid kit should be standard equipment on any river trip. Minor injuries are inevitable, even on easy rivers, but can often be treated immediately by someone trained in first aid. Take the time to consider the type of trip you're undertaking and the location of the nearest medical assistance when you assemble the first aid kit. Consult the appendix for a partial list of suggested items to include in your first aid kit.

Group Travel

LEAD AND SWEEP KAYAKS

River trips are safer when two, three, or more kayaks participate. The extra boats and paddlers can provide assistance in emergencies and can make the difference between a successful rescue and a disaster. In groups of three or more kayaks, it may be helpful to choose a *lead* boat to run at the front of the pack and a *sweep* boat to bring up the rear. The lead kayak usually contains the most experienced and knowledgeable paddler, acts as a scout or probe in rapids, and renders assistance to other kayaks when everyone pulls over to scout. The sweep boat also contains an experienced paddler but lags slightly behind the pack so it can help if a problem arises.

GROUP SCOUTING AND RESCUE

It is often helpful to scout difficult rapids as a group and to follow the SAFE plan (Scout, Analyze, Formulate, and Execute—see Chapter 6). Try to get everybody involved and listening to the group discussion—that way everyone will know the group's game plan.

In easy rapids, a rescue plan is rarely needed. However, more difficult rapids demand special consideration and extra precautions. If the rapid is too difficult for your skill level, portage around it. If you plan to run it, position a couple of kayakers with throw bags at key points along the rapid to render assistance in case you flip or swim. Practice *redundant safety,* which simply means having both a main plan and a contingency plan for everything that could go wrong.

Portaging

Rapids evoke a broad spectrum of emotions—from excitement to outright fear. Your mind's inner voice usually provides a good gauge of your chances of success. For those of us who like to ignore our *mind's* inner voices, we can listen to our *bodies*—a sudden desire to urinate or the inability to spit are pretty good indicators that the rapid's going to present a heck of a challenge.

Portaging is commonplace on whitewater rivers. Whenever a stretch of the river exceeds your skill level, shoulder your kayak and start walking. If there is a shallow route around a rapid, you can float your kayak in front of you while you hold it from the upstream end. Whatever you do, don't let your peers, ego, or disdain for portaging put you in whitewater that exceeds your skill level.

Self-Rescues

River-based rescues fall into two categories: *self-rescues* and *assisted rescues*. In self-rescues, kayakers are essentially left to attend to their own well-being; in assisted rescues, land- and water-based rescuers contribute to the relief efforts with throw lines, extra boats, and physical support. In both types of rescues, one aspect of river safety reigns supreme: People come first!

Inflatable kayaks are amazingly stable—up to a point. Once you pass that last point of stability, your kayak flips and you go for a swim. If you can stay with your kayak and hold onto your paddle, you can reboard and keep paddling. This is called the *kayak self-rescue*.

Before deciding to self-rescue, quickly analyze your predicament. It is often safer to stay with your kayak than it is to swim to safety, but let the river tell you what to do. While a kayak provides tremendous flotation and visibility for rescuers, it can pin you if you get trapped between the kayak and an obstacle. Be prepared to abandon your boat if you will be better off swimming to safety.

If you are near your kayak and it is upright, kick your feet and swim over the nearest tube back into the cockpit. By twisting your torso forward or rolling over into the cockpit, you can quickly regain your normal seating position and start paddling as soon as you're ready. Try to enter your kayak from the upstream side so you don't get smashed by your boat, but sometimes it is better just to get into the kayak as fast as you can.

If your kayak is upside down, reach across the floor, grab the far tube or drain holes, and flip the boat back upright. (You can also use the thigh straps, seat, or footbraces to flip the kayak over.) Once the boat is upright, pull yourself back aboard and get ready to paddle again.

If you find yourself swimming a particularly rocky rapid next to your upside-down kayak, you may have one other option: climbing onto the floor of the kayak. Overturned kayaks may be mounted and used like a giant piece of inflatable armor to keep you from getting beaten up by rocks and boulders. If you make it through a rapid like this, you can flip your kayak and board it properly when an opportunity arises.

GRAB STRAPS

Some kayakers attach a 2- to 3-foot strap to the stern before running difficult rivers and let it trail on the

This kayak self-rescue started with an upside-down kayak. The swimmer righted the kayak by pulling the bottom tube toward him while pushing the other tube upward.

Once the kayak was upright, he then kicked his legs to swim over the near tube. Notice that he didn't lose his paddle.

To regain his seat, the paddler flopped his butt into the seat while kicking his legs forward.

In a matter of seconds, the kayak self-rescue was completed.

surface behind the kayak. This short safety strap can give you something extra to grab after a flip before your kayak drifts away. Keep in mind, however, that any extra line or webbing increases your chances of becoming entangled. So choose your setup wisely.

THE ESKIMO ROLL

The Eskimo (or *IK*) roll—a complicated combination of sweep strokes and body rotations—is one of those feats that separates hardshell kayaking from inflatable kayaking. When a skilled kayaker flips a hardshell kayak upside down, he can use his paddle to do a sort of inverted sweeping brace to right himself. Once an inflatable kayak flips, on the other hand, the paddler inevitably swims. That is, unless the paddler is one of the lucky few who have mastered the Eskimo roll.

Only a few modern inflatable kayaks combine the small tube diameters, narrow widths, and customized cockpits that are needed to make the roll possible. Even with the best designs, it is extremely difficult to roll an inflatable kayak.

The easiest way to learn an IK roll is first to learn how to roll a hardshell kayak. (Books describing hardshell techniques are listed under "Recommended Reading" in the appendix.) The techniques will be almost identical, with only minor variations: First, rolling an inflatable kayak is easier if you slide your hands down the paddle shaft so that the sweeping blade extends farther out from the boat (kayak instructors call this the "extended paddle position"). Also, it takes a lot more patience and strength to roll an inflatable kayak than it does a hardshell kayak.

SWIMMING

Swimming a rapid, much to the surprise of many beginners, is nothing like swimming in a lake or a pool. Strong currents can overwhelm and quickly fatigue even experienced swimmers. However, once swimmers learn about the forces involved—either by swimming easy rapids or from prior experience—they can relax and rationally set out to swim to safety.

Unless you intentionally jumped into the river, your first reaction to swimming will be one of surprise. Most of the time you'll pop back to the surface instantly, cussing the cold and aiming your lips toward the sky. Survey the river and banks the moment your vision clears, and look downstream for calm pools or major hazards. Hold onto your paddle unless releasing it increases your chances of a quick rescue.

ACTIVE SWIMMING

If you find yourself too far from your kayak or rescuers, you should be prepared to actively find a way to the safety of an eddy or the bank. Start off by getting yourself to the surface. (Now, I don't really expect you to ask yourself what the first goal is—your lungs will remind you in a hurry!) In violent hydraulics it can be pretty difficult to find the surface. Relax for a second and look around. Head toward the light or follow the bubbles. When you know you're heading in the right direction, keep a cool head and tight lips until you can breathe again.

Once back at the surface, aggressively spot and avoid hazards and prepare to swim toward shore when an opportunity arises. Swimmers in shallow, boulder-strewn rapids should lie on their backs, feet held high and pointed downstream. By assuming this *human shock absorber* position it is possible to fend off rocky collisions with your feet and to use backstrokes and leg kicks to ferry yourself toward safety.

With your feet floating ahead of you, a new hazard

When swimming a rapid, you can use your legs like giant shock absorbers to avoid painful collisions with obstacles. Keep your legs and feet near the surface, but ball up if you're going to go over a steep drop. When an opportunity arises, swim actively toward safety.

Can an expert roll an inflatable kayak? You bet!

presents itself—*foot entrapment.* To avoid this peril, never try to stand up in rapids. Instead, wait until the current has subsided or you are in the calm of a gentle eddy.

In any swimming situation, let the river dictate your actions. In deeper, more powerful rapids, you may be better off turning onto your stomach and swimming aggressively toward shore. In steep, bone-bruising rapids, the *cannonball* position—your knees pulled into your chest—may be a good short-term way to protect your limbs (and other vital parts) from injury. Always strive to keep enough air in your lungs. Swimmers should breathe only in the calm troughs between wave crests, and should turn their heads to the side to avoid inhaling any spray or foam.

HOLES AND DAMS

The upstream surface currents of large holes and lowhead dams can recirculate swimmers indefinitely, and once you are caught in these traps, your lifejacket may not have enough flotation to float you above the aerated water. Accordingly, holes and dams sometimes demand special techniques for quick escapes.

Keep in mind that most holes are too small to be keepers. So if you find yourself stuck momentarily in the backwash, relax for a second, breathe when you can, and try to swim sideways out of the hole. If you can't escape sideways, remember that the falls contains a powerful downcurrent that can be used to push you under the hole and out. Swim right into the falls, ball up in the cannonball position, and hang on for the ride. If you come up on the boil line, be sure to swim aggressively downstream to avoid being recirculated.

Lowhead dams contain the most deadly of all holes, and the ones most difficult to escape. ***Don't run them!*** If you ever *do* find yourself swimming a dam, you may recirculate in the backwash many times. Try to save your energy and work your way toward shore. Swimming into the falls may be enough to push you out under the backwash, but be prepared to make many attempts at self-rescue. Above all, *don't give up!*

STRAINERS AND SWEEPERS

Some of the worst hazards facing kayakers are downed trees (sweepers) and boulder sieves (strainers). Since these obstacles don't impede the current entirely, sweepers can snag lifejackets and hold a swimmer underwater, and strainers can wedge swimmers into tight subsurface pockets.

If you find yourself swimming toward one of these hazards, try to swim around it with all the power you can muster. If a collision with a downed tree or log is inevitable, turn onto your stomach and face downstream, concentrating on the approaching log or tree. A split moment before you reach the log, begin kicking your legs and pull your body *over it head first* using any handholds you can find. Give it all you've got! If you can't make it over the log, try hanging on until you can be rescued. If you absolutely have to go under the strainer, first feel for snags with your legs. Remember, going underneath a strainer is the last thing you want to do! Do it only as a last resort.

Assisted Rescues

ASSISTED KAYAK RESCUE

A kayaker in his boat can often assist a swimmer by offering a tow or a place to sit in the stern. In many situations, a swimmer can grab a stern handle or tube with one hand, hold the paddle with the other hand, and kick while the rescuer tows him to safety. On rare occasions, the swimmer can crawl into the stern compartment and lay low while the rescuer paddles to safety. This latter technique is difficult, however, because it usually overloads the kayak and makes effective paddling extremely difficult.

ROPE RESCUES

Throw bags—also called *throw ropes, rescue ropes,* and *rescue bags*—can provide a lifesaving umbilical cord linking a swimmer with a rescuer, but it takes a lot more than just aiming and tossing a throw rope to carry out a good rescue. It takes frequent practice to land a throw rope where a swimmer can reach it, and it takes keen knowledge of currents and river forces to finish off a rescue once a swimmer actually grasps the rope.

GETTING ROPES TO SWIMMERS

Before throwing a rope to a swimmer, evaluate the situation. The most effective rope rescues are those that

Log jams and sweepers are extremely dangerous. Though still in a precarious position, the kayaker got to shore before his kayak pinned on a barely submerged log.

were anticipated before the swim. By stationing rescuers where the swimmer actually has an opportunity to see a throw bag coming, rescuers have a chance to establish the *first goal* of rope rescues: *eye contact* with the swimmer. By stationing a rescuer slightly downstream of where a flip might occur, the swimmer has a chance to get back to the surface and clear her vision before the rope toss is made. Then, with a strong yell from the rescuer ("ROPE!"), the swimmer has a chance to look at the rescuer and see the rope coming.

The rescuer's *second goal* also involves proper bank positioning, this time taking into account the power of the main current and downstream obstacles. Position the rescuer so that the first toss angles *45 degrees upstream* toward the swimmer. That way, the current can actually *help* push the swimmer toward the rescuer as the rope is pulled in. (Also, by throwing the rope upstream to the swimmer, the rescuer may have a chance at a second toss if the first one misses the mark.) If there are calm currents or gentle pools below a likely flip spot, the rescuer can use the rope to pendulum the swimmer into shore. Never, however, pull a swimmer into a worse situation than he or she is already in. Make sure that the rescue path is free of boulder sieves, sweepers, and other hazards that might be best avoided by letting the swimmer swim a few more yards downstream.

The rescuer's *third goal* is to get the rope *to* the swimmer. Depending on your dexterity, and on surrounding obstacles like overhanging cliffs or branches, your best toss may be underhand, sidearm, or overhand. Though it helps to be adept at all three types of throws, most rescues are done with an underhand toss. When aiming your throw, try to land the rope *at or just downstream* of the swimmer. That way, the swimmer can reach the rope even if it is a few feet away. (If you aim upstream of the swimmer, the slower surface current will slow the rope's descent

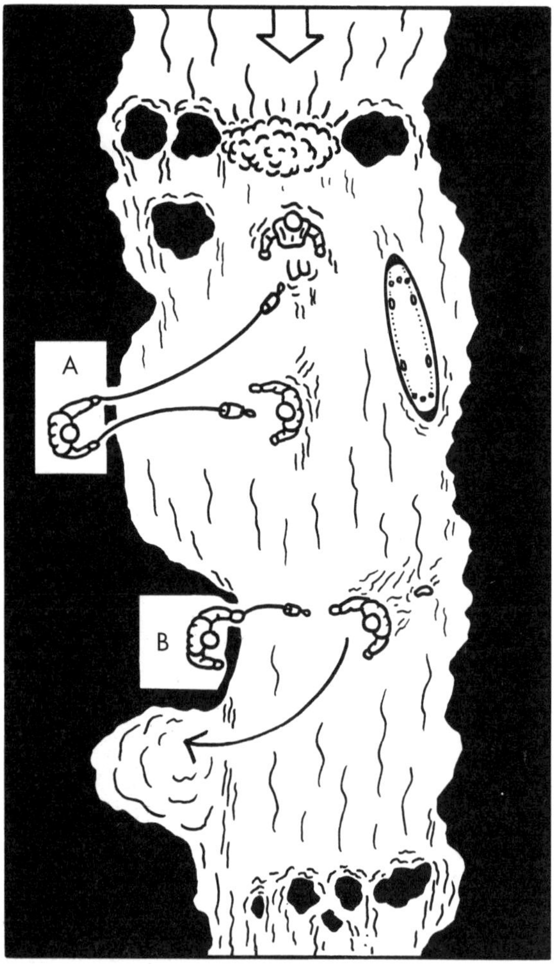

Position rescuers where they'll do the most good. Here, rescuer A can toss a throw line 45 degrees upstream toward the swimmer after a flip, and can get in a second toss before the swimmer heads downstream. Rescuer B can pull the swimmer into a calm eddy before he floats into a dangerous boulder sieve.

while the swimmer accelerates downstream in the deeper, faster currents.)

A swimmer has to be able to help himself just as much as the rescuer helps him. Presuming that the rope reaches the swimmer, the swimmer must be prepared to grab the rope with one or both hands and turn onto his back, faceup. (It is important to grab the rope, not the bag!) In this position, the swimmer's body will plane toward the surface and offer less resistance to the current. Swimmers should never wrap the rope around their hands, limbs, or bodies!

Swimmers should hold the rescue rope over their shoulders and lie on their backs. That way, they'll plane toward the surface and have an air pocket over their faces. Never wrap the rope around your wrist, arm, or body!

BELAYS

Once the rescuer and the swimmer are holding either end of the rescue rope, it is time to work the swimmer toward shore. Both people should pull the slack out of the rope and prepare for a powerful jolt as the rope pulls tight. There are two ways to pull the swimmer ashore: The rescuer can pull the swimmer in from a stationary position with a *static belay* or can run downstream with the swimmer in a *dynamic belay*.

In a static belay, the rescuer pendulums the swimmer toward the shore from a stationary point on the bank. The rescuer can step on the end of the rope if she's worried that it will pull free or can use a belay anchor, such as a tree stump or boulder. In using a belay anchor, the rope is wrapped one-half to one full turn around the anchor. (If you wrap the rope more than once around the anchor, it will take longer to unwrap it.)

In strong currents, a *dynamic belay* is better since it reduces the counteracting forces, which could jar the rope from the swimmer's hands. In a dynamic belay, the rescuer walks or runs down the bank with the swimmer, pulling him in gradually with light rope pressure. This technique, as you can imagine, works only if there is an open corridor along the river bank.

There are two more tips that will make rope rescues easier. First, don't pick a rescue position too high above the river as this will make the working length of rope both shorter and less versatile. Second, use the best type of throw you can. Depending on where you're standing, the throw bag or rescue rope may have to be thrown underhand, overhand, or sidearm.

The rescuer can use a static belay (A) or a dynamic belay (B) to assist the swimmer. In case a dynamic belay becomes necessary after a static belay has already started, never wrap the rope more than one turn around an anchor.

OTHER ROPE RESCUES

There may be times when a swimmer is caught against a midstream boulder and a throw rope or a boat-based rescue is simply impossible. If someone has to reach the swimmer to render assistance, one technique that might work is the *strong-swimmer rescue.*

The strong-swimmer rescue is a paradox in rescue procedures—it increases the risk that the rescuer could be hurt or drowned by placing the rescuer *inside* a rope-loop while working in the current. Nonethe-less, there may be times when nothing else works and the increased risk is justified by trying to save a victim's life.

The strong-swimmer rescue requires—minimally—a swimmer, a belayer, and a strong rope. A large, *very loose* loop is tied into one end of the rope and placed around the rescuer's chest. (The loop must be loose enough to push free if the rescuer runs into any trouble.) Once in the loop, the rescuer can be pendulumed to the victim from the far bank (this works only in narrow streams) or lowered downstream to the victim from an upstream boulder or island.

A slightly safer alternative to the strong-swimmer rescue is an offshoot of the fixed horizontal line (discussed on page 94). In rescue situations, a fixed horizontal line can be rigged with one end anchored and one end loose. By slowly letting rope out from one of the belay anchors, the rescuer can walk downstream while leaning at waist height against the line, and can be set free in an emergency by somersaulting away from the line or having a belayer release one end of the rope.

River Crossings

It is sometimes necessary to walk across shallow rivers without a rope. This can be done solo in gentle currents, or as a team in stronger currents. No matter which technique is used, the same basic concepts apply: All shallow water crossings are premised on maintaining *three points of contact* with the

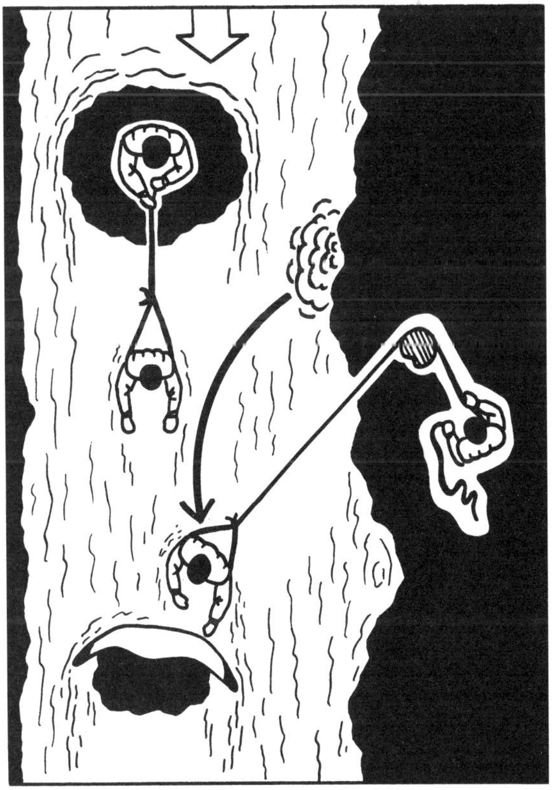

Strong-swimmer rescues: The rescuer can be pendulumed down to the victim from the bank, or can walk downstream from an island.

When doing a solo crossing, use a paddle, pole, or sturdy branch to brace yourself. The paddle and your feet provide three points of contact with the riverbed. By leaning forward and moving just one point of contact at a time, you are much more stable than you would be otherwise.

river bottom, and are done slowly and methodically to avoid foot entrapment. Also, one crossing method may outweigh another depending on the speed of the current and the depth of the river.

SOLO CROSSINGS

When crossing a river by yourself, use a sturdy paddle, pole, or tree limb as a brace. (The brace and your two feet provide three points of contact.) Face upstream and jam one end of the paddle into the river bottom and tilt it 30 degrees back toward your shoulder. At the same time, brace your shoulder against the paddle and lean your body 30 degrees upstream against it. Maintaining this 60-degree triangle, you can slowly sidestep your way across the river, moving one point of contact at a time.

GROUP CROSSINGS

The most basic group crossings are mere variations of solo crossings: The solo crosser carries someone *piggyback* from one bank to the other or a second individual follows the lead person across the river pressed tightly against his back and the back of his legs.

If more people are to be added to the group, each new person can step toward the outboard shoulder of the person in front of him, effectively forming a *wedge* formation. A *line astern* formation works by placing additional people directly behind the point person. The secondary people add stability to the system by pressing down on the point person's shoulders, effectively increasing the pressure on his feet and the river bottom.

If there are three people in your group, you can also arrange yourselves in a triangle and lock your arms around one another's shoulders. With the heaviest person on the downstream end of the triangle, facing upstream, the group can lean into one another and form a pyramid. With one person moving his feet at a time, the group can work its way across the river.

Another way to shuttle people across the river is with a *fixed horizontal line*. The fixed horizontal line is a rope that is stretched taut just a foot or so above the river. The crosser simply stands upstream of the fixed line, holds the rope against her waist, and walks sideways across the river. If something goes wrong, all she has to do is somersault over or swim under the rope to break free. Since there is always a possibility that the crosser could snag a lifejacket buckle or carabiner on the line, the line shouldn't be anchored on both banks. Instead, use belay points on both banks or just tie one anchor off while belaying from the opposite bank.

Wraps

A wrap is one of those river ordeals that you'll never forget. It either provides an exciting opportunity to apply all of your rescue skills and ingenuity, or else leaves you tapping your booties together and chanting, "There's no place like home, there's no place like home, there's no place . . ."

When a kayak wraps around a rock or obstacle, hun-

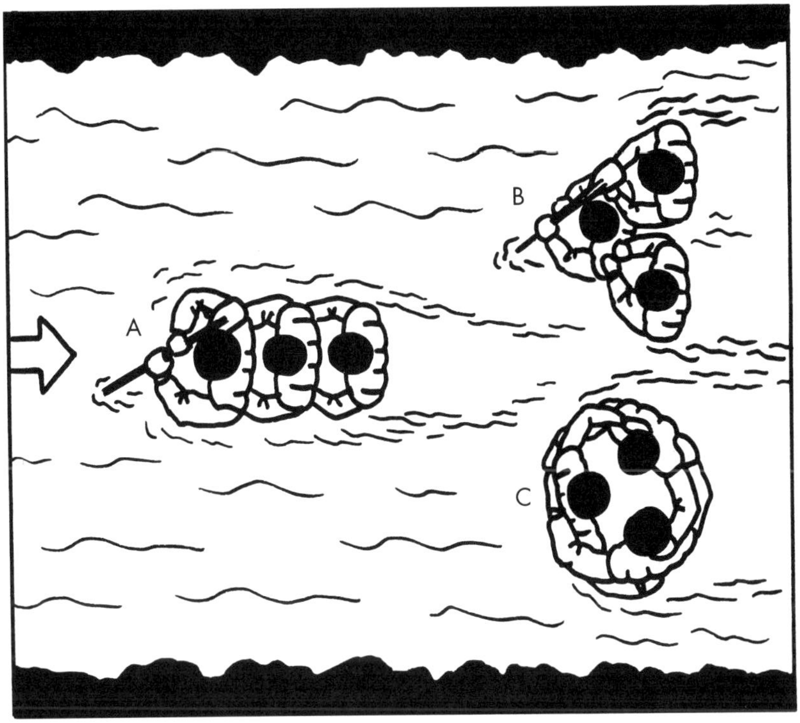

Three ways to cross a river with a small group: Group A is standing in a line astern formation; group B is using a wedge formation; and group C is using a triangle formation. Each technique relies on the downward pressure exerted by each individual to stabilize the entire group.

dreds or thousands of pounds of water hold it securely in place. Overcoming such forces takes muscle, sturdy equipment, and a bit of streamside engineering.

A horizontal line supports the crosser, but allows him to dive over or under the line in an emergency. Don't anchor the ends of the rope—you may have to let one end go if the crosser gets caught on the rope.

Some river runners look at wraps as an outstanding opportunity to whip out all their rescue paraphernalia, blanket the landscape in ropes and hardware, and set up intricate retrieval systems. While some wraps require just that type of action, it is usually more efficient to select the most basic system that will retrieve the kayak quickly without any complication.

SURVEY THE SCENE

Before setting up any ropes, survey the scene. Which bank is the kayak facing? What obstacles await downstream once the kayak is freed? How much of the kayak is left showing? How accessible are anchor points on the kayak and along the banks? Will the kayak be easier to remove in one direction than another?

Then, appoint someone to direct the rescue operation. The director should be a member of the shore crew unless the only one who knows how to unwrap the kayak is still sitting in the middle of the river. By putting one person in charge, rescuers can work together as a team under the guidance of one coach. Keep in mind that the rescue process set out below is flexible and should be tailored to meet the needs of your situation.

THE ANCHORS

Start the rescue operation by securely attaching one end of a strong rope to the kayak. (Don't use your throw-bag rope on a severe wrap, unless that's all that you have available. It could easily snap under stress and injure a rescuer.) If the kayak was left in a precarious position after all its passengers washed free,

A close look at this picture reveals a kayak wrapped around a barely submerged boulder. (Photo by Bryan Cavaness)

of force—more force than most D-rings and handles can withstand. Since these attachments have a tendency to blow free unexpectedly, consider other anchoring options. In self-bailing kayaks, try tying your rope around an exposed tube by threading it through the floor's drain holes; in standard-floor kayaks, tie ropes to thwarts or multiple D-rings.

BASIC ROPE SYSTEMS

The first way to pull a kayak loose is simply to join your fellow paddlers in a riverside version of tug-of-war. The tug-of-war develops only a 1:1 mechanical advantage, but can pull lightly wrapped kayaks free. A variation on this is the vector pull: Rather than pulling on the end of the rope, you tie the end to an anchor point and attach a second rope to the center of the first rope at a 90-degree angle. Depending on which direction the second rope is pulled, a slightly higher power ratio can be transferred to the kayak.

To double the power of your pulling system, anchor a pulley or couple of carabiners to the kayak and run the rope through them. Then, with one end of the rope tied to an anchor point on shore, you can pull on the loose end of the rope and create a 2:1 mechanical advantage.

Z-DRAGS

The Z-drag is one of the most popular rescue systems available. In a simple Z-drag system a 3:1 mechanical advantage is developed, and more complex Z-drag systems can generate much greater leverage.

It takes little more than some strong rope to build a rudimentary Z-drag system, but carabiners and

reaching the kayak could be very difficult. Proceed with great caution and choose the approach that is lowest in risk. That might mean that you'll have to set up a horizontal-line or a strong-swimmer rescue to reach the boat. Once at the kayak you may be able to stand on the obstacle holding it in place or to sit on the exposed tube. If an anchor point is submerged, try to have an assistant hold on to the rigger to keep him from getting pinned or swept beneath the surface.

Some rescue systems develop a tremendous amount

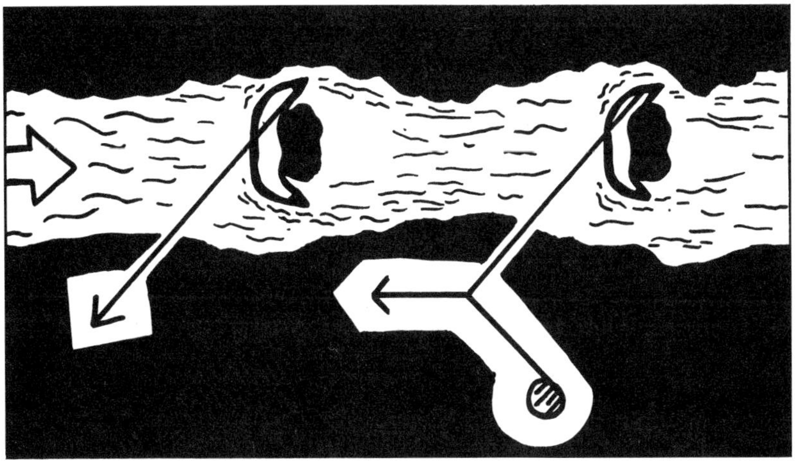

The tug-of-war (left) and the vector pull (right) provide two basic ways to unwrap a pinned kayak.

pulleys will lower rope friction wherever the rope makes a turn. (If you don't have carabiners or pulleys, use a figure eight or butterfly knot in their place. These knots are shown in the appendix.)

The first step in setting up the Z-drag involves anchoring the rope to the kayak just as you would for tug-of-wars and vector pulls. At the same time, tie a sturdy tubular webbing sling or rope around a shore-based anchor and clip a carabiner and a pulley (if they're available) into the webbing.

To set up a 2:1 system, run the rope from an anchor to the kayak and back to shore. For every pound of pressure exerted on the end of the rope, 2 pounds of pull will transfer to the kayak.

Next, tie a figure eight or butterfly knot in the rope between the kayak and the anchor loop. Since this knot will move toward shore when you start pulling on the rope, it is important to set the knot close enough to the kayak so that it won't jam into the shore anchor. (If you're standing on the shore far from the kayak, you might want to tie the figure eight or butterfly knot *before* you anchor the rope to the kayak.) If you have another carabiner and pulley handy, clip them into this knot.

Then it's time to complete the system. Take the rope's loose end and thread it through the shore anchor carabiner or pulley, back through the figure eight or butterfly knot, and back to shore. If you've done this correctly, the system will form a backward Z. To operate the system, just pull the free end of the rope.

Some rescuers add a *brake prussik* (the prussik loop is illustrated in the appendix) to the shore anchor loop by wrapping the prussik loop around the pulling rope as shown in the appendix, then clipping the prussik loop to the anchor loop with a carabiner. The brake prussik lets rescuers rerig the system if a knot approaches the anchor loop, and stops the rope from traveling backward through the system. Second, additional lines to the kayak can be used to ease the burden on the Z-drag. A *rollover line* can also be used to help tug the kayak free. The rollover line runs over the top of the exposed tube, down around the back of the kayak, and attaches to the submerged D-ring or thwart. When pulled from upstream, this rope helps the kayak dump water and lessens the pressure on the Z-drag.

Z-drags can be rigged in many ways. By adding a 2:1 pull to the system, the mechanical

The basic Z-drag system: For every pound of pressure exerted on the end of the rope, 3 pounds of pull will transfer to the kayak.

advantage grows to 6:1, and by doubling the Z-drag, the mechanical advantage grows to 9:1. If nothing works—including one of the high-advantage Z-drag systems—it may be time to relieve the resistance caused by the floor. In self-bailing kayaks with laced-in floors, cut the floor line and let the floor flap open. This may make the kayak much easier to pull free. In standard-floor kayaks, cut a hole at the point of greatest pressure, but beware the consequence of doing this: The whole floor might tear out. Although arguably tubes could be deflated to assist in the rescue, this lets water enter the tubes, which eventually damages the kayak. The deflated tubes are also more likely to conform to the obstacle and make the wrap even worse.

A rollover line can be used to help drain water from a pinned kayak. A rollover line can be used alone or together with one of the other rope systems.

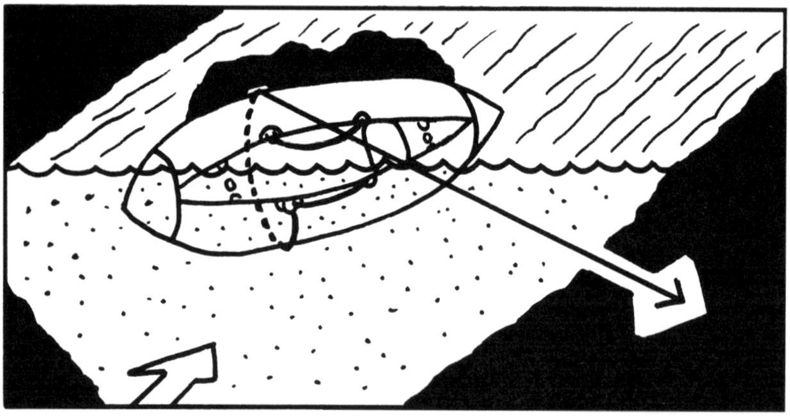

First Aid

As in any other form of outdoor recreation, kayakers may get injured. Fortunately, small cuts, bruises, or bouts with poison ivy are about as bad as any first aid provider will see. In any event, it is important to be prepared for any type of first aid situation, from broken bones to near drownings.

Take the Red Cross basic first aid and CPR courses and strive for higher levels of first aid certification. Know your physical limitations before embarking on a trip, and inform others of medical conditions that may affect patient care decisions. Also, have at least one member of your group carry a first aid kit on every trip. On longer wilderness rivers and remote streams it is important not only to *have* every item necessary to provide first aid, but to *know how to use* them effectively.

HYPOTHERMIA

The same water that provides a thrilling roller coaster ride can become a dangerous enemy for swimmers or underdressed passengers. Hypothermia—cooling of the body temperature—can happen whenever a swimmer is immersed in water for any length of time or when cool air and spray drain the body's ability to stay warm. Hypothermia affects your judgment and can be life-threatening in its advanced stages. So, it is important to avoid hypothermia with proper preparation and to know how to reverse its effects once it sets in.

Warm clothing, adequate food consumption, and constant activity provide the first line of defense against hypothermia, but one quick swim can drain even the heartiest kayakers of

By adding a second line, the mechanical advantage of this Z-drag has increased to 6:1

internal warmth. If a kayaker winds up in the river, get him or her out quickly. Water can drain body heat 20 to 30 times faster than air does, making even a short swim in very cold water dangerous.

It is important to know hypothermia's warning signs and how to treat a victim once these signs are present. In the initial stages of hypothermia, the victim may shiver vigorously, act cold, and appear pale. Treatment is easiest and most effective at this stage. Get the victim away from the river, into dry clothes, and near a source of heat, such as a car heater or a campfire. If nothing is available, walk the victim along the bank until he warms up and stops shivering. Left untreated, a victim will progress into the next stage of hypothermia.

As the body's core temperature drops to 90 to 95 degrees Fahrenheit, a hypothermia victim may become confused, clumsy, and sluggish, and shivering may slow down. Speech may become slurred and eyes may become dull. By the time these symptoms appear, the body has lost its ability to rewarm itself, and the basic treatment regimen won't work—an external source of heat is necessary. In a fix it may be necessary for a couple of people to climb into a sleeping bag with the victim and establish full-body skin-to-skin contact, letting their body warmth gently warm the victim. If a strong fire is available, seat the victim close to the heat with a backdrop of blankets or sleeping bags for insulation. Whatever is done, it has to be done before the victim loses any more heat.

As the victim's core temperature drops further, the muscles will become rigid; the patient will become unconscious and might suffer a cardiac arrest. Immediate evacuation and hospitalization is mandatory in this situation.

8

ADVANCED KAYAKING

PADDLING ON THE CUTTING EDGE

Three-Dimensional Paddling

How many times have you stood above a rapid, shoulder to shoulder with fellow kayakers, saying things like, "I'm going left of that hole, then to the right of the big boulder, then back to the center of those waves?" With minor variations, I've heard myself talk like that hundreds of times.

Subtle as it may seem, the myopic thought process going into scouting rapids was always two-dimensional, locked into directions like upstream and downstream, left banks and right banks. Advanced paddling forces you to explore new paddling techniques. It forces you beyond the two dimensional world you're become accustomed to and into *whitewater's third dimension.*

Whitewater's third dimension is the river's vertical world. A world of steep waves, sharp holes, exposed rocks, and swelling boils. Up to now you have thought of many surface features as *obstacles*—things to be avoided or overcome. But now you can begin to think of them as natural tools—tools that provide an extra link with gravity, friction, or hydraulic forces; tools that enhance your ability to outmaneuver a tough

Class V paddling is not for the weakhearted!

rapid; and tools that can make seemingly impossible rapids runnable.

In this chapter you'll explore the techniques and mind-set necessary to kayak difficult rivers. You'll discover specialized techniques for running everything from steep creeks to giant rivers. To the novice and intermediate kayaker, a lot of these concepts will sound insane. After all, who in their right mind would *intentionally* slide their kayak over rocks, drop off the lip of waterfalls, or surf holes to stop and scout a rapid?! But the advanced kayaker knows that these techniques not only exist, *they work!* If you're willing to step beyond conventional wisdom and to use every part of the river to its fullest potential, you'll walk away with a broadened perspective of your kayak's capabilities . . . and your own.

Preparation

Class IV and V rivers present challenges rarely found on gentler streams. Whether these challenges manifest themselves as endless boulder labyrinths or minefields of boat-swallowing holes, the consequences of human miscalculations or equipment failure can be catastrophic. Accordingly, Class V rivers mandate that paddlers and their equipment be up to the rigors the river will present. Any kayakers preparing to run a Class V river should already have two things going for them . . . the skills and confidence born of many hours on the river. These are not skills well suited just to a particular river or set of rapids, but skills that will translate well in any river situation: the ability to read and run confusing currents, full knowledge of the Z-drag and other rescue systems, the ability to recover quickly after a flip, experience in swimming rapids, and an understanding of emergency medical procedures.

A Class V rapid is *not* the place to learn about advanced kayaking. Instead, practice flipping and reflipping kayaks in Class III rapids with safe pools. Swim Class II rapids, trying to catch eddies by swimming back and forth across the current. Do everything that *could* happen in a Class V rapid in a controlled setting and get *good* at fast rescues long before your first Class V adventure.

In addition to the obvious skills needed to survive difficult whitewater, advanced kayakers should be in good physical condition. By being in shape your body will withstand the stresses of powerful rapids. You'll have the strength to power swamped kayaks around in pushy hydraulics, the ability to hold your breath during long swims, and the dexterity to lean and brace if your kayak collides with a menacing boulder.

Finally, advanced kayakers should surround themselves with top-quality equipment. Today's self-bailing kayaks provide an enormous safety margin for intrepid river travelers. Their ability to shed water quickly makes them much more nimble in long, difficult rapids than their standard-floor counterparts. Paddles, helmets, lifejackets, throw bags, and rescue gear should also be able to stand up to the rigors of the most demanding rapids. Still, kayakers should check and recheck their gear for flaws. Spare equipment should be carried whenever possible to replace whatever breaks down, and enough rescue and first aid gear should be carried to meet or exceed the needs of any emergency situation. This means carrying extra throw bags, static lines, carabiners, pulleys, expeditionary medical kits, and much, much more.

STOWING GEAR

The combination of extra gear and kayak-flipping rapids can be lethal. Catching a foot in a loose rope during a wrap might be all it takes to turn an adventure into a disaster. Pack gear as lightly and compactly as possible, remembering to leave safety gear readily accessible. Lash it tightly to the kayak in places that won't interfere with the positioning or movement of kayakers. Also avoid carrying solid items, like ammo cans, if possible. Soft-sided dry bags may work just as well, and won't rearrange valuable body parts in the event of a collision.

THE CLASS V ATTITUDE

The first sentence of the definition of Class V rapids says, "Extremely long, obstructed, or very violent rapids which expose a paddler to above-average endangerment." Scary, huh? You bet! Try paddling a long Class V rapid—even after scouting it thoroughly—and you're likely to be on the edge of your seat until you're resting safely in a pool below.

Class V rapids take both a different mind-set and a different approach. First, don't stare at one or two objects in the river, such as a big rock or a wave. You'll end up getting tunnel vision and lose sight of everything that is going on around you. Strive to broaden your peripheral vision and expand your senses. Relax, take a couple of deep breaths above the rapid, and try to breathe normally once you're in the whitewater. You'll have a much better feel for the rapid, and be able to react better if things go wrong.

It is important never to give up trying to navigate your kayak upright through a rapid until it flips or wraps. If you're suddenly confronted by a big boulder or the largest hole of the day, it is often better to keep maneuvering than to hold on. Your last-ditch effort might provide just enough momentum to bust through a hole, or just the right move to slip through the tight spot unscathed.

Finally, don't just run Class V rapids in one mad dash, dissect them into bite-size portions. Rather than blasting downstream, use a zigzag approach. Jump from eddy to eddy, concentrating on the next eddy as you head downstream, then regrouping and reassessing your plan once you arrive in the eddy. Use powerful ferries in the main channel to counteract the current, and avoid turning broadside to the current. Using this piecemeal approach to rapids, you'll have more control, more time to react, and additional time to mold your strategies.

Helpful Hydraulics

WAVES

The same gravitational forces that pull rivers downhill help kayakers *surf* in place on a standing wave. By pulling your kayak against the current on the upstream face of a wave—or in the trough between two waves—the kayak will stall out dramatically. This is not only fun, it can buy some extra time to execute maneuvers.

The first time you use a wave to slow down, keep your kayak parallel with the current. This will give you an extra second to make your next move. Once you get used to the feel of stalling on a wave, turn your kayak slightly, set a ferry angle, and back-ferry. The wave will magnify the intensity and trajectory of your ferry—in fact, by using medium-size waves (not waves large enough to flip your kayak), some seemingly impossible ferries can be achieved.

Waves can also act as *turntables,* making turns much easier. As your kayak approaches the crest of a wave, the bow and the stern become unweighted, and for a split second the kayak will spin easier than it does in wave troughs. Since a turn started in the trough between two steep waves often produces nothing until the kayak reaches a balancing point on the tip of the wave anyway, start your turns high on the wave to save a lot of unnecessary effort.

Once you get comfortable with wave moves, it will be easy to use them on other vertical features—large pillows, surging boils, and small breaking waves. Gravity acts as a maneuver turbocharger in all these situations.

HOLES

You first trip through a hole may have brought some big surprises. The powerful upstream current of the backwash may have kicked you sideways or stopped you in your tracks. However, experienced paddlers can tell which holes to run and which ones to avoid. They know that they can bob over small holes and that they have to hit big holes with precision and momentum.

Since small (smaller than your kayak) holes rarely meet the textbook definition of a *keeper* (most provide an easy escape route at one end or the other), they can be surfed in place or cross-river just like waves. In fact, small holes sometimes present the only stopping point in the midst of a long rapid.

The same concepts you just learned for wave surfing apply equally well to hole surfing, with some minor modifications. As you approach a hole, look for the direction of its *kick*—the direction it will toss your kayak as you plow into its backwash, then be prepared to brace to keep the kayak upright. If you are going to hit the hole fairly sideways, you can brace on the backwash for stability. If you plan to hit the hole straight, reach through the backwash and grab the solid current flowing downstream.

Remember, not every hole is runnable. If you think that impeccable bracing is all that stands between you

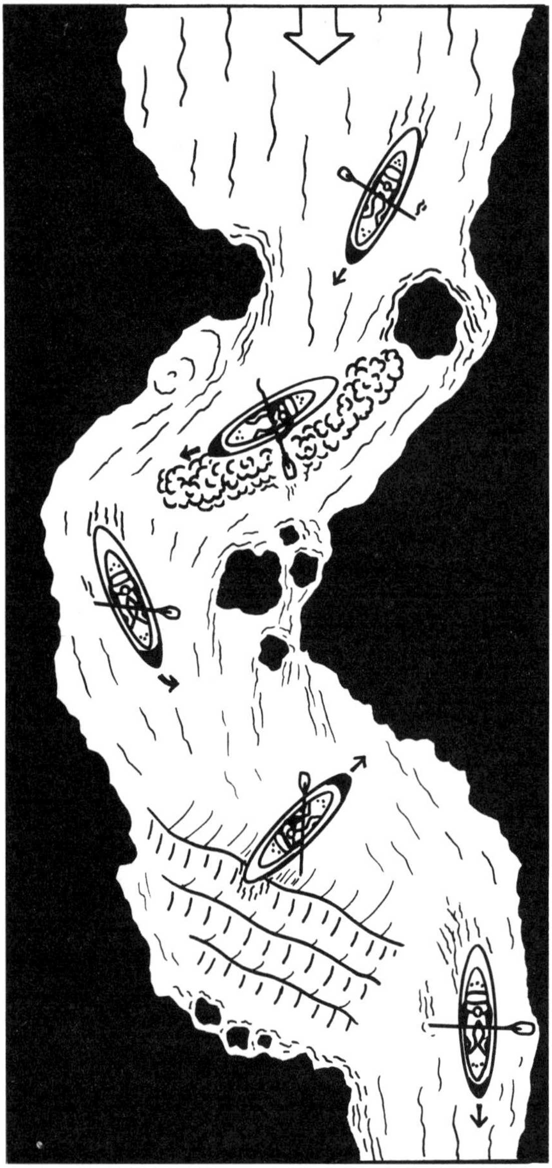

You can surf diagonal holes and ferry on the upstream face of waves to make dramatic cross-river moves.

and a swim, you probably shouldn't run the hole in the first place.

EDDIES

You have already acquired the basic skills needed to enter and exit eddies. You have also learned that eddies house a variety of useful currents—some of which flow upstream, some of which swirl downstream faster than the main current, and some of which suck downward. Now you can expand your knowledge of eddies and tap into these currents for some dramatic maneuvers.

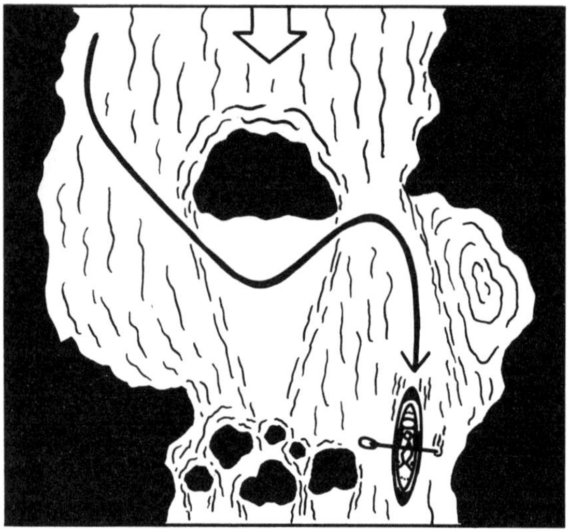

S-turns: Eddies can be used to accelerate your kayak cross-river or upstream. By linking eddies, you can even use S-turns to ascend rapids!

A kayak that begins ferrying in the main current will find its lateral momentum greatly magnified by conveniently placed eddies. As the kayak crosses the eddy, the eddy's upstream current will slingshot you upstream against the main current faster than when it entered the eddy. The turbocharged effect of the transition from one side of the eddy to the other and back into the main current is very exciting and can make some big, powerful moves possible. Try practicing it in a familiar rapid until you can get the kayak to make S-turns back and forth across the river.

Boulder-Choked Rapids

Early in my kayaking career I treated solid obstacles as enemies—the nemeses of ill-fated kayakers. I respected and avoided rocks and boulders and portaged rapids that were too boulder-choked to be considered runnable. It took a bona fide Class V kayaking adventure to change my perspective of these notorious river features.

In some instances, shallow rocks and boulders provide midriver brakes when there are no eddies to be

High-quality kayaks can slide over shallow boulders with ease.

found. By running the kayak onto partially submerged boulders (lean downstream and don't pivot sideways!), the kayak can be dragged to a halt, then spun off the boulder to continue downstream. Even if you don't want to stop completely, you can use the boulder to help make quick turns. This can be a real boon in the middle of a long Class V rapid. Also, shallow, wet boulders might provide the only feasible route through an otherwise impossible rapid. If the main channel is hopelessly boulder-choked, it would be senseless to try to kayak it. On the other hand, wet boulders can be *boofed* with some momentum. In boofing, stiff, slick-bottomed kayaks are paddled full speed across the tops of wet boulders and into the safety of the eddies below (see Angling and Boofing, on page 107).

Steep Creeking

Steep creeks are small, high-gradient streams that combine big drops with extremely difficult rapids. Most steep creekers categorize creeks as *steep* when the gradient begins to exceed 100 to 150 feet per mile, even though much steeper creeks have been paddled. Also, the *creek* part of steep creeking denotes rivers in the 150 to 1,500 cfs range, although some larger streams still fit the definition of steep creeks.

Steep creeks are a haven for adrenaline addicts. Though I've hammered kayaks over scores of waterfalls, I've yet to figure out a way to suppress the butterflies I get staring out over a thundering, foam-spewing horizon line. In fact, occasionally all that has stood between me and predrop hysteria were the right choice of runnable waterfalls and the techniques described in this section. They haven't stopped me from being eaten alive in a couple of big drops, but they have increased my confidence in my kayak and gotten me through a couple of close calls.

You have already learned how to use small holes, waves, and boulders to run hard rapids. Those same techniques apply on steep creeks. It's time now, however, to take the vertical world of three-dimensional

Steep creeks are a haven for adrenaline addicts. (Note the kayaker in the middle left portion of this photo.)

paddling to the extreme. It's time to learn about the tactics steep creekers use to run big ledges and waterfalls.

SCOUTING

The first key to successful steep creeking is knowing which ledges and falls *not* to run. Check out the face of the falls. How far does it drop? Does the falls pour freely off a ledge or slide downward at an angle? Are there rocks in the falls that are going to throw the kayak off course before it even hits bottom? A tall free-falling waterfall might flip your kayak end over end, while a slanted falls might feel like little more than an exciting carnival ride. Next, check out the hole at the base of the falls. Is it free of boulders and debris? Will the kayak have enough momentum to break through the backwash, or will the river be too powerful? What if you're swimming? Can you break free of the hole or will it be a keeper? Examine all these features carefully before you decide to run any waterfall, and always have a rescue team set up in case anything goes wrong.

PLANNING

Ask yourself how you're going to know where to enter the falls. After all, you're going to see nothing but a big horizon line from your kayak. Pick distinctive landmarks along the bank that will help tell you where your line is ("I'll enter ten feet left of that big boulder"). Other useful signposts are obvious hydraulic features ("I'll nick the right of that hole with my left tube, then drop over the falls") or downstream landmarks that can be used as a gunsight ("Paddle straight toward the tree"). No matter what signposts you use, make sure you can see them from upstream or they won't do you any good! Walk upstream and look back down at the falls from a distance. Is your landmark still visible? If not, pick another one.

Remember that there's more to a waterfall than paddling over the lip. You have to land safely, too. Sometimes that means paddling straight off the falls with a lot of power, and other times it may mean paddling diagonally into softer hydraulics to the side of the falls.

Three types of waterfalls: The waterfall on the left slopes gradually. If there are no holes or sharp rocks in this slide, it may be runnable. The middle waterfall forms a rounded dome. If it isn't too tall, you may be able to jump over the hole and paddle away upright. The waterfall on the right drops steeply over a ledge. If it is tall enough, you'll have to have luck on your side to avoid a flip.

ANGLING AND BOOFING

Shallow landings and powerful holes await at the bottom of many waterfalls. However, you can sometimes avoid these obstacles by angling your bow one way or the other, jumping out over the shallow landing, or keeping your bow high enough to land fairly flat. These techniques keep your bow from penciling toward the river bottom and help get you into safer water.

Angling works in two ways: It keeps your bow from diving straight down and effectively shortens the length of your kayak. This may help you avoid crashing into shallow river bottoms, and may help keep your kayak from stalling out and flipping in big holes. Keep in mind, however, that you'll have to paddle hard to jump out past recirculating hydraulics.

Angling across a waterfall to avoid the worst part of the hole.

Plant your last forward stroke at the lip of the waterfall and pull your legs upward to keep the bow high.

wanted to see exactly what I was getting myself in to and which way I was going to go once I was in it. Later on, as my river-reading skills developed, I spent less time on the bank and more time in my kayak. Piloting a kayaking through Class II and III rapids became as comfortable as piloting my feet along rocky forest trails, but Class IV and V drops still kept me ferrying toward the bank.

While shoreline scouting is the best way to go in *any* rapid, it isn't always possible. In fact, on some really high-gradient, steep-walled rivers, bank scouting might be plumb out of the question. So a whole new set of river-reading skills has to come into play, skills that will let you read blind drops without scouting them from shore.

An unbroken horizon line followed by standing waves will give hints as to the cleanest path over the falls. As you learned in Chapter 4, the waves usually show up wherever the current flows clear and unobstructed. So if you had to place a bet on where to run the drop, the best bet would be to head straight for that part of the drop that leads into the waves. If there's a hole visible beyond the horizon line, see if one end angles downstream. The current will kick toward the hole's downstream end, which may provide an easy escape route. (Remember to brace into the hole!)

Check out the diagram on page 110 and try to match it to a drop you've seen before. Still scout whenever possible, but keep these ideas in mind for the time they're really needed.

Boofing off falls—also called *pancaking* or *airplane jumping*—is a technique used to achieve a flat landing. Boofing an inflatable kayak can be pretty challenging. You must combine speed with a dramatic upward pull of your legs to lift the bow as you leave the lip of the falls. One of the keys to a great boof is to take your last power stroke right at the lip of the falls. This gives your bow some extra lift as you begin your descent. Some kayakers boof by leaning back as far as possible. That technique may also work for you, provided you still pull your legs up as you start your descent.

Whichever way you decide to run a waterfall, decide how you're going to handle your paddle. Although your paddle will give you the power you need to clear the falls, it can cause injuries if it gets caught in the fall's hydraulics. Most paddlers hold the paddle slightly to one side and stab the base of the falls, although others hold it slightly over their heads. Either technique may work fine for you, although the over-the-head technique increases your risk of shoulder dislocations.

READING AND RUNNING

When I first started kayaking I scouted *everything!* I didn't care whether a rapid was Class II or Class IV, I

Low-Water Techniques

Low-water trips demand a special style of river running—one that won't leave you high and dry on a gravel bar trying to bribe fishermen to pull you out of a canyon. Rivers change at low water—the river moves

The author probing a 30-foot waterfall in Washington State. (Photo by David Prange)

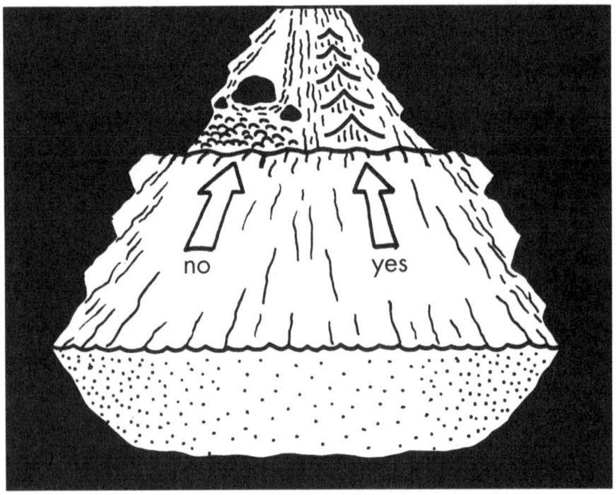

There may be times when you are forced to run a rapid that you can't scout. Look for clues—like a clean set of standing waves—to mark the best point to approach the horizon line, and be prepared to alter your course quickly.

slower and has less push, there are more obstacles to avoid, and there may be many shallow channels to select from. Slow currents decrease the possibility of a wrap but increase your need to maneuver.

There are many ways to make low-water kayaking enjoyable. Start by picking a river that actually has enough water to float your kayak, not one that is bone dry. Even if you are forced to line or portage a few rapids, pool-drop rivers are more fun at low water than rivers with continuous gradients because the pools hold water. Low-water trips are also easier when you use small, sturdy kayaks—ones that fit through tight slots and are easy to pull over shallow bars. Finally, think about your feet. Sooner or later you'll run aground and have to pull your kayak free. A solid pair of tennis shoes or hiking boots—even if worn over neoprene socks—will save your feet from the inevitable bashing inflicted by slippery rocks and hidden potholes.

When running rivers at low water your primary goal is to stay in the deepest channels. Here are a few hints that will make your task easier:

1. Look for slick surfaces or long, even waves among smaller, choppier waves. These features reveal deeper, more forgiving channels.
2. Use the deep eddies behind big boulders to make cross-river maneuvers around shallow shoals. When a shallow bar is impossible to avoid, build up some momentum to help you slide over it and into deeper water.
3. Lean to one side to lessen the amount of floor actually touching the water. The unweighting of one tube might be just enough to get the kayak through a narrow slot.
4. Don't be afraid to spin or pivot your kayak to and fro. Since the kayak will inevitably snag rocks and shallow obstacles, pivots might get it off the rock before you have to jump out and pull it free.

Big-Water Techniques

When rivers bloat and swell after heavy rains or big snowmelts, their moods can become downright cantankerous. The current speeds up and eddies disappear, and holes become deeper as waves surge higher. It takes a dedicated paddler, a level head (figuratively speaking, of course—my friends have oval heads, just like yours!), and strong river skills to match wits with big, powerful currents.

High-water runs require some additional safety precautions. You should be a good swimmer and experienced in self-rescue, and there should always be kayaks close by to help out in rescue situations. You should also consider paddling rivers with nearby roads and easy evacuation routes in case the river turns out to be too dangerous.

On the river, the techniques used during high water are the same as those used during any river trip, only more exact: Keep your paddle moving to keep your senses well tuned to the river's moods; keep the bow pointed squarely at waves and holes, not necessarily square with the current; keep standard-floor kayaks bailed; and paddle hard through waves and holes to avoid stalling out in their troughs. If you find yourself on a collision course with a mighty hydraulic, maintain your momentum and hit it straight on. Also, don't try to pull off dramatic ferries in front of big haystacks or holes—you're likely to drift broadside into the hydraulics and flip.

High-water kayakers need to know when to paddle and when to portage. You are much more likely to spend

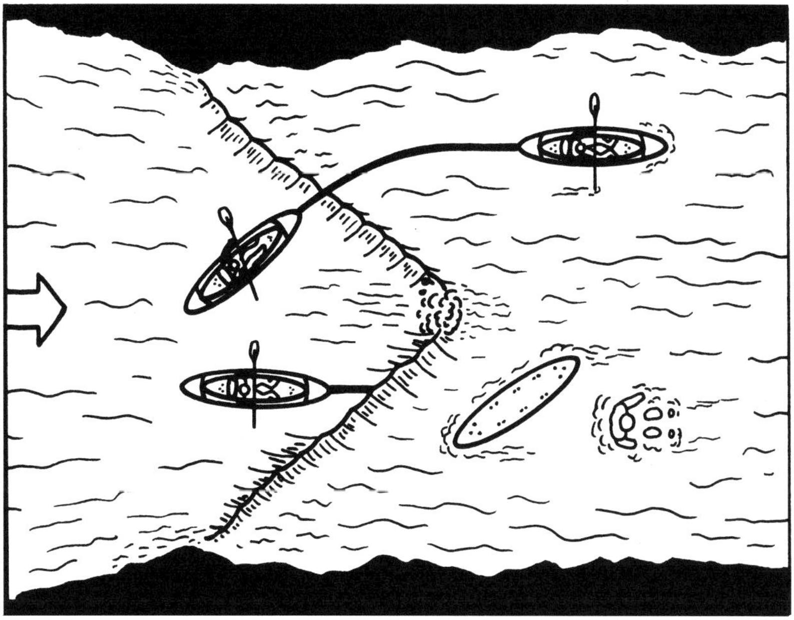

When hitting big waves, drive straight through the wave. Here, the top kayak paddled perpendicular to the wave and had a successful run. The bottom kayak stayed parallel with the current and flipped when it hit the wave broadside.

some time swimming during high-water runs than you are during ordinary trips, so your ability to recognize long, dangerous rapids may keep you alive.

Another difference between high- and low-water rivers involves scouting. During high water, rocks and shoreline landmarks might be invisible or moving too fast to be of much help. However, features like individual holes or waves become more significant and can provide just as good signposts as riverside landmarks.

No matter what you do, *avoid rivers at flood stage!* Flooded rivers are unpredictable and dangerous. Powerful downcurrents can hold you under for dangerous periods of time, and tree-lined banks can pose serious threats to swimmers attempting to escape the river's grasp. If the river has water in it now, it will have water in it another day. But if you run it now, you might not be around to run it another day.

Rivers become wild and unpredictable at extremely high flows.

9

PLAYBOATING
DANCES WITH RIVERS

Look how far you've come! Your kayak feels like an extension of your body, and you're paddling white-water with style and poise. Kayaking is a blast whether you're floating big, meandering rivers or darting through steep boulder gardens. Along the way, you've seen other kayakers surfing waves, riding holes, or popping up out of ledges. Now that's what you want to do.

Welcome to the world of playboating, a world where surfing, spinning, and blasting are the norm. A world where hydraulics turn into amusement parks, and you control the ride.

In this chapter we're going to discuss the standard playboating tricks and lay down the foundation for more advanced tricks.

We'll talk about where to try surfing and how to get comfortable in holes, where to try blasting and how to execute your first enders. You can take this stuff with you every time you paddle the river and spend the rest of your days honing your playboating skills.

No matter what you do, this chapter will add to your paddling repertoire, improve your understanding of rivers, and open a new realm of kayaking opportunities.

Getting Ready

EQUIPMENT

A self-bailing kayak is a must for playboating. With a standard-floor kayak, the cockpit will flood, and you'll become heavy and unmaneuverable. Also, a stiff, highly rockered kayak tends to outperform flexible kayaks in just about all play conditions.

If you're planning to play in holes, consider using thigh straps. They'll give you more leverage over your tubes and keep you aboard when the kayak is bouncing around. Also, unload any unnecessary gear and make sure there are no loose items or ropes in your kayak. Bare kayaks make better playboats because they're lighter and more stable. Finally, make sure that you've got your helmet and lifejacket securely fastened and that you're wearing enough insulating outerwear to survive a few dunkings. As you will soon discover, swims are a part of playboating!

NECESSARY SKILLS

Before you think about playing around on waves and holes, learn to distinguish forgiving hydraulics from nasty keepers. By knowing what the river is likely to do to your kayak ahead of time, you'll be able to anticipate the river's actions and adjust accordingly. Since flips are common when playing, you must be comfortable righting a flipped kayak and swimming out of holes. If you're one of the lucky few who can roll your kayak, now's your moment in the spotlight. Pulling off an Eskimo roll after flipping out of a hole is sure to impress your friends! Finally, you should be adept at maneuvering your kayak in powerful hydraulics.

Surfing Waves

FRONT SURFING

Surfing a river wave relies on the same gravitational force that drags surfers down the face of ocean waves.

Cutting from an eddy out to a V-shaped surf spot.

Surfing a standing wave.

But while surfboards are streamlined and light, kayaks are heavy and sluggish. So to surf a wave, you first have to overcome the friction created by the kayak.

An ideal beginner's wave will be medium size (about 2 to 4 feet high) and close to a large eddy. Your goal is to ferry out of the eddy, slide onto the face of the wave, and stall out. If you don't catch the wave on your first attempt, the eddy gives you a chance to paddle back upstream and give it another try.

Check out the current between the eddy and the wave. You'll often find a small diagonal wave or depression that feeds off the eddy line into the trough of the wave. This diagonal current is the swinging door that either lets you enter the wave or pushes you back toward the eddy. Start paddling forward up the eddy, matching your speed and ferry angle to the intensity of this diagonal current. As you cross out onto the wave, keep a shallow ferry angle to avoid spinning downstream. When you find the magic balance between your boat and the current, you'll stall comfortably in the wave's trough with your kayak gliding endlessly down the face of the wave.

If you start veering one way or the other, use sweep strokes and stern rudders to keep yourself aligned with the current. If you have a fast boat and are planted on the wave, stern rudders may work. Slower inflatable kayaks may slow down and slide off the wave, so keep some strong forward sweeps in your stroke repertoire.

Once you've established your position, keep your boat flat or lift the upstream tube slightly. If you lean too much, your boat will dig into the wave and you'll peel off downriver. If you rudder, do so on the downstream side so that your paddle doesn't catch against the upstream tube. Finally, watch the water in front of you. If your bow starts diving, lean back. If you're sliding backward off the wave, lean forward and paddle forward.

Once you have front surfing figured out, you can try it anywhere you find waves. If there are no eddies nearby, you can drift down to a wave, point your bow upstream, then stall on the wave by paddling hard forward. It's tougher to catch a wave this way because you can't see where you're going and your momentum becomes your enemy. On the other hand, mastering this technique will open up a whole new realm of surfing opportunities.

BACK SURFING

Back surfing is the same as front surfing—just backward. While the principles are all the same, the technical aspects of back surfing are a lot tougher! Your pivot point moves toward your bow as you lean forward, the river disappears from view behind your back, and the most familiar strokes begin to feel backward when done in reverse.

To start your back surf, either ferry out of the eddy backward (stern pointed upstream) or stall out midriver while floating downstream by back-paddling hard against the current. If you practice this every chance you get, your back-surfing skills will grow quickly.

With a little practice, you can stay perfectly balanced while side-surfing small holes.

Hole Riding

PLAYING HOLES

Small holes make perfect play spots: Their backwash creates natural kayak catchers and eliminates the need to keep perfect angles as you would on waves. In holes, all you have to do is stabilize your kayak, then set about spinning, side-surfing, and eventually busting free of the hole.

SIDE-SURFING

You can jump into holes much the same way you get onto waves, with some minor changes. First, start parallel or just upstream of the hole and ferry across to it. Next, turn your kayak sideways before you hit the hole, and get ready for some excitement. Lean downstream and brace on the backwash (keep that high brace *low*). If you have thigh straps, lift your upstream knee to keep your cockpit high and dry. Otherwise, just keep leaning downstream.

Finally, the things you do *in* the hole depends on its *size* and *shape*. Find your balance point and wait until you feel pretty stable in the hole. In almost any small- to medium-size hole, you should be able to sit upright while shifting your weight slightly downstream. Sitting sideways in the hole and bracing on the backwash is called *side-surfing*. It's the most basic trick in the book, and a great way to learn hole riding.

SPINNING

Once you get the feel for side-surfing, move toward the shoulder of the hole and try to spin. Let the downstream currents out past the shoulder of the hole grab your bow and spin you around 180 degrees. Rotate the stern back into the middle of the hole and voilà . . . your first *180!* Next time, try to spin *360 degrees* by staying high up on the backwash until your bow and stern spin all the way around. Once you get the feel for 180s and 360s, you can start linking them up in quick succession and spin until you've had enough.

BLASTING

One of the most dynamic hole-riding moves you can try is called a *blast,* or *blasting*. In blasting, you sink your stern beneath the recirculating foam and point the bow upstream into the air. Done correctly, you can stall your kayak in the hole just as if you were front-surfing on a wave. The big difference will be the wall of boiling water now crashing into your stern and over your back.

Blasting works best in well-defined holes formed by low-angle sliding ledges. These low-angle holes make blasting easier by providing plenty of space for your

To start a spin, use the currents passing the shoulder of the hole to grab your bow or stern. Here, the kayaker has already paddled toward the shoulder of the hole and has readied his paddle and body to start a 180- or 360-degree spin.

bow. In steeper holes, your bow will dive into the falls, making blasting difficult or impossible.

EXITING HOLES

Riding big holes can rattle your bones and shake your brain. When you've had enough, exit the hole by slipping sideways over the shoulder of the hole. If you're really getting worked over by the hole, the only way to exit may be to rock back and forth across the face of the hole until you squirt free. Use alternating forward and back strokes to get your sideways momentum going, and keep working until you slide out over the shoulder of the hole. If all else fails, have someone on shore toss you a throw bag and pull your kayak free.

When blasting, the hole's backwash fills up your stern while your bow points straight upstream.

Enders and Pirouettes

If the river is deep, safe, and has a big pool in which to reclaim your gear, you can try a classic play move: the *ender*. Whether called *enders, endos,* or *pop-ups*, this move uses the hole's hydraulic power to sink the bow and shoot the kayak straight up in the air.

FRONT ENDERS

The best ender spots don't have to be big holes. Any hole or small ledge with a powerful, vertical falls and a deep pool will work. When you find a spot like this, paddle straight upstream into the falls and let the water falling over the ledge submerge your bow. Your stern will fly upward as the buoyancy stored in your bow provides the energy to launch your kayak skyward. You may pop up at a 45-degree angle, ender at 90 degrees, or cartwheel forward into the falls. If you want to stay upright, lean back hard before your kayak reaches 90 degrees. Otherwise, be prepared for a dunking, and get ready to roll or self-rescue.

The key to clean enders is alignment. Aim for the deepest, most powerful part of the hydraulic and keep your kayak perpendicular to the falls. (All of the wave-surfing practice

In a front ender (or "pop up"), the river pushes your bow underwater while your stern flies into the air.

comes into play here!) As your kayak launches upward, use your paddle and body English to stay straight. It may take some practice and experimentation to get it right, but it'll feel awesome when it finally clicks!

BACK ENDERS

Back enders are simply front enders in reverse: You bury your stern in the falls to shoot your bow up in the air. The trick to back enders is getting lined up properly. Look over one shoulder or the other as you approach the falls, and lean back as the stern catches the down current. If you keep leaning back, your kayak can cartwheel wildly overhead; or you can lean forward again to stall your ender and land upright.

PIROUETTES

Once you get the feel for enders, you can move on to the next level of aerial acrobatics—the pirouette. A pirouette starts like an ender but adds a spin when the kayak becomes vertical. You can initiate the pirouette by looking in the direction you want to spin and adding a draw stroke across your bow. The closer you keep your body to your kayak, the faster you'll rotate.

Variations on the Basics

Playboating is a form of self-expression: one paddler and one kayak flowing together in controlled motion. Once you learn the basics of playboating, you can perfect your moves and fire up your imagination.

Instead of bracing in a hole, try side surfing while spinning your paddle. On your next ender, hold the paddle with one hand while waving with other. You can even link front and back enders in spectacular combinations if you're fast enough. Playboating is an endless stream of challenges and rewards.

A back ender.

10

MULTIDAY TRIPS

THE OVERNIGHT TRAVELER

Camping and kayaking make great travel companions. In fact some paddlers have gone so far as to say that the river is little more than a liquid highway to be traveled before the next campsite. Though few kayakers would downplay the joy of river running, most kayakers would agree that camping is a ton of fun.

Riverside camping has a special air about it. There are no RVs parked in the next space, no pop machines or laundromats nearby, and, if you're lucky, no humans for miles around. Everything that's in camp was put there by Mother Nature or carried there in your kayak. But that doesn't mean that river camping demands a Spartan existence. Kayaks can carry sleeping bags, tents, stoves, food, and enough clothing to keep you quite comfortable.

This chapter gets you ready for your next overnight adventure with inside tips on gear, storage techniques, campsite selection, and more.

Planning Ahead

Long before you start your river outing, consider what you'll need to bring. Will you be on the river one day or three? Will a few pairs of shorts and T-shirts constitute your entire wardrobe or will you need some heavy outerwear to stay warm? Do you plan to take prepared freeze-dried meals or exotic riverside feasts? No matter how long a trip you plan or what type of conditions you expect to encounter, the mere fact that you'll be *kayaking* will change the type of food and equipment you'll have to carry.

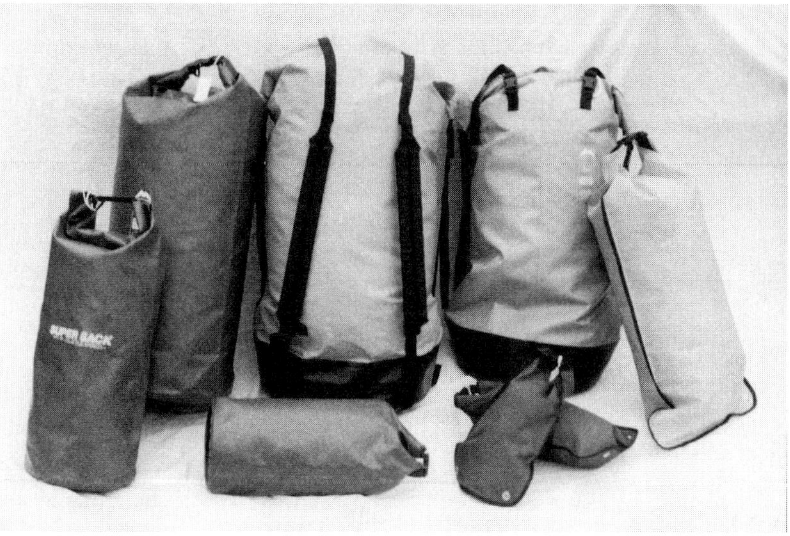

Dry bags are durable waterproof sacks. They're perfect for keeping your clothes and camping gear dry.

Let's start with some simple presumptions. They may not always be correct, but they work. First, no matter how hard you try, the river is going to jostle your equipment and attack your gear cache. If you're carrying down sleeping bags, cotton clothing, or canvas tents, you're risking a long, damp night in camp. Polyester and nylon gear, on the other hand, repels water and works well even when wet. Synthetic sleeping bags—filled with Hollofill, Quallofill, Polargaurd, or other space-age insulators—provide some warmth if they're wet, and fleece clothing dries quickly once you squeeze out most of the water. Second, the more gear you carry, the heavier and less maneuverable your kayak will become. Your trip will be more enjoyable if you think like a backpacker. Consider carrying minimal kitchen gear, one-burner stoves, and dehydrated meals. Layer your clothes for efficiency, and leave the excess baggage at home.

Waterproof Containers

Even though improperly packed gear is destined for a soaking, a number of modern technological wonders have made kayaking drier and more enjoyable than ever. You really *can* keep your gear dry on the river—most of the time.

Dry bags are durable, specially designed waterproof sacks. When properly sealed shut—usually with foldover or self-sealing closures—dry bags keep their contents totally dry. Most of the time. For some extra insurance, seal your gear in small plastic trash bags *before* inserting them in dry bags. Smaller items can be separated into sandwich- and freezer-size self-sealing bags before putting them into dry bags. Not only will this help keep small things dry, it will make finding them in camp much easier.

Some items—such as cameras and video equipment—are especially vulnerable to water and jostling and should be accorded special attention. Waterproof boxes—such as Pelican cases—have O-ring seals and solid walls to keep water out of their interiors. For the inflatable kayaker, these boxes come in a variety of sizes

Waterproof boxes—like the Pelican cases shown at left—keep cameras and other valuables dry. The ammo cans on the right have sharp corners that can damage your kayak.

and usually have rounded corners, which ensures that you can find a waterproof box that will fit in your kayak without damaging the tubes.

Stowing Gear Safely

Veteran kayakers take great pride in their ability to pack oddly shaped items within the small confines of an inflatable kayak. Some of you might be wondering why you can't just throw gear in the cockpit and run a bunch of rope around it. The answer is: Someday you're gonna flip. That's right! Sooner or later all the gear standing high *above* the tubes will be hanging far *below* the tubes as your kayak floats away upside down. And the longer it hangs there, the more likely you are to lose it. Stow your gear as if you're actually going to flip, and keep in mind some standard principles:

1. Keep the kayak's center of gravity low by lashing all gear down with a low profile. Keep heavier items closer to the floor.
2. Keep the kayak balanced fore and aft.
3. Pack items in the bow carefully! Leave plenty of room for your legs and feet, and beware of items that could entangle you.
4. Protect your floor. Keep hard-sided items off the floor, and don't overload your kayak. Try to pack as light as possible.
5. Lash everything down tightly. Make sure every item is securely fastened to the kayak with strong webbing. Use the best anchor points available—whether they're D-rings, bailing holes, or seat straps.

Campsite Selection

Some canyons offer a wide variety of terrain and campsites, while others contain few if any hospitable camping niches. Before you start your trip, peruse the local guidebooks for camping opportunities, or ask some friends who have run the river what to expect. If the river is unexplored, check topographic maps for broad valleys that may offer level, comfortable sites. There may even be a government agency that preassigns designated campsites to river travelers. If you are able to find out about campsites ahead of time, try to preselect sites that fit your travel plans. If the trip is two days long, pick a site midway so that both river days are enjoyable.

Whether or not you've learned about campsites before leaving the put-in, make sure that you're looking for a feasible site in daylight. There is nothing more petrifying, disheartening, or dangerous than traveling downriver after dusk! If the riverbank offers many ideal settings, you're in luck. You can choose campsites that will be sunny early in the morning or late in the day; campsites that slope gently into the water, or involve a short hike away from the river; and campsites that offer shade or unobstructed vistas.

Even though this kayak appears to be heavily loaded, the gear is strapped down tightly out of the way of the paddler. Also, the gear is evenly distributed to keep the kayak trim.

RISING WATER

One thing you certainly don't want is a riverside campsite that might disappear if the river comes up! If there is any chance that the river will rise—whether from heavy runoff or dam releases—pick a site high above the waterline that offers easy escape, even in the dark of night. Unload kayaks in the evening and carry the gear and kayaks high up on the shore. If the river rises a few feet, you can still spend the night resting peacefully.

WIND

There's one other thing to think about when you make camp for the evening: *wind*. If you've spread your paddle jackets, dry suits, T-shirts, and hats all over the rocks so that they can dry out, they might not be where you left them come morning. Canyons have a way of focusing and amplifying local air currents, especially late in the afternoon. Make sure you secure all your belongings each time you *make* camp so that you'll still have them each time you *break* camp.

THE ENVIRONMENT

Conscientious kayakers strive to minimize their impact on the riparian environment. Thick, grassy banks or beaches lined with delicate shrubs are especially susceptible to human harm. On the other hand, broad sandy beaches and pebble-strewn bars can camouflage and erase your presence soon after your group leaves. Pick a site that has been used many times before or one that won't record your presence, and treat it with respect.

One trick to preserving the habitat is to use nothing but freestanding gear. Utilize tents that don't have to be staked out and small stoves that can be set up on a large rock. Avoid building campfires or clearing brush to make your camp more comfortable. If you must have a fire, build a small one below the high-water mark away from immovable boulders and logs. Provided you dismantle the fire in the morning, the scars will vanish with the next freshet.

Human Waste

Sooner or later you're going to have to answer the call of nature. Unfortunately, kayakers are caught between a rock and a hard spot when it comes to human waste. Many federally regulated rivers have strict rules regarding the disposal of human waste, landfills are prohibited from accepting human waste in plastic bags, and river runners are often required to pack their waste out of the river. A number of companies build portable latrines that meet the federal regulations, but they're too bulky to carry in a kayak. Even the large ammo cans often used as latrines by rafters are too big to carry in a kayak.

This leaves kayakers three choices: Bring a support raft to carry a latrine, use a small ammo can to capture human waste, or go au naturel on rivers that are not federally regulated. Although admittedly I've dashed behind a thousand trees in my day, I don't profess it to be the best way to do things.

Instead, the best way to do things *naturally* is to dig a single hole 6 to 8 inches deep at least 100 feet from the river and to dispose of human waste there.

Cookery

Kayaking—like any other form of outdoor recreation—burns calories. And if you're anything like me, much of your time will be spent figuring out how to restore those calories while keeping your taste buds amused. After a long day on the river, a tasty meal provides a soothing transition into the lazy hours after dusk, and bountiful lunch spreads will give you all the energy you need to get you down the river.

Riverside meals can be simple or elaborate, depending on your budget, kitchen paraphernalia, carrying space, and gastronomic preferences. They can be simple one-pot meals, cheese and salami, or extravagant banquets. Riverside dining is limited only by your culinary creativity.

MENU

Menu planning begins long before you make your first lunch stop or reach your first night's camp. In fact, it starts before you get to the local supermarket. Planning your river menu is only slightly different than planning your menu at home. Of course, you are restricted by considerations of weight, carrying space, refrigeration, and cooking utensils. Create a menu that will make everyone happy, and get everyone involved in selecting meals either by having them list items they do and don't like or by having them rotate menu responsibilities.

Try to plan meals around the length of the trip, your level of patience, and the amount of cookware available. On lengthy trips, select durable, long-lasting foods that won't spoil quickly. Most perishables are bulky and rot quickly without a cooler, but dehydrated food items are light and long-lasting. Consider easy meals like one-pot stews, pasta dishes, and Mexican dinners. Also, anticipate the season and weather. Do you *really* want to stand outside slow-simmering that special stew in the middle of a rainstorm?

PACKING YOUR FOOD

Food storage techniques depend on the length of your trip, the number of people going, and the amount of food you're carrying. On a one-day jaunt, with no more than a handful of kayakers, you may be able to get by with string cheese, apples, and high-energy bars packed into a small dry bag. Heartier eaters can pack bigger meals. On multiday journeys, even the chilly compartment of a friend's cooler might not be enough to keep food fresh and edible. In this case, some creative menu planning and packing becomes necessary.

River runners tend to be an inventive and resourceful lot when it comes to packing foods. The tricks of the trade are many. Since eggs break easily, they are better off broken ahead of time and stored in plastic bottles, ready for use in your morning omelette. Bagels and hard rolls last longer than soft loaves of bread. Durable fruits and vegetables—such as potatoes, apples, and cucumbers—are easier to keep fresh and undamaged than other types of produce and can be stored in tough bags. Canned meats, powdered milk, and freeze-dried items can be used to replace fresh goods—they'll last longer and they come in their own protective containers.

THE KITCHEN

Just about any manually powered tool you have in your home kitchen will work in your riverside kitchen. Kayaking stoves, however, are different from those you find at home.

There are many compact camping stoves on the market today, with those powered by white gas, propane, and butane leading the market. Though all of these fuel-burning stoves work fine, some rivers restrict the type of fuel kayakers can use in camp. So check out the local regulations well in advance.

Once in camp, set up the kitchen away from the gear pile. That way, people won't constantly pester the cook.

WATER

It is disheartening to think that almost every kayakable river poses a potential risk to humans if used for drinking water. Even the clearest streams can carry industrial pollutants, dangerous bacteria, and a nasty little bugger called *Giardia lamblia*. Nonetheless, it is important to maintain your level of hydration by drinking enough water every day. So, fresh, safe drinking water demands some special attention.

The most obvious way to guarantee fresh drinking water is to carry your own supply. However, water is heavy, so you often have to produce potable water during your river trip.

There are three common ways to treat water for most living organisms. The first way is to boil the water for 10 to 20 minutes. (For every 1,000 feet you gain above sea level, add 1 minute of boiling time.) The second method is to use chemical purifiers such as halizone, iodine, or bleach. Halizone and iodine tablets come with instructions for proper dosages. However, if you're using tincture of iodine (2 percent), use 5 drops per quart of water and let it sit 30 minutes. (Double the time if the water is cold, and double the dosage if the water is cloudy.) Bleach is generally added to water at the rate of 8 drops per gallon, and takes about 30 minutes to kill living organisms. None of the chemical treatments are foolproof, and each requires some patience and caution. Remember that it takes a bit of time to kill the organisms, and that just one drop of untreated water can spoil the whole batch.

The third water treatment method—filtration—is the only one that can remove pesticides, solvents, and other artificial contaminants as well as living organisms. Portable filtration units (water filters) actually strain water through microscopic pores in the unit's filter element and eject potable water out the tail end of the system. Kayakers should carry large enough water filters to supply adequate water for everyone on the trip and bring replacement filter elements in case one clogs or breaks.

11

FAST AND WILD

RIVER EXPLORATION AND WHITEWATER RACING

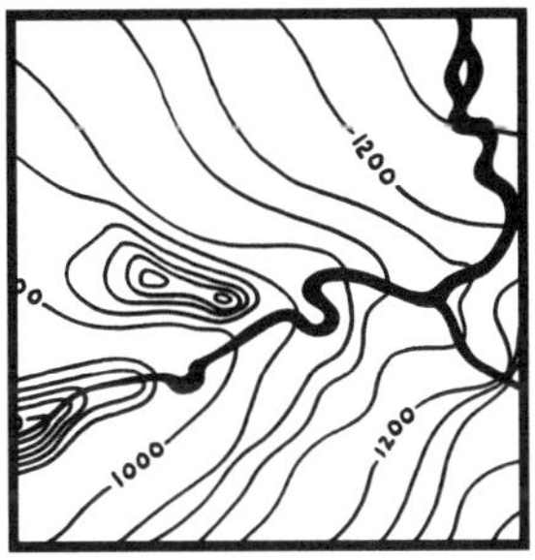

Adventurous kayakers can expand their whitewater horizons far beyond the limits of everyday river running. For those willing to accept new challenges, there await new rewards.

This chapter opens the door to two new interesting ways to look at rivers. It explores the basics of planning and carrying out exploratory trips and delves into the exciting sport of kayak racing. It presents yet another chance for those kayakers whose abilities are advancing to take another giant step forward, and for seasoned veterans to brush up on some rusty skills.

River Exploration

Exploring an unnavigated river can be an extraordinary experience. Some kayakers feel an irresistible draw to these types of trips, just as some travelers prefer rustic backroads over popular highways. In many ways, exploratory descents mark the apex of all whitewater endeavors. Such trips provide the ultimate test of kayakers' skills, judgment, and river prowess since many aspects of these adventures start as unknowns. First descents can combine the reverence of traversing untouched wilderness with the personal challenge of negotiating unnavigated canyons.

THE RESEARCH PHASE

Few exploratory descents—successful ones at least—take place without an enormous amount of preparation. In fact, pretrip planning often takes much longer than the trip itself, beginning weeks, months, or even years ahead of time. By learning everything possible about the river and the surrounding terrain ahead of time, many of the risks inherent in wilderness exploration can be minimized.

Any exploratory descent should begin with a survey of all available information resources. Start with a copy of the region's best guidebooks, review paddling magazines and paddling newsletters, and call around to local whitewater clubs. It is quite possible that your exploratory trip is really a second, third, or twentieth descent! Next, check out topographic maps. For North American paddlers, the United States and Canadian Geological Surveys maintain detailed topographic maps covering any river you can find, and these maps can be a kayaker's single most valuable resource.

When purchasing topographic maps, select the smallest scale possible. Large area maps (with a scale of 1:100,000 or 1:250,000) usually offer too little detail to provide much information. However, smaller-scaled maps—particularly the 1:24,000 or 7.5-inch maps—are quite useful. Many of these maps have contour intervals of 20 to 40 feet, which can at least forewarn the presence of large waterfalls and box canyons.

Begin reading the map by looking at the width of the blue line denoting the river. Is it a *thick* blue line, indicative of a large-volume river, or is it a *narrow* line, indicating a small stream? Next, note the contour intervals (change in altitude between lines) and the mileage scale. Look at the section of river you wish to explore and break it down into ½-mile or 1-mile sections. By counting the number of times the contour lines cross the river in a 1-mile section and then multiplying by the contour interval, you can get the average gradient in feet per mile.

Knowing how to interpret gradient is important. Many popular streams drop 10 to 100 feet per mile. More extreme whitewater rivers drop 100 to 200 feet per mile. On rare occasions, kayakers have even descended rivers with gradients exceeding 300 feet per mile. Always keep in mind that topo maps don't tell you everything. Even low-gradient rivers might descend very gradually, then suddenly drop many feet over unrunnable falls!

One way to figure out whether your venture is worth the risk is to compare the river's gradient to the canyon's surrounding terrain. If the land adjacent to the river shows closely spaced contour lines, the river is in a canyon. This can be a genuine hazard if there are waterfalls, severe whitewater, or unrunnable rapids. A narrow canyon with a steep gradient is not the place to be unless you've scouted everything out from the air or the land ahead of time! However, put that same steep river on a map showing widely spaced contour lines traversing the adjacent land and it may be possible to portage anything.

While examining your map, look for obvious escape routes in the form of broad contour lines departing the river's edge. Note obvious landmarks such as giant peaks, cliffs, or major tributaries that will be visible from the river. These will let you monitor your progress. Also figure out the total mileage between put-ins and take-outs to get a rough estimate of your expected river time.

Topographic maps are your guidebook during exploratory descents, so take good care of them. Keep them securely fastened and stored in waterproof containers when not in use, and keep a duplicate set on another kayak in case one set of maps gets lost or destroyed.

Once you have an imaginary picture of the river, set about gathering more information. If you can, go to the river and scout as much of it as you can see. Many first descents started with long, arduous hikes along canyon rims to view the rapids below or with airplane and helicopter flights over the river to view hidden corridors. Talk to the locals—anglers, hunters, and hikers—and store whatever information they're willing to share with you.

The final research task is to obtain information on water levels. While the mental picture imparted by that thick blue line might be accurate, a gauge will tell you a lot more. Check with the local Geological Survey

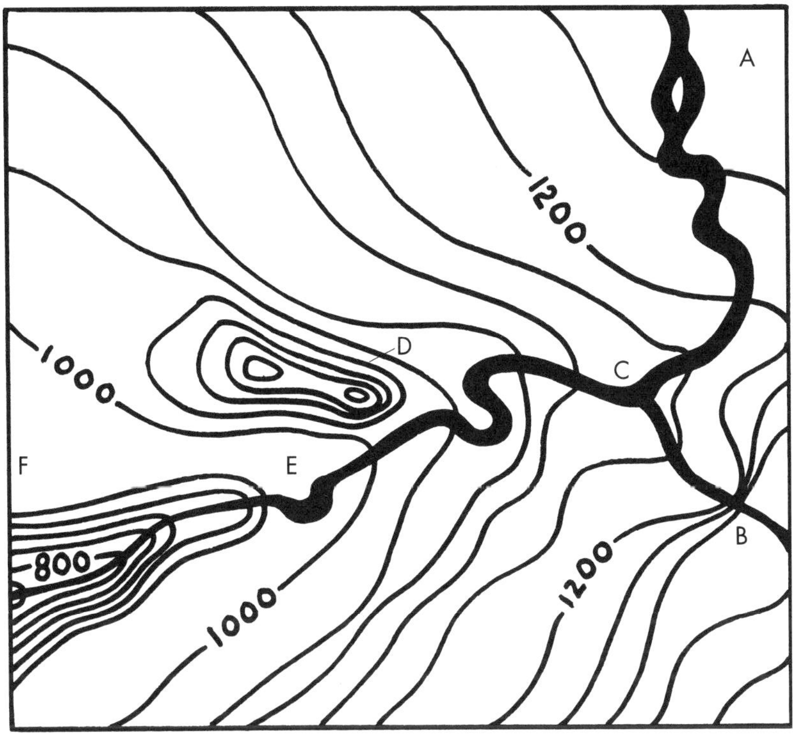

Topographic maps can provide a lot of valuable information. Here, the river winds through a broad valley while gradually descending through braided channels (A). A tributary descends over a big waterfall (B) before joining the main river (C). A big hill (D) might be seen from the river. If you did your homework, you'd know that the big eddy (E) signals you that the river will soon steepen and enter a narrow canyon (F).

office, weather services, or water districts to see if the river has a gauge, then monitor the river level periodically. The Geological Survey can also provide historical watershed and drainage area information and flow data. When combined with information on local weather patterns and a Water Supply Outlook (available from the USGS), this information gives a strong indication of the river's reaction to things like rain and snowmelt.

PUTTING TOGETHER A TEAM

In North America almost anything that *could* be kayaked *has* been kayaked. Accordingly, it is usually the most difficult and challenging rivers that remain unexplored. Meeting that challenge requires a team of kayakers who are compatible in both their personalities and their tenacity. It takes much more than a positive mental attitude to confront and survive unknown dilemmas. Each team member should be comfortable with treacherous whitewater and should bring to the team a solid set of wilderness skills and useful technical abilities. By including kayakers with medical expertise, rock-climbing skills, and intimate knowledge of the adjacent terrain, the team will have a broad range of useful skills, and will be better prepared to handle difficult situations.

EQUIPMENT AND SUPPLIES

Since you'll be traversing unknown canyons, portaging with greater frequency, and relying on your equipment much more than ever before, it is imperative that your equipment be of top quality and in excellent shape. Take some time before the trip to double-check your kayak. Pump it up tightly and check for leaks. Repair any loose seams and seal any noticeable abrasions. Examine all the gear you plan to bring for flaws. If an irreparable defect shows up, don't risk bringing the item along!

The most important part of assembling the equipment for the trip is trimming weight. It is far easier to portage a light kayak than one fully loaded with expendable luxuries. That *doesn't* mean that you shouldn't bring all the gear that is—or may be—*necessary!* You will be depending more on your gear now than you ever have, so bring everything that is essential to the success of your trip. Trim extra clothing by using layers of polypropylene clothing and waterproof shells, and plan menus the way a backpacker does. Bring freeze-dried food, one-burner stoves, and single pots rather than large stoves and fresh foods.

SAFETY

One place you don't want to shave weight is in your safety gear selection. Bring extra safety gear (climbing ropes, carabiners, throw bags, break-apart paddle, etc.) in case an emergency arises. Also carry a fully equipped first aid kit with a detailed medical handbook. The more remote and dangerous the trip, the more you should consider carrying a two-way radio. Also, notify rangers, families, and friends of your itinerary before you leave, including your expected time of return. That way, if something does go wrong, a search party can be sent to find and help you.

Slalom races provide a great way to develop your river-running skills.

GETTING TO THE RIVER

Many first descents and exploratory trips have been overlooked simply because of the difficulty of access to put-ins or take-outs. If you're willing to carry your gear long distances over adverse terrain, you may just find a whitewater paradise awaiting at the end of the trail.

Keep in mind that additional gear—sleeping bags, riverwear, safety gear, and food—also has to be carried to the river. If the hike down to the put-in is only a mile or two long, consider spending one day hiking back and forth to transport everything to the river. On the other hand, if you have time to make only one hike, load your gear into backpack-style dry bags. They carry a heavy load and won't interfere with carrying the kayak on your shoulders.

RUNNING THE RIVER

Whenever you're in a new canyon or on an unknown section of river, run more conservatively than you would otherwise. Make sure your gear is tied down with bombproof straps or knots. Take a moment to ask yourself "what if . . ." before running blindly around a bend or over a horizon line. On remote rivers, a mistake could be costly and a serious injury could go untreated for days. Don't succumb to paranoia, but take a slight step back from your normal river bravado. By the time you reach civilization, the descent will take on heroic proportions anyway.

Racing

Kayak racing is a dynamic and exciting sport for competitors and spectators alike. From wildwater races to slalom competitions, the thrill of running rivers is magnified when every move becomes critical. In their effort to go fast and minimize errors, racers become totally focused. All the skills learned before—from kayak control to route finding—come to a head. Sound skills shine, and deficiencies become glaringly apparent.

It is in this process that another aspect of kayak racing appears: Kayakers who make good racers make good river runners! The same precision that goes into running gates carries into running rapids, and despite philosophical differences among paddlers as to what river running is all about, racing and recreational kayaking accent each other magnificently.

TYPES OF RACES

Kayak races have varied over the years as much as the rivers that have hosted them. Today, most races involve two events: *slalom* and *wildwater* (also known as *downriver*) *races*.

Slalom competitions are the most dynamic and fascinating of the kayaking events. They entail maneuvering kayaks through a series of gates while racing against the clock. Slalom racers must balance speed with perfect technique because each tapped pole or missed gate adds significantly to the final time.

In regular slalom competitions, there may be 20 to 30 gates set up over a short section of river. Once the boats are in the gates, the action is fast and furious. Rather than progressing downstream at tremendous speed, kayaks have to maneuver back and forth from gate to gate, sometimes turning into eddies to drive through upstream gates.

Wildwater races are the purest forms of kayak racing. They are the sprints and marathons of the whitewater world, with no poles or gate judges to add penalties to raw time. They are purely races against the clock, in which the fastest overall time wins. It takes both physical conditioning and solid river-reading skills to compete effectively in a wildwater race. The idea is to maintain fast, powerful strokes throughout the race, while sticking to the fastest currents.

PRERACE TIPS

A whole book could be written on kayak racing, including chapters on technique, physical preparation, and equipment. But, in many ways, racing merely builds upon the techniques, fitness, and equipment one already possesses. To improve your racing results, hone these techniques to build muscles and wind, and choose the fastest kayaks available.

Before any race begins, spend enough time to learn all the rules and to study the course. Check your starting time, then go scout the river. Look for strong currents, currents that will assist you with turns, and fast routes from gate to gate. Finally, form an indelible mental image of the course so you can imagine every stroke ahead of time.

SLALOM TIPS

Since the racer's goal is to make the run as fast and as penalty-free as possible, it can be difficult to relax at the starting line. Before the starter says, "Go," set your paddle in the catch position so you can make the first stroke immediately. Keep your grip relaxed so you don't waste any energy, and keep a vision of the course in your head.

Paddling in the gates is no different from normal river running. However, you should concentrate on short, fast, and powerful strokes using your torso muscles for drive. Since the tail end of the forward stroke delivers little energy to the kayak, chop it off and begin each stroke's recovery phase sooner than usual. Keep your head up to widen your field of vision.

In slalom events, the fastest way to run the course is to keep the kayak running *smoothly* from gate to gate. This means avoiding momentum-draining corrective strokes and choppy turns, and running minimally offset gates with subtle draw strokes or sweep strokes to shift the kayak's position. When making turns, turn *above* or *in* the gates so you don't have to struggle to change the kayak's direction after the gate. Also, as you enter each gate, figure out which pole you should run closer to, watch the poles and your kayak's tubes to make sure there are no touches, and always concentrate on the next gate downstream.

WILDWATER TIPS

Prepare for wildwater races the same way you do for slalom races: Review the rules, check your starting time, and scout the river. Find the fastest currents and the cleanest route through rapids and choose a course with the straightest line and fewest maneuvers. An ideal course will require no backstrokes and few, if any, turning strokes.

When running the river, avoid eddies, holes, and pockets of shallow, slower-moving water. Although wave trains generally signify fast water, run the shoulders of waves rather than their peaks. (The peaks will increase your vertical motion, slap your kayak around, and make it tougher to paddle, all of which will slow you down.) If you get back onto the right path, you may even catch up to the kayak in front of you. Plan to overtake the front kayak carefully. Don't waste energy trying to pass in slower water. Pick a broad, fast channel with even currents, announce your intentions, and pass only when legal.

12

THE BIG WIDE OPEN
SURF AND SEA KAYAKING

For every drop of fresh water that can be paddled, there is an infinitely greater amount of salt water available. Salt water covers most of the earth, and provides a recreational wonderland for inflatable kayakers.

Saltwater paddling takes on many forms. Whether you're paddling along a gentle coastline or riding through a pounding surf, salt water can provide as much variety as river running . . . possibly more.

In this chapter we'll briefly explore surf kayaking and sea kayaking and examine the specialized equipment and techniques that can make your next outing exciting and memorable.

Surf Kayaking

Riding ocean waves in an inflatable kayak is a thrilling form of whitewater boating. It combines all of the paddling techniques you've already learned with some simple adjustments for surviving the surf. Riding ocean waves can also be hazardous business for the uninitiated. Powerful riptides, rugged headlands, and pounding waves can take their toll on boats and boaters alike.

Before jumping into moderate surf, make sure that you have strong swimming skills, a durable self-bailing

There's a world of adventure waiting just beyond the shoreline.

kayak, and enough skill to run Class III rapids. Later, you can progress to bigger, more challenging waves as you refine your skills and develop a keen sense of how the surf works.

WAVES

Surf waves often begin hundreds or thousands of miles offshore where storm winds whip the ocean's surface into corduroy patches of irregular waves. Gradually, these waves transform into ocean swells as they travel away from the storm center. When these swells reach shallower waters, they begin to drag on the beach bottom (this is called *shoaling*) until they begin to spill shoreward.

If the beach descends steeply into deeper water, the waves will rise and plunge steeply; gentler beaches produce gradually spilling breakers that can roll for hundreds of yards before reaching land. Also, particulars like tides, winds, swell size, and shoreline shapes will affect the way waves behave.

The best waves for inflatable kayaking are small spilling breakers in the 2- to 4-foot range (measured from crest to trough). Bigger waves can punish paddlers and bust up gear, so start small and work your way up. If you can find waves that roll left or right from a sandbar, reef, or point, you may have found a perfect kayaking zone. By keeping just in front of the breaking part of the wave, you can stay on its steep, smooth part and enjoy a long ride.

CURRENTS

Beach currents can hold some big surprises for paddlers more used to kayaking rivers. *Longshore currents* flow parallel to the shore and can travel much faster than you can paddle. *Rip currents* can suck violently out to sea, carrying unwary paddlers or swimmers as much as a half mile offshore before letting them go. Finally, *nearshore currents*—which push surface waters toward the beach—can form amid shoaling waves.

Undertows—which really aren't currents at all—form at many beaches. Here, the surface water pushed up on shore from breaking waves dives to the bottom as it works its way back out to sea. This backwash can pull a swimmer underwater for a short period of time, then pop her back up many yards off the beach.

Paddle straight out through oncoming waves wherever they're small and weak.

Of all the currents just mentioned, rip currents can be the most hazardous. You can identify rip currents by choppy surface water, turbid water, or streaks of sea foam. If you get caught on these currents, your best escape is to swim or paddle perpendicular to the current until you break free. This can take some time and perseverance in big surf.

PADDLING OUT

The first trick to surf kayaking is breaking through the waves on the way out from the beach. Before you enter the surf zone, watch how long it takes each set of waves to build, break, and rebuild. Also check the water for hazards like strong currents or shallow reefs.

There will often be patterns in the surf. Areas of slack water and gentle highways will open up amid towering breakers. Envision the opportunity where the waves are least powerful and paddle toward that window aggressively. Success usually involves direction and timing. Point your bow straight into oncoming waves and time your approach so that you hit the waves after they have already expended their energy. Paddle all the way through the wave, grabbing as much of the solid water on the back side of the wave as possible.

HANDLING BREAKERS

If a big wave is about to crash in your face, you've got two choices: Paddle like mad or brace. Frequently, a series of powerful forward strokes will propel you over the face of a wave, into the air, and onto the flat water behind the wave. Other times, forward stroking is an effort in futility.

If there's no way to bust through a wave, plan B is to turn sideways, lean hard into the wave, and brace into the wave. If you're lucky, you'll squirt out in front of the wave—still sideways—and side-surf the wave in to shore. If you're unlucky, you'll get creamed and have to start all over again.

DROPPING IN

Ocean waves are quite similar to river waves and holes, with some interesting differences. In the ocean, the waves move while the water stays put. In rivers, the water moves while the waves stay put. Either way, wave surfing is the same. You slide onto the face of the wave, let gravity pull you downward, and surf away. If the ocean wave breaks, simply switch to the hole-riding techniques you learned in Chapter 9 and side-surf, ender, or blast your way to the beach.

A good ride starts with wave selection. Relax out beyond the surf zone and watch how the waves form. Generally there will be a set of nicely shaped waves followed by a series of duds. Each wave will steepen and begin to break in the same area. This is where you'll want to drop into your first wave.

The steep part of the wave next to a breaker can be a great place to surf.

Once you find a wave you like, paddle into position. Find the location where the wave will be steep enough to carry you forward and begin paddling toward shore. As the wave picks you up, forward-stroke just enough to keep your momentum going. Use your rudder and sweep strokes to keep yourself on the cleanest part of the wave and watch that the breakers don't swallow you up. If all goes well, you'll spend your day catching the good waves and paddling back out through the duds.

SURF TRICKS

Depending on the type of kayak you're paddling, you can ride just the smooth face of the waves (you can back off the wave before it begins to break), blast the breakers by leaning back into the whitewater, or even lean forward and paddle off the lip of a breaker to do front and back enders. All the tricks you learned about playboating in Chapter 9 apply equally well in the surf.

Sea Kayaking

Kayaking along open coastlines and secluded harbors may seem less intimidating and simpler than river kayaking, but the sea should never be underestimated. It is big, powerful, and moody. Invisible currents and strong winds can push you offshore and leave you stranded. Still, treated with respect, the ocean can be a wonderful place to paddle.

EQUIPMENT

The same equipment you have been using on the river can work equally well on the ocean. However, many river kayaks tend to move slower and spin easier than their oceangoing counterparts. Inflatable sea kayaks tend to be longer and more stable than river kayaks, and can come with V-shaped hulls, rudders, or skegs to help them track straighter and faster.

Sea kayaks can transport you to pristine bays and breathtaking harbors like this one in the British Virgin Islands. (Photo by Mark Lisk/Lisk Studios, Boise, ID; Courtesy of AIRE, Inc.)

THE BUDDY SYSTEM

The prudent kayaker rarely paddles alone. Companions can lend a helping hand if you have any trouble. They can help you right your boat after a flip, render first aid if a medical problem arises, or lend a floating platform in case your kayak needs a quick repair.

Always consider paddling with friends. If you decide to go alone, make sure you have the skills necessary to get yourself out to sea and back again. Also, let someone know where you're going and when you will return.

HANDLING WIND

Powerful winds can slow your progress and force your bow off its intended path. In and of itself, a gentle wind is nothing to fear. You can just paddle harder, constantly check your sights, and adjust your strokes to stay on course. Strong winds, on the other hand, can blow you off balance or cause big waves to lurch in your direction. Strong winds can also force you onshore or into rocky surf zones.

The best advice for sea kayakers is to avoid gusty days. The exception to this rule is when the wind is at your back. If you are an experienced kayaker and comfortable with the vagaries of your ocean setting, you can fly along the water's surface, propelled forward by wind and waves.

HANDLING WAVES

Waves are almost always present on big bodies of water. Fortunately, they come in all shapes and sizes, from small ripples to cresting whitecaps. You can often handle smaller ocean waves much the same way you paddle river waves. In fact, some of the same rules apply: Paddle straight through the waves or lean and brace into them. You can even spin on the top of waves much as you do on the river.

Waves start to become more exciting or dangerous—depending on your point of view—as they grow. Big waves can crest over your bow, jostle your kayak, or knock you into the water. If you find yourself in large swells, keep your paddle moving and always lean slightly in the direction of oncoming waves. Keep an eye on all members of your group, since they'll tend to disappear momentarily if you drop into different troughs.

TIDES AND CURRENTS

There is much more to sea kayaking than floating along on calm seas. Tides and currents can present forces to be reckoned with. They can impede or stall your progress and can even force you far off your desired route.

Before leaving protected bays and harbors for the big ocean, take some time to learn how to read tide and current charts. Once you understand the complex array of maps, arrows, and tables that fill these charts, you will be able to plan your trips so that you harness the ocean's power. You can find invisible currents that will carry you where you're going and avoid the currents that lead to long, frustrating days on the water.

LEARNING MORE

There is much more to sea kayaking than could ever be described in this chapter. For a more complete introduction to ocean paddling, read David Seidman's *The Essential Sea Kayaker* (Ragged Mountain Press, 1991) or any of the other fine sea kayaking books available at your local paddle shop. Remember, knowledge and safety go hand in hand!

Specialized sea kayaks can have V-shaped hulls, rudders, and long, sleek tubes.
(Photo by Mark Lisk/Lisk Studios, Boise, ID; Courtesy of AIRE, Inc.)

13

STAY IN SHAPE
GEAR MAINTENANCE AND REPAIR

Inflatable kayaks are built to withstand abuse: collisions with rocks, chafing from poorly loaded gear, the damaging effect of ultraviolet rays. But owner abuse—poor maintenance, careless storage, or improper use of gear—will greatly shorten the life expectancy of almost every item in your kayaking arsenal.

It takes only a little bit of care and common sense to keep your equipment healthy and kicking long after the warranties expire. In this chapter we'll not only look at how to maintain inflatable kayaks and paddling accessories, we'll explore ways to repair gear once it breaks down.

Caring for Your Inflatable Kayak

There are a multitude of ways to damage or destroy a kayak, but most kayak damage results from overinflation, tears, abrasion, ultraviolet decay, and water damage. Here are some simple guidelines to follow every time you use your kayak:

1. Rinse sand and dirt from shoes and gear when boarding a kayak so they don't grind their way into the fabric or valves.

2. Don't step on a deflated kayak. There may be rocks or sharp objects on the ground that could puncture the boat.
3. Carry—don't drag—a kayak while putting in, taking out, or portaging.
4. When pulling a kayak ashore, pull it to a point where it won't rock or rub against the bank.
5. Don't overload a kayak or load gear directly on the floor (light gear can be loaded on a self-bailing floor).
6. Don't overinflate a kayak, and check periodically for the correct air pressure—especially on hot or sunny days.
7. When transporting a kayak, make sure it isn't rubbing against the sides of the trailer or the interior of the trunk or truck bed.

TAKEDOWN AND ROLLING

A surprising amount of damage can occur after the kayak trip is over—damage that won't show up until the kayak is blown up again before the next outing. To avoid this type of damage, take a few extra minutes after each trip to prepare the kayak for storage.

At the take-out, unload all your gear from the kayak and remove the floor. Rinse the kayak thoroughly with clean water and lean it up on its edge to dry (unless, of course, it's raining). After the kayak is dry, gently wipe off any residual dirt and lay the kayak back on the ground. If there are wet ropes still tied to the kayak, remove them so the water doesn't damage the boat when it is in storage.

To roll up your kayak, first press or pump all the air out of the chambers. Then roll the kayak from the end without valves toward the other end (with the valves) as you would roll up a sleeping bag. When you're done, use a strong strap to hold the roll closed tightly, being careful to avoid chafing. When you're finished, your kayak will be rolled just like the one shown in the photograph on page 21, Chapter 3.

STORAGE

Most kayak manufacturers recommend that you store your kayak completely dry and semi-inflated. A kayak left with just enough air to maintain its shape is less likely to suffer the fabric stresses and delamination problems that go with being rolled up. A perfect storage spot is out of the way of direct heat, sunlight, chemicals, and sharp objects.

Field Repairs

I'd like to tell you that you'll never have to use the following information on kayak repair, but I'd probably be wrong. Just by looking at the number of sharp rocks in a typical river, and applying the law of averages, you'll see that sooner or later your kayak is going to get a hole.

If you're lucky, the only time you'll puncture your boat is at the take-out after a trip. That way, you can apply a clean, permanent patch at home under controlled conditions. However, many tears and punctures happen far from the nearest take-out. On-river repairs lack the dry, controlled workplace of home repairs and must be done more quickly. You often have to improvise in the field to make your repairs work, or else utilize a temporary solution like the *Ram Patch.*

The Ram Patch is an amazing little tool that seals small tears by squeezing the kayak's fabric between two rubber-faced disks—one for the inside of the tube and one for the outside of the tube. A specially designed key is used to tighten the Ram Patch in place and a miniature razor blade is included to make small holes large enough to accept the disks.

If the Ram Patch won't work—or if you want to make a more permanent repair—the traditional methods are described below.

Home Repairs

The first step in repairing a kayak is figuring out where the hole is. Though big tears are easy to find, pinhole leaks can be deceptive. In fact, sometimes they go unnoticed for years! The best way to find a pinhole leak is first to listen for the telltale whistle of escaping air, then to rub the suspected tube with soapy water. The water will bubble when it hits the leak. Once the leak is spotted and marked with a ballpoint pen, it'll be easier to figure out what type of patch is necessary.

THE THREE-STEP PROCESS

An easy way to think about the patching process is to divide it into three stages: (1) selecting the materials you'll need, (2) preparing the workplace, and (3) applying the patch.

MATERIALS

Patching materials include glues, solvents, and fabrics that match your kayak's fabric. There are a number of one- and two-part glues available. One-part glues require no catalyst, but can soften and lose their grip in temperatures as low as 150 degrees Fahrenheit (which can occur on a hot day). Two-part glues require the addition of a catalyst, but they remain stable at higher temperatures and cure faster. Unfortunately, the working time of many two-part glues is frustratingly short, so you must be prepared to place your patch as soon after mixing the glue as practical.

Ask your kayak dealer what type of glue your kayak needs. Also, buy your glues from your kayak dealer—they'll probably be more suited to kayaks, and may be of higher quality than those you'll find in a hardware store. When buying glue, purchase small cans and replace them at least once a season. If a can has been opened it may last as little as 30 days, so always have a fresh batch handy.

Solvents are used for thinning glues, cleaning the kayak, and breaking down the kayak's surfaces in preparation for receiving a patch. Typical solvents include toluol, which is used on Hypalon and neoprene kayaks, and MEK (methyl ethyl ketone) which is used on PVC and urethane kayaks. **Note that all solvents and glues are extremely toxic**. Use them only in well-ventilated areas while wearing nitrile gloves and safety goggles. If you're around kayak solvents a lot, you should consider wearing a breathing mask with an activated-charcoal filter.

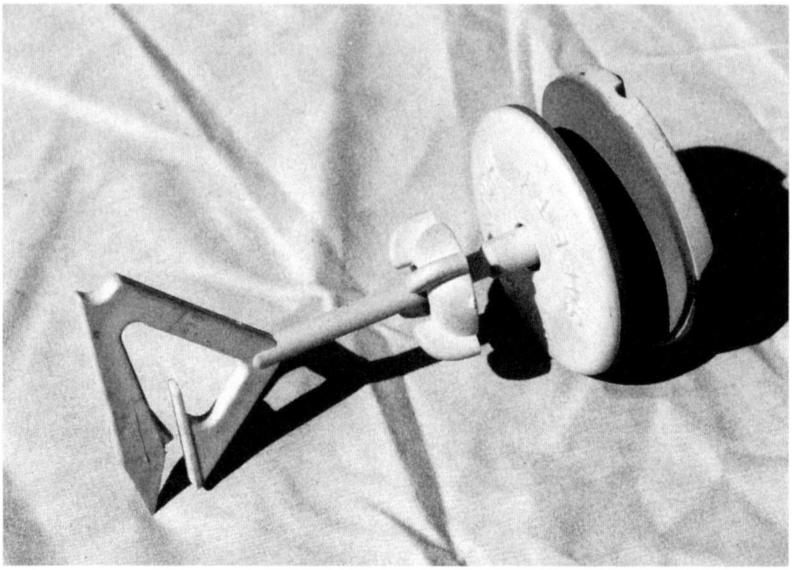

The Ram Patch seals small tears by squeezing the kayak's fabric between two rubber-faced disks. One disk folds in half before slipping inside the tube, and the long-stemmed key is removed once the disks are tightened into place.

The fabric used for the patch will be the same as the fabric of the kayak. Cut loose pieces of fabric into patches large enough to overlap the edges of the hole by at least 1.5 inches. Also, round and bevel the edges and the corners of the patch so they won't pull up later. Since really large tears *are* a possibility, it is a good idea to carry along as large a swath of fabric as your repair kit will hold. For additional items to use in making repairs, see the checklist in the appendix.

THE WORKPLACE

The ideal workplace is clean and windless, with low humidity and an ambient temperature between 50 and 80 degrees Fahrenheit. Set up the workplace by laying out all of your tools (listed in the appendix) and preparing the glues, kayak surfaces, and patches for use.

Patches should be cut to overlap holes or tears by at least 1.5 inches on all sides. Lay the loose patch on the tube over the hole and trace it with a pen so that you remember where to apply the glue. If the kayak is constructed from Hypalon or neoprene, sand the tube and one side of the patch. Roughening the fabric

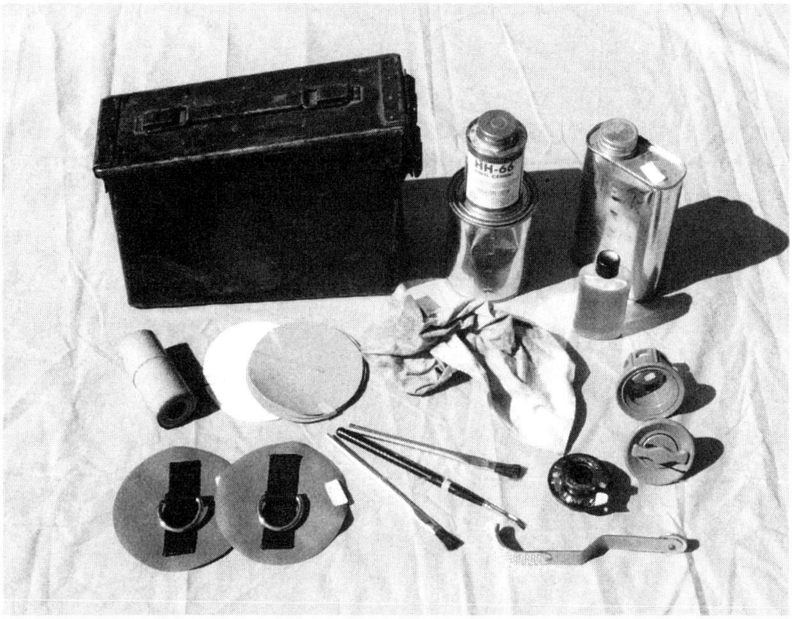

A well-stocked repair kit.

surface will greatly increase the strength of the bond. Remove excess grit with a clean cloth (cheesecloth works best) soaked in toluol. PVC and urethane don't require sanding (although some urethane is so tough that sanding or vigorous rubbing with MEK is necessary). Instead, just wipe them vigorously with MEK to soften the coating. Finally, prepare the glue following the manufacturer's directions. If the glues are not prethinned, thin them by adding a bit of the solvent you'll be using.

APPLYING THE PATCH

There are seven steps in applying patches:

1. Arrange and mark the patches so that you'll remember which one goes where.

2. Wipe the patch and the kayak surfaces clean with a clean cloth soaked in solvent.

3. Apply a very thin first coat of glue, overlapping the patch outline by ¼ inch, and let it dry completely. (Use long, quick strokes when applying glue to avoid its balling up, and don't touch glued surfaces—body oils will affect the bond!)

4. Apply a second thin coat of glue and let that coat dry completely.

5. Reactivate the glue by wiping it quickly with a cloth wet with solvent. Wait about 15 to 30 seconds.

6. Carefully match up the patch and the outline, press the patch against the kayak, and firmly press it down with a roller, making sure to force all air bubbles out from under the patch.

7. Clean up any excess glue with solvent or a hard eraser, and let the patch dry completely (24 hours).

Note that many kayakers shorten steps four and five by pressing the patch into place when the second coat just becomes tacky rather than reactivating the glue with solvent.

PATCHING TIPS

Moving beyond the basics, there are some tips and shortcuts that can make the patching process easier.

Try presanding patch surfaces and prethinning glues at home. That way, they'll be ready for on-river repairs. To avoid glue splatter, outline the mark you drew on the kayak with masking tape before you start painting on any glue. This will keep the glue from running away from the edges of the patch.

Really big rips can be particularly tough to repair. In times past, many kayakers used an awl and heavy-duty thread to sew the tear closed first, using a baseball stitch. Though this is still done periodically, the thread causes an irregularity in the patch, making it tougher to mend the surfaces together flat. If you need to repair a big rip, start by thoroughly drying out the torn chamber. Use bias tape or radiator-hose repair tape inside the tube to bring the torn edges back together. Working on a flat surface, carefully insert the tape inside the tube through the tear with the sticky side up, then work the rip down against the tape. This will make laying the outside patch much easier. Similarly, an inside patch can be used in place of the tape and applied in the same way as any other patch. Once the inside patch cures, you can apply an outside patch too.

Major Repairs

Major repairs include tears near seams and blown baffles. Although it is usually best to leave these repairs to the pros, both types can be done by experienced amateurs.

Repairing seams differs little from other patch jobs, except that the seam may have to be peeled away from the kayak to make effective repairs to adjacent materials. To save some big headaches, start off these types of repairs by giving your manufacturer a call. Chances are you'll get sound advice and some technical guidance. Next, buy a hot-air gun to heat the seams and to loosen the glue.

To begin the repair, hold the hot-air gun 4 to 6 inches from the seam and warm up the seam very gradually, taking care not to melt the fabric coating. Check the seam every couple of minutes to see if it can be pulled away from the remaining material (use a pair of pliers to grab and pull the seam). Once the seam is pliable, peel it back and proceed with your repair in the same manner as for any other patch.

WELDING

As kayaking technology evolves, glues and solvents are disappearing. There are already some handheld fabric-welding units that can be used to make bombproof kayak repairs at home. Since welding actually melts the patch right into the kayak's fabric, the patch becomes part of the kayak rather than just adhering to it. If you have a choice, have your major repairs welded to ensure that they'll last the life of the kayak.

D-RINGS

Hot-air guns are also needed to heat and loosen torn or blown D-rings. Again, heat the D-ring gradually to avoid melting the surrounding material and try to pull the D-ring free with a pair of pliers every couple of minutes. Once the D-ring has been pulled loose, replace it with a similar D-ring using the same gluing methods as you would to patch your kayak.

VALVE REPAIRS

Depending on the type of valve used in your kayak, valve repairs can be a quick, efficient chore or a real nightmare. However, most of the newer valves are designed for easy replacement with little more than a few tools.

Many military-style and AD-1 valves fit into a recessed boot on the kayak and are fixed in place with screws. To replace these, just undo the screws, remove the damaged valve, and screw a new valve in place.

Halkey-Roberts valves consist of two pieces, and are held in place by screwing male and female parts together. To replace the outer face of a Halkey-Roberts valve you will need a specially designed valve tool. This tool fits inside the valve face and is used to unscrew the outer half of the valve while you hold the valve's inner half in place. When the two halves separate, pull the face free of the kayak. Hold the female half in position inside the tube by pinching the tube with your free hand and use the tool to tighten a new male half into the female socket. (If the entire valve breaks, you may need to head to the local repair shop.)

If valve replacement makes you nervous, let a professional handle it or give your manufacturer's representative a call.

Riverwear

Drysuits, wetsuits, paddle jackets, and booties see an enormous amount of abuse on river trips. Twigs and snags can rip the fabrics, body oils start to stink up your neoprene items, and ultraviolet rays slowly chisel away at the life span of nylon.

Neoprene clothing—such as wetsuits and booties—should be hand-washed with mild soap and water. There are even some special detergents on the market for eliminating the telltale neoprene smell that follows many river runners around. Drysuits, on the other hand, demand some special care.

First, never try to zip a rear-entry drysuit by yourself—have someone do it for you. (The zippers are very expensive and can easily be damaged if tugged or bent the wrong way.) Next, take good care of your drysuit's neck, wrist, and ankle seals and cuffs, which are particularly vulnerable to drying, splitting, and tearing. Swab the seals with generous amounts of *seal saver* (a food-grade silicone) or *303 protectant* before or after each trip. Don't use anything on the seals that contains petroleum and avoid spilling solvents on them.

DRYSUIT REPAIRS

If a drysuit seal or cuff ever tears, it can be replaced by the factory or by some whitewater shops. If you want to do it yourself, here's how:

1. Tear off the old cuff, making sure to get rid of all the excess latex and glue.
2. Find a container large enough to fully expand the opening where the cuff will be mounted and insert it inside that opening.
3. Apply a thick coat of *Aquaseal* (a special glue for use in water) to the outside of the drysuit opening where the new cuff will go, being sure to add an extra ¼ inch of Aquaseal past the cuff line.
4. Stretch the new gasket with your hands and lay it over the glued opening of the suit.
5. Hold the seal in place with tape and let it dry for 24 hours.

Repair tears to drysuits with vinyl bond—a general-purpose glue—and a small patch made of the same material as your drysuit, or simply use a dab of Aquaseal for small jobs.

WETSUIT REPAIRS

Wetsuits start seeing abuse the moment you go to use them. Neoprene can tear if stretched or pulled too hard, so use care when you're putting it on and taking it off. If a rip does develop, repair it before it spreads. The easiest way to repair damaged suits is to use an iron-on neoprene patch (available at scuba diving shops). However, neoprene cement and Aquaseal work better and don't leave an elevated section of material. Both Aquaseal and neoprene cement come in small cans with simple directions for gluing the torn edges back together.

To keep a wetsuit clean and strong, wash it periodically. Use a special wetsuit detergent instead of a harsh detergent and clean it by hand. It is possible to wash your wetsuit in a washing machine on the rinse cycle, but be careful to avoid damage. Once the suit is dry, sprinkle it with talcum powder and store it in a dry place.

Other Equipment

LIFEJACKETS

Lifejackets are tough survivors if properly maintained. The key to their longevity is not using them for other purposes, such as seats, cushions, or rags. Don't stuff them in small spaces, and strive to keep them clean. When not in use, keep them away from ultraviolet rays and heat.

PUMPS

Manual pumps have moving parts that work better and last longer when lubricated. Keep the cylinders of hand pumps clean and lubricate them in accordance with the manufacturer's specifications (waterproof grease often works well). Electric pumps will last a longer time if they're used only to pump kayaks up to shape, but they'll die fast if they're used to top the kayak off.

APPENDIX

Manufacturers of Inflatable Kayaks

Achilles Inflatable Craft, 1407 80 Street S.W., Everett, WA 98203; (206) 353-7000

AIRE, Inc., P.O. Box 3412, Boise, ID 83703; (208) 344-7506

All River Equipment (distributor for Star Inflatables), 232 Banks Road, Traveller's Rest, SC 29690; (803) 836-2800

B & A Distributing Co. (distributor for Riken, Momentum, and Eurocraft kayaks), 201 S.E.Oak Street, Portland, OR 97214-1079; (503) 230-0482

Custom Inflatables, P.O. Box 80, Albright, WV 26519; (304) 329-2359

Demaree Inflatable Boats, P.O. Box 307, Friendsville, MD 21531; (301) 746-5815

Duckworks, P.O. Box 277, Rowlesburg, WV 26425; (800) 872-7238

Hyside Inflatables, P.O. Box Z, Kernville, CA 93238; (619) 376-3723

Incept, 3347 Highway 8 East #7, Moscow, ID 83843; (208) 882-2844

Jack's Plastic Welding, 115 S. Main, Aztec, NM 87410; (505) 334-8748

Maravia Corporation, Box 404, Boise, ID 83701; (208) 322-4949

Northwest River Supplies, 2009 S. Main, Moscow, ID 83843; (800) 635-5202

Osprey Whitewater, 561 Merlin Road Merlin, OR 97532; (503) 474-7656

Sevylor (distributor for Sevylor, Sevymarine, and Jumbo kayaks), 66511 E. 26 Street, Los Angeles, CA 90040; (213) 727-6013

SOAR Inflatables, 507 N. 13 Street, #409, St. Louis, MO 63103; (800) 280-SOAR

So-Cat, 56741 Stellar Drive, Bend, OR 97707; (503) 593-1009

Vista Recreation, P.O. Box 147, Almond, NC 28702; (704) 488-8594

Waterwolf, P.O. Box 3341, Telluride, CO 81435; (800) H20-WOLF

Whitewater Manufacturing, 1700 S.W. Nebraska Avenue, Grants Pass, OR 97527; (503) 476-1344

Manufacturers of Sit-on-Tops

New Wave Kayak Products, 2535 Roundtop Road, Middletown, PA 17057; (717) 944-6320

Ocean Kayaks, Inc., 2460 Grandview Road, Ferndale, WA 98248; (800) 8-KAYAKS

On The Edge, Inc., 1446 127 Place N.E., Bellevue, WA 98005; (206) 453-8846

Pacific Northwest Designs, Inc., Bellingham, WA 98226; (800) 433-1969

Perception/Aquaterra, P.O. Box 8002, Easley, SC 29641; (803) 859-7518

Prijon/Wildwasser Sport, P.O. Box 4617, Boulder, CO 80306; (303) 444-2336

Recommended Reading

Bechdel, Les, and Slim Ray. *River Rescue,* Second Edition. Appalachian Mountain Club.

Bennett, Jeff. *The Complete Whitewater Rafter.* Ragged Mountain Press.

Gullion, Laurie. *Canoeing and Kayaking Instruction Manual.* American Canoe Association.

Harrison, David. *Sea Kayaking Basics.* Hearst Marine Books.

Hutchinson, Derek. *Eskimo Rolling,* 2nd Edition, Ragged Mountain Press.

Lessels, Bruce. *Whitewater Handbook.* Appalachian Mountain Club.

Nealy, William. *Kayak: The Animated Manual of Intermediate and Advanced Whitewater Technique.* Menasha Ridge Press.

Seidman, David. *The Essential Sea Kayaker.* Ragged Mountain Press.

Snyder, Jim. *The Squirt Manual.* Menasha Ridge Press.

U'ren, Steve. *Performance Kayaking.* Stackpole Books.

Walbridge, Charlie and Wayne Sundmacher. *Whitewater Rescue Manual.* Ragged Mountain Press.

Periodicals

American Whitewater, American Whitewater Affiliation, P.O. Box 85, Phoenicia, NY 12464

Canoe & Kayak, 10526 N.E. 68, Suite 3, Kirkland, WA 98033

Currents, National Organization for River Sports, Box 6847, Colorado Springs, CO 80934

Paddler, 4061 Oceanside Boulevard, Suite M, Oceanside, CA 92056

Outfitters Organizations

America Outdoors, P.O. Box 1348, Knoxville, TN 37901; (615) 525-4765

Ministry of Tourism, Queen's Park, Toronto, Ontario, Canada M7A 2R9

National Organization of Canoe Liveries and Outfitters, R.R. 2, Box 249, Butler, KY 41006-9674; (606) 472-2205

North American Paddlesports Association, 12455 North Wauwatosa Road, Mequon, WI 53092; (414) 242-5228

The Quebec Outfitters Association, 2900, Boulevard Saint-Martin Quest, Laval, Quebec H7L 2J2

TravelArctic, Yellowknife, N.W.T. X1A

Yukon Outfitters Association, Bag Service 2762, Whitehorse, Yukon Y1A 5B9

Private Boaters' Organizations

American Canoe Association (ACA), 7432 Alban Station Blvd., Suite B226, Springfield, VA 22150; (703) 451-0141

The American Whitewater Affiliation, P.O. Box 85, Phoenicia, NY 12464

The National Organization for River Sports, Box 6847, Colorado Springs, CO 80934

Safety Instruction Organizations

Rescue 3 International, P.O. Box 519, Elk Grove, CA 95759; (800)-45RESCU

Rescue 3 Northwest, 12112 N.E. 195, Bothell, WA 98011; (800)-234-4644

Rescue 3 Canada, 5075 Angus Drive, Vancouver, B.C., Canada, V6M 3M6; (604) 263-3580

For additional safety instruction programs, contact one of the outfitters, kayaking schools, or rafting schools in your area.

Checklists

BASIC GEAR FOR DAY TRIPS

___ Kayak, with seat and floor
___ Paddles
___ Pumps
___ Lifejackets
___ Helmets
___ Straps
___ Wet- or Drysuit
___ Booties
___ Paddle jacket or dry top
___ Rescue/safety gear (separate list)
___ First aid kit (separate list)
___ Repair kit (separate list)
___ Waterproof containers
___ Water and food
___ Other:

REPAIR KIT

___ Patch materials (6" X 48")
___ Glue and catalyst
___ Solvent (MEK or toluol)
___ Mixing cup
___ Small paintbrush
___ Roller
___ Rag (cheesecloth)
___ Sandpaper or scuffing tool
___ Pen and hard eraser
___ Nitrile gloves
___ Safety goggles
___ Pliers
___ Scissors
___ Large needle and cord
___ Wire cutters
___ Screwdrivers
___ Halkey-Roberts valve tool
___ Spare parts
___ Other:

RESCUE/SAFETY GEAR

___ Carabiners (5)
___ River knife
___ Throw bags (1 for each raft)
___ Pulleys (2)
___ Whistle
___ 2" Pulleys (3–4)
___ Web slings
___ Break-apart paddle
___ Static rope
___ Prussik loops (3–4)
___ Z-drag crib cards
___ Anchor slings (3–4)
___ Paddle hook
___ Other:

CAMPING AND COOKING GEAR

___ Waterproof containers
___ Tent or tarp
___ Sleeping bag
___ Ground pad
___ Lantern/fuel
___ Pillow
___ Clothing
___ Toiletries
___ Camera gear

___ Stove/fuel
___ Matches/lighters
___ Forks, knives, and spoons
___ Pots and pans
___ Cups, plates, and bowls
___ Can opener
___ Water containers
___ Spatula
___ Seasonings
___ Scouring pads
___ Biodegradable soap
___ Trash bags
___ Food
___ Water purifiers/filters
___ Other:

FIRST AID KIT

___ First aid book
___ Band-Aids
___ Adhesive tape
___ Gauze (4" x 4")
___ Roll Gauze (2")
___ Compresses
___ Ace bandages
___ Paramedic shears
___ 10% proridine-iodine solution
___ 19% hydrocortisone cream
___ Neosporin ointment
___ Small tweezers
___ Knife
___ Needles
___ Safety pins
___ CPR face shield
___ Hypothermia thermometer
___ Disposable gloves
___ Alcohol swabs
___ Small package liquid soap
___ Large syringe/rubber bulb
___ Oral glucose/sugar/candy
___ Powdered sports drink
___ Penlight
___ Moleskin
___ Venom extraction kit
___ Space blanket
___ Tylenol or ibuprofen
___ Lomotil
___ Ex-Lax
___ Dramamine
___ Robitussin-DM
___ Prescription medications
___ Triangular bandages (optional)
___ Sam splint (optional)
___ Total sun block
___ Waterproof carry case
___ Other:

(NOTE: Consult a physician before taking any prescription medications. Many of the items included in this list require some expertise to use effectively. Obtain adequate first aid and CPR training through the Red Cross or other certified medical training programs.)

TRIP PLANNER

___ Assemble group of paddlers
___ Consult regional guidebooks for details about rivers
___ Pick a suitable river based on season, access points, rapids, etc.
___ Gather additional information from local boaters or outfitters
___ Call government agencies to see if permits are required
___ Acquire any river and camping permits you may need
___ Check additional government regulations (i.e., regarding toilets, gear, etc.)
___ Arrange and plan shuttles
___ Plan menu
___ Check basic gear list (above)
___ Check safety/rescue gear list (above)
___ Check first aid kit list (above)
___ Check camping and cooking gear list (above)
___ Buy or rent any missing items or kayaking gear
___ Check river levels
___ Check weather forecast
___ Have fun!
___ Other:

(This checklist is primarily designed as a basic guideline for inexperienced kayakers. There are many more steps that go into a pretrip agenda. As your river experience grows, so will your ability to assemble groups of kayakers and plan river trips quickly.)

Knots

bowline

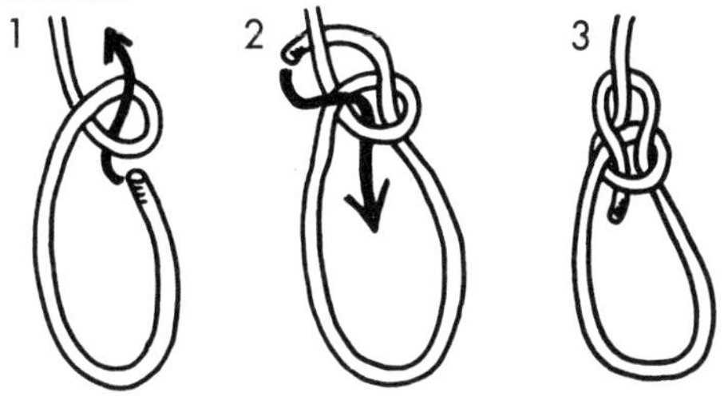

butterfly knot

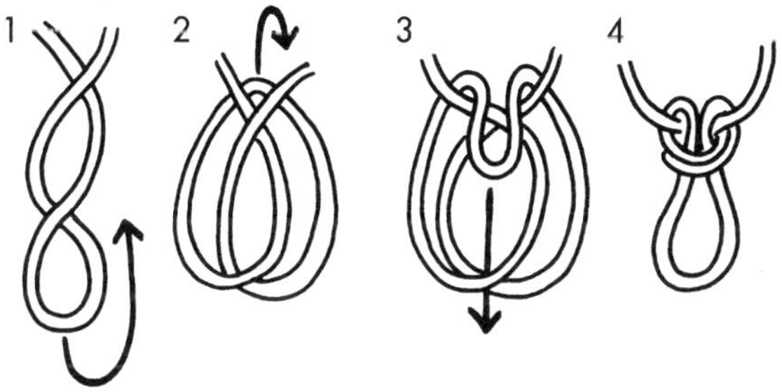

double fisherman's knot

prussik loop

trucker's hitch

water knot (ring bend)

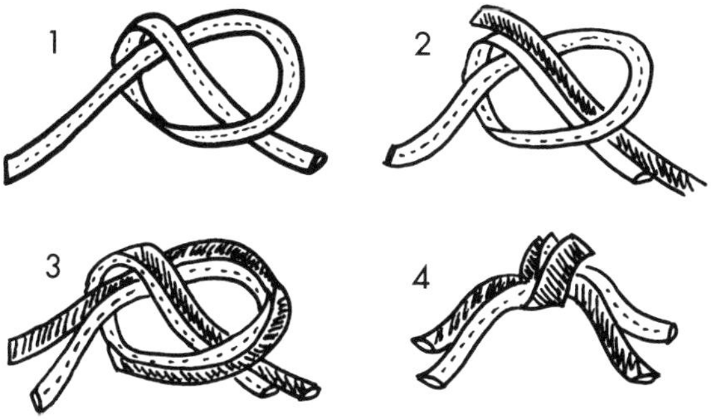

figure-eight knot

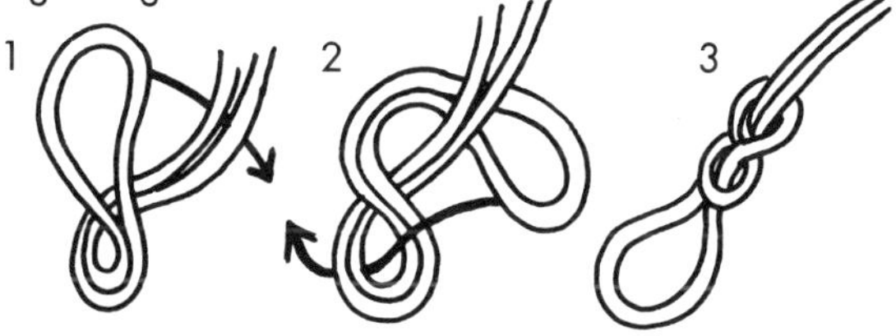

double half hitch

square knot

GLOSSARY

Baffle: A diaphragm that divides the interior of tubes into separate compartments.

Bank: The river's shore.

Bar: A shallow part of the river channel consisting of sand, gravel, or small rocks.

Belay: A method of slowing or stopping a rope from sliding.

Big water: Refers to rivers with large volume and powerful hydraulics.

Blade: The wide, flat part of a paddle or oar.

Boat: Kayak.

Boater: Kayaker.

Boils: Ascending currents that rise above surface level unpredictably.

Boulder garden: A rapid densely strewn with boulders.

Bow: The front or nose of a kayak.

Bowline: The rope tied to the front or nose of the kayak (also a type of knot).

Brace: Using the paddles to assist a paddler in staying in the kayak or to prevent the kayak from flipping over.

Breaking wave: A standing wave that falls upstream.

Bulkhead: See *baffle.*

Cfs: Cubic feet per second. Measures the current's velocity past a fixed point in the river (35.3 cfs equals 1 cubic meter per second).

Cms: Cubic meters per second.

Carabiner: A metal clip used to attach lines to kayaks, to secure gear, or to substitute for a pulley.

Chamber: One interior compartment of a kayak tube.

Chute: A narrow, constricted portion of the river.

Clean: A word used to describe a route free of obstructions.

Classification: A system for rating the difficulty of whitewater rapids.

Confluence: The point where two rivers or streams meet.

Current: Moving water.

Cushion: See *pillow.*

D-ring: A steel ring attached to the kayak and used as a tie-down point.

Diaphragm: See *baffle.*

Downstream: The part of the river to where the current flows (a.k.a. *downriver*).

Draw stroke: A stroke used to move the kayak sideways by placing the paddle out to the side of the kayak and pulling it back to the kayak.

Drop: A steep, sudden change in the level of the river bottom. Drops taller than 6 to 7 feet are frequently called waterfalls.

Dry bag: A waterproof bag designed to keep its contents dry.

Drysuit: A waterproof suit that encloses a paddler in impermeable layers of fabric. Designed to be worn over insulating layers of clothing.

Eddy: A pocket of water downstream of an obstacle that flows upstream or back against the main current.

Eddy line: The interface between the eddy current and the main current (a high eddy line is called an *eddy fence*).

Entrapment: A situation in which a kayak or kayaker gets pinned against an obstacle by the river's current.

Falls: A drop where the river plummets steeply over boulders or broken river bottom. Can refer to a waterfall, or to the upstream side of a hole.

Feather: To turn a paddle or oar blade horizontal to the water.

Ferry: A maneuvering technique used to move a kayak back and forth laterally across the river.

Flip line: A short rope used to flip a kayak upright.

Foot cup: A loop, cone, cup, or stirrup mounted on the kayak's floor and used to brace the foot.

Gradient: A term used to measure a river's descent in feet per mile or meters per kilometer.

Haystack: A large, unstable standing wave.

Helmet: Rigid headgear designed to protect a kayaker's head from impact.

Hole: A swirling vortex of water wherein the river pours over an obstacle and drops toward the river bottom leaving a pocket behind the obstacle that is filled in by an upstream surface current.

Hypothermia: A lowering of the body's core temperature.

Keeper: A large hole or reversal that can keep and hold a kayak or a swimmer for a long period of time.

Lifejacket: A personal flotation device designed to float a swimmer in water.

Psi: Pounds per square inch. A way of measuring air pressure in a kayak.

Pillow: A cushion of water that forms on the upstream side of obstacles.

Pivot: To turn the kayak in place.

Pool: A flat section of river with no rapids.

Pool-drop: A type of river that has intermittent rapids followed by long, easy sections of calm water.

Portage: To carry a kayak around a rapid.

Power face: The side of an oar or paddle blade that normally pulls against the current.

Put-in: The place where a kayak trip begins.

Rapid: A place where the river leaves its two-dimensional state and enters a three-dimensional state complete with faster currents, rocks, and various types of liquid surface features.

Reversal: See *hole.*

Riffle: Shallow, gentle rapids caused by rocks or streambeds.

River left: The left side of the river when you are looking downstream.

River right: The right side of the river when you are looking downstream.

Roller: A big curling wave that falls back upstream on itself.

Rooster tail: A fountain of water that explodes off a submerged obstacle in a fan pattern.

Scout: To walk along a bank to inspect the river.

Section: A portion of river between two points.

Self-bailing: A type of kayak that lets water drain out through the floor.

Shaft: The long cylindrical tube between the blades of a paddle.

Sneak route: The easiest route through a rapid (a.k.a. *cheat route*).

Standard-floor: A type of kayak that does not let water drain back into the river.

Standing wave: A stationary river wave.

Stern: The back end of a kayak.

Stopper: A hole, reversal, or breaking wave capable of stopping, holding, or flipping a kayak or a swimmer.

Strainer: An obstacle, such as logs or boulders, that lets water flow freely through it but catches swimmers, rafts, and debris (a.k.a. *sweeper, logjam, boulder sieve*).

Sweep stroke: A turning stroke in which the blade is swept in an arc pattern fore or aft.

Tail wave: Standing wave that forms at the base of a rapid.

Take-out: The place where a kayak trip ends and kayaks depart from the river.

Technical: A type of river that has many obstacles and therefore requires constant maneuvering.

Throw bag: A bag that holds a long coiled rope, used as a rescue device to be tossed to swimmers.

Thwart: The cross-tube of a kayak.

Tongue: A smooth V of fast-moving water that frequently appears at the top of a rapid.

Undercut: An overhanging rock or ledge with water flowing underneath it.

Volume: The amount of water in a river.

Waterfall: See *drop.*

Wave: A hump in the river's flowing water.

Wave train: A series of standing waves.

Whitewater: Rapids (a.k.a. *fun!*).

Wrap: A kayak pinned flat against an obstacle by river currents.

Z-drag: A pulley system used to rescue pinned or wrapped kayaks.

INDEX